The Ignoble Savage

Photograph courtesy of the National Gallery of Art, Washington, D.C.

THE IGNOBLE SAVAGE

American Literary Racism, 1790-1890

LOUISE K. BARNETT

Contributions in American Studies, Number 18

Greenwood Press
WESTPORT, CONNECTICUT • LONDON, ENGLAND

Library of Congress Cataloging in Publication Data

Barnett, Louise K
    The ignoble savage : American literary racism, 1790-1890.

    (Contributions in American studies ; no. 18)
    Bibliography: p.
    Includes index.
    1. ' American fiction—19th century—History and criticism. 2. Frontier
and pioneer life in literature. 3. Indians in literature. I. Title.
PS374.F73B3   813'.03   75-16964
ISBN 0-8371-8281-6

Library of Congress Catalog Card Number: 75-16964
ISBN: 0-8371-8281-6

First published in 1975

Greenwood Press, a division of Williamhouse-Regency Inc.
51 Riverside Avenue, Westport, Connecticut 06880

Printed in the United States of America

For Robbie and Gregory

The Indian way of consciousness is different from and fatal to our way of consciousness. Our way of consciousness is different from and fatal to the Indian. The two ways, the two streams, are never to be united. They are not even to be reconciled. There is no bridge, no canal of connection.

D. H. Lawrence, MORNINGS IN MEXICO

CONTENTS

ACKNOWLEDGMENTS

Any student of white American attitudes toward Indians owes a large debt to Roy Harvey Pearce's *The Savages of America: A Study of the Indian and The Idea of Civilization* (1953), revised as *Savagism and Civilization: A Study of the Indian and the American Mind.* This seminal work has been followed by a number of other important studies, notably Edwin Fussell's *Frontier: American Literature and the American West* (1965) and Richard Slotkin's *Regeneration Through Violence: The Mythology of the American Frontier, 1600-1860* (1973).

I am grateful to Roger W. Cummins for reading my work and offering valuable suggestions, to Betty Jo Sheirich, Fackenthal Library, Franklin and Marshall College, for service above and beyond the call of duty in procuring books on interlibrary loan, and to the staff of the Rare Book Room, Van Pelt Library, University of Pennsylvania, where many of my primary materials were to be found. The Philip H. and A. S. W. Rosenbach Foundation gave me a generous welcome when I needed their resources. A fellowship from the American Association of University Women financed much of the research for this study, and a grant from the Madge Miller Fund of Bryn Mawr College paid for the preparation of the manuscript. My typist, Maria Cattell, did a superb job, and Stephen L. Kennamer read the manuscript with care.

The National Gallery of Art kindly granted permission to reproduce the frontispiece illustration, Benjamin West's portrait of Colonel Guy Johnson, from the Andrew W. Mellon Collection. *Art in America* has courteously allowed me to reproduce portions of the John Lefeather poem, "Hi, Paleface!" In a slightly different form Chapter 5 of this study originally appeared in *The South Atlantic Quarterly*, which has given permission for its inclusion here.

I am grateful beyond my powers of expression to three people: to Arthur P. Dudden, for good advice and generous encouragement; to Henry Mayer, who gave unstintingly of his time, knowledge, and critical ability; and to my husband, who has been an unfailing resource—as he still is—twenty-four hours a day.

The Ignoble Savage

INTRODUCTION

SOME PRE-FICTIVE IMAGES
OF THE INDIAN

ABORIGNES. n. Persons of little worth found cumbering the soil of a newly discovered country. They soon cease to cumber; they fertilize.

Ambrose Bierce, THE DEVIL'S DICTIONARY

1

As the original inhabitants of the new world, Indians have been figures for all generations of Americans to react to, first as curiosities and physical threats, later as objects of pity and guilt, and always as foreign phenomena to be assimilated somehow to prevailing white ideas of civilization and morality. From the beginning of the American experience there must have been little doubt in the collective white mind that its superiority—conceived of as moral and religious but tangibly exhibited to the Indian in the form of firearms and numbers—must eventually triumph over the aborigines. Ralph Waldo Emerson's characterization of an early Indian war could serve for any other white-Indian conflict equally well: "We know beforehand who must conquer in that unequal struggle. The red man may destroy here and there a straggler, as a wild beast may; he may fire a farm-house or a village; but the association of the white men and their art of war give them an overwhelming advantage . . . ."[1] White civilization might be proffered to the Indians by random enthusiasts from time to time, but this ultimately had little impact; the Puritan

3

paradigm for white-Indian relations was adhered to with little variation: first, white dispossession of the Indian from his lands, then war, and finally subjugation of the Indian remnant. John Robinson's pious wish—"How happy a thing had it been if you had converted some before you had killed any"[2]—would aptly sum up the extent of Christian charity toward the Indian in the historical overview.

It may be argued that the Indian was a fictive character long before he appeared in a work of fiction, the very name "Indian" constituting the first fiction imposed on him by the white man. Indeed, one of the best known and most typical Puritan "historical accounts" of the white-Indian confrontation, Cotton Mather's *Decennium Luctuosum* (1699), could serve as the prototype for countless early nineteenth-century novels. The providential framework, which, in Mather's view, encompasses the action of King William's War, undergoes secularization in the nineteenth century, but whether God is invoked or not, the fictive outcome remains Matherian: the whites "bravely Conquered the Salvages."[3]

The action which Mather focuses upon as the central experience of white-Indian relations, the captivity of white settlers by Indians, remains the major plot action in the pre-Civil War frontier romance. In reality, the occupation of Indian land by whites and the consequences thereof must surely rank as the historically significant aspect of the interaction between these groups, but it is readily apparent why Mather and later white writers preferred to dwell on the captivity. Although settlers quickly provided rationales for their usurpation of the continent, there was obviously room for sympathy for the Indian in the land transaction.[4] The captivity, on the other hand, cast the Indian in a totally unsympathetic role as gratuitous persecutor of whites, perpetrator of numberless atrocious deeds which provoked pity for his victims' suffering and admiration for their endurance. As Mather describes the captives' lot:

> Truly, the Dark places of New-England, where the Indians had their Unapproachable Kennels, were Habitations of Cruelty; and no words can Sufficiently describe the Cruelty undergone by our Captives in those Habitations. The Cold,

and Heat, and Hunger, and Weariness, and Mockings, and
Scourgings, and Insolencies Endured by the Captives, would
enough deserve the Name of Cruelty; but there was this also
added unto the rest, that they must ever now and then have
their Friends made a Sacrafice *[sic]* of Devils before their
Eyes. (*Decennium Luctuosum*, p. 208)

As a vehicle for a whole range of unsavory excitements and as an
apology for white brutality toward the Indian, the captivity
format functioned successfully for almost two centuries.

Similarly, Mather's descriptions of the Indians furnished a
crude portrait which early writers of fiction might refine and
elaborate on without finding it necessary to change the essentials.
The helpful ministrations of Squanto and Massasoit forgotten,[5]
Mather uses synonyms for Indian which range from animal to
devil. They are wolves, tigers, dragons, serpents infesting the
garden, "horrid Sorcerers, and hellish Conjurers and such as
Conversed with Demons" (*ibid.*, p. 242). When the word "Indian"
itself is employed in *Decennium Luctuosum*, it is seldom without a
qualifier on the order of fierce, formidable, furious, or terrible.
Mather's epithets for Indians, the numerous changes which he
rings on the description of cruelty and devilishness, recur in
romance after romance of the pre-Civil War period. More subtly,
perhaps, but to similar purpose, white Americans followed
Mather's example of dehumanizing the enemy and thus robbing
him of any appeal to just treatment as he was gradually pushed
aside or exterminated. Whatever the New England tribes of
1689-1699 were like, Mather's emotional rhetoric tells us only of
their effect on a white consciousness, or rather, of the effect of an
idea of them, a subjective response to subjective evidence.

With unctuous self-satisfaction Mather concludes a grisly
episode of captivity horrors in *Decennium Luctuosum* by instruct-
ing the reader:

A Modern Traveller assures us, that at the Villa Ludovisia,
not far from Rome, there is to be seen the Body of a Petrified
Man; and that he himself saw, by a piece of the man's Leg,
Broken for Satisfaction, both the Bone and the Stone
Crusted over it. All that I will say, is, That if thou canst Read

these passages without relenting Bowels, thou thyself art as
really Petrified as the man at Villa Ludovisia.

Nescio tu quibus es, Lector, Lecturus Ocellis;
Hoc Scio quod Siccis scibere non potui (p. 213).

None of Mather's tears, nor those he hoped to draw from his
readers, were for the exterminated Indians. Although one is
tempted to ascribe a bloodthirsty temperament to this ferocious
prelate, the immediacy of the conflict, and the conviction that the
Indians were divinely intended to provide opportunities for
Puritan heroism, go far to explain Mather's single-mindedness.
The discernible difference between his typically Puritan view of
the Indian as devil's agent and implacable enemy[6] and the equally
inimical savage of the pre-Civil War frontier romance is that from
a position of far greater physical security and a diminished confidence in man's ability to fathom God's plan, the nineteenth-
century authors could afford to shed some tears for the aboriginal inhabitants of what was now so firmly their country. The fact of
the Indian's passing was, of course, the controlling condition
governing the appearance of the elegiac theme; the positive value
of the white triumph remained unquestioned. In practice, then,
where Mather dutifully recorded the grievances which the Indians advanced before the war broke out and then dismissed
them without refutation, the nineteenth-century writers often
admitted that the Indians had just cause, but approved the
ultimate white victory nevertheless.

In building his history of King William's War around captivity
episodes, Mather emphasized the significant mythic experience
of the early white-Indian relationship.[7] Few whites would actually
be captured by Indians, but the imagined possibilities of such an
event were of interest to all; the many living in exposed settlements or pushing the frontier westward could find the worst
hazards of their own situation actualized in the captivity
narrative—literal extinction at the hands of the enemy or
metaphoric extinction through adoption by him. Those who were
safe from the threat of captivity could vicariously enjoy supposedly true adventures which were not geographically far
removed from their own lives. For the sober-minded seventeenth

century, the captivity theme provided the pleasures of fiction without frivolity.[8]

In the standard seventeenth- and early eighteenth-century captivity narrative, the first person point of view generally precludes any larger perspective on events than the author's own experience.[9] Typically, the narrative begins with an Indian raid in which some whites are massacred, usually in brief but revolting detail, and some, including the author, are carried away. The main body of the account is devoted to the hardships of the captivity period, which concludes with the author's return to civilized society. In captivity narratives of this period, the Indians are invariably the one-dimensional, satanic beasts of Matherian depiction, whose chief characteristic is wanton cruelty. There is seldom an indication that Indian aggression was provoked by whites in any way; ordinarily a captivity begins, as the *Narrative of the Captivity and Restauration of Mrs. Mary Rowlandson* (1682) does, with the Indians swooping down on a dwelling or settlement: "On the tenth of February 1675, Came the Indians with great numbers upon Lancaster."[10] The account continues with the massacre scene and arbitrary cruelties inflicted along the line of march. Except for noting that a captive was unable to keep up or had tried to escape, the author-victims of captivity accounts offer no explanation for the sudden dispatching of prisoners, but convey the impression that such acts, like the gratuitous attack on an innocent civilian population, were examples of a capricious bloodlust:

> There was one who was chopt into the head with a Hatchet, and stript naked, and yet was crawling up and down. It is a solemn sight to see so many Christians lying in their blood, some here, and some there, like a company of Sheep torn by Wolves, All of them stript naked by a company of hell-hounds, roaring, singing, ranting and insulting, as if they would have torn our very hearts out. (Rowlandson, pp. 120-121)

Given Mrs. Rowlandson's view of her captors as inspired by the devil, her failure to speculate on a reasonable motive for their behavior is understandable. Both her precarious existence on a survival level and the Puritan reduction of Indians to subhuman status explain the flat report: "My Mistresses Papoos was sick, and it died that night, and there was one benefit in it, that there was more room" (*ibid.*, p. 144). Her underlying assumption that white Christians should thrive and Indians disappear from the earth sometimes finds forthright utterance in a direct emotional response: "I cannot but take notice of the strange providence of God in preserving the heathen" (*ibid.*, p. 131).[11] On other occasions she can dutifully voice the accepted Puritan rationale that "our perverse and evil carriages in the sight of the Lord, have so offended him, that instead of turning his hand against them, the Lord feeds and nourishes them up to be a scourge to the whole Land" (*ibid.*, p. 160).

While some good treatment of captives may be recorded in captivity narratives, it is not named as such or attributed to Indian kindness. Mrs. Rowlandson writes:

> As we went along, they killed a Deer, with a young one in her, they gave me a piece of the Fawn, and it was so young and tender, that one might eat the bones as well as the flesh, and yet I thought it very good. When night came on we sate down; it rained, but they quickly got up a Bark Wigwam, where I lay dry that night. I looked out in the morning, and many of them had line [*sic*] in the rain all night, I saw by their Reaking. Thus the Lord dealt mercifully with me many times. (*ibid.,* p. 146)

The evil of the captive's situation proceeds from the Indians, the good from the Lord. Similarly, Mrs. Rowlandson merely states that her son's new master "told me he loved him: and he should not want" (*ibid.*, p. 144), without commenting on either the Indian's kindly disposition or her own peace of mind on being reassured that her son would be well treated. In reporting such incidents Mrs. Rowlandson is limited not only by her conception of the Indian as devil's agent, but by the sheer weight of physical suffering so vividly recollected in tranquility.

For all that he habitually mortified the flesh with fasts and vigils, Cotton Mather could not duplicate the feeling of a day-today battle with exhaustion or the delight in a scrap of unwholesome food which Mrs. Rowlandson's simple language communicates, but he was able to equal the moral fervor and the fearful substance of her narrative. Mather's scope was larger than that of any individual seventeenth-century captivity writer, but their attitude toward the Indian was the same, their terms interchangeable. All could accept the description advanced by the anonymous author of the introduction to Mrs. Rowlandson's narrative: "Atheisticall, proud, wild, barbarous, bruitish (in one word) diabolicall creatures" (*ibid.*, p. 116). The idea held by Roger Williams, John Eliot, and Daniel Gookin—that Indians were at least inferior human beings—was only a historical footnote to the portrait painted by Puritan New England.[12]

2

Other early pre-fictive pictures of Indians exist, such as those created by the more tolerant men who settled Virginia. From the founding of that colony, Virginia's government regarded Indians as worthy opponents rather than demons. However popular the gothic Indian engendered by the Puritan chroniclers, another image of the Indian, which would establish itself in nineteenth-century thought, originated in the Virginia tradition. In the writings of Captain John Smith and his men, Powhatan was habitually and seriously referred to as "the great King" or "Emperor": "With such a Majestie as I cannot expresse, nor yet have often seene, either in Pagan or Christian."[13] In action as well as in title, the king proved to be as wily as a European monarch, alternating eloquent discourse about peace with plotting against and attacking the colonists. Smith's writings maintain a dual attitude of respect and distrust toward Powhatan, just as they combine a judgment that Indian culture is essentially inferior with a recognition that it functions well in its own terms: "Although the countrie people be very barbarous, yet have they amongst them such government, as that their Magistrats for good commanding, and their people for du [*sic*] subjection and obeying, excell many places that would be counted very civill."[14]

A century after Smith's *True Relation,* Robert Beverley's *The*

History and Present State of Virginia (1705) attempted a thorough explication of all aspects of Indian life. What emerges is a noble savage concept of Indians before their contact with the English: "Happy . . . in their simple State of Nature, and in their enjoyment of Plenty, without the Curse of Labour."[15] Understanding the impossibility of Indians returning to that felicitous natural state, now that the English "have introduc'd Drunkenness and Luxury amongst them, which have multiply'd their Wants,"[16] Beverley recommends intermarriage as the best way to acquaint the Indians speedily with the benefits of civilization and to minimize Indian troubles for the colonists. Had this been the policy from the very beginning, he speculates, "I can't but think it wou'd have been happy for that Country [Virginia] had they embraced this Proposal."[17]

William Byrd's *History of the Dividing Line* (1737-1738) advances views similar to Beverley's. Writing at a time when the approximately five thousand Virginia Indians John Smith had observed had been reduced in a century's time to two hundred, Byrd was able to appreciate, like Beverley, the deleterious effect of the English presence on the native inhabitants.[18] And, like Beverley, he believed that only the race death of radical assimilation could halt the literal death of the Indians:

> There is but one way of converting these poor infidels and reclaiming them from barbarity, and that is charitably to intermarry with them. . . . All nations of men have the same natural dignity, and we all know that very bright talents may be lodged under a very dark skin. The principal difference between one people and another proceeds only from the different opportunities of improvement.[19]

Byrd's was an enlightened view, indeed, but several circumstances qualify his optimistic theory of racial difference. First, although the cause is environmental rather than inherent, the Indians as they exist—either in isolation or in contact with the English—are barbarians, clearly inferior to whites. They may be saved only by ceasing to be Indians in any discernible way: Byrd conjectures that had the first settlers been willing to intermarry, the Indians' heathen worship *and* their dark complexions would already be conditions of the past. With a tolerant approach and a different theory, Byrd arrives at a conclusion scarcely more satisfying to the Indian *qua* Indian than the Puritan position. His more open attitude and good will, so characteristic of this group of prominent Virginian writers, is, of course, more palatable to the modern temper than the bigotry of the Puritans, but either view—definition as devil or as savage—led to the same end: a being identifiable as an Indian must cease to exist. Once this idea became widely accepted, the choice was, in the the words of General Sullivan's Revolutionary War toast: "Civilization or death to all American savages."

It was the optimistic hope of Thomas Jefferson that American Indians would be civilized rather than destroyed.[20] The best-known explication of this position, whose outline is at least apparent in the Virginian writings already discussed, is found in Jefferson's *Notes on the State of Virginia* (1784). Like Gray and Byrd, Jefferson explains aspects of Indian life environmentally: "They raise fewer children than we do. The causes of this are to be found, not in a difference of nature, but of circumstance."[21] Differences in behavior did not deprive the Indian of an essential humanity in Jefferson's eyes, as they did in Mather's, but the problem of the Indian as Other and as Inferior still persisted under this more charitable dispensation. After remarking that it took Europe many centuries to produce a Newton, Jefferson hastens to add: "I do not mean to deny that there are varieties in the race of man, distinguished by their powers both of body and mind. I believe there are, as I see to be the case in the races of other animals."[22] What was formulated by the Puritans in religious terms now became national: Americans saw the Indian, in Roy Harvey Pearce's words, as "bound inextricably in a primitive past, a primitive society, and a primitive environment, to be destroyed by God, Nature, and Progress to make way for Civilized Man."[23]

3

In spite of the development of a concept of the Indian as merely inferior rather than evil, the great popularity of the captivity narratives, coupled with the Indian role in the French and Indian and Revolutionary wars, reinforced the Puritan image of the devilish heathen sent to plague the settlement of the new world.[24] Before the idea of savagism could have a meliorating effect on literary images of the Indian, the one-dimensional "bad" Indian passed from the flourishing genre of the captivity narrative into fiction.[25] The initial and continued success of this figure is attributable to the employment of the captivity episode as the central plot action of fiction containing Indian characters. Guilty as they were of ravaging homesteads, massacreing settlers, torturing and abusing captives and threatening them with loss of identity through assimilation, Indians who captured whites could only be evil.

Throughout the period of American literature when fiction prominently featuring Indians was standard fare, this Indian of the Puritan imagination endured, elaborated upon but not basically altered.[26] Whatever the Indian might have been in isolation—and a number of authors could grant him to have been a noble savage—once the fatal confrontation of the two cultures had taken place, the bad Indian became the stereotype of what Indians must be for whites. This was inevitable because "civilization or death" proved to be, as Byrd's unconscious logic demonstrated so inexorably, no choice. From the destruction of the praying Indian communities during King Philip's War and beyond the Cherokee Trail of Tears to Wounded Knee, history repeatedly negated white fantasies of civilizing the Indian in any viable or permanent way.[27] The desire of "the most grasping nation on the globe"[28] to dispossess the Indian was simply stronger than the proselytizing impulse.

The amount of freedom from real events which historical fiction enjoys was insufficient to rewrite American history with a happy ending for the Indian, nor could white authors really wish to do that. History, Progress, Nationalism, Civilization, Religion, and Race all found the Indian unacceptable, and in addition, plot exigencies demanded that he play the role of evil captor. Nevertheless, the counterimage introduced by the Virginians and reiterated by prominent students of the Indian, in conjunction with the passing of a real Indian presence from the Republic, produced a sympathy for the Indian which most of these writers exhibit. What they could do within their fictive worlds to express this attitude was to succeed, as conspicuously as life had failed, in civilizing individual Indians. Provided that certain rigid requirements were adhered to, fiction could partially approve of the Indian in the sense of a "good" counterstereotype: he must only be the exception to the rule of the evil captor Indian and, in spite of all his virtues, go down to defeat in the end. In fiction as in life, there was little hope for the integrity of Indian identity.

NOTES

1. "Historical Discourse at Concord," *Miscellanies*, vol. XI of *The Works of Ralph Waldo Emerson* (Boston, 1878), p. 62.
2. Letter to Governor Bradford in William Bradford, *Bradford's History "Of Plimoth Plantation"* (Boston, 1901), p. 197.
3. *Decennium Luctuosum*, in *Narratives of the Indian Wars 1675-1699*, ed. Charles H. Lincoln (New York, 1913), p. 184. Further references will appear in the text.
4. The commonplace justification both early and late in American history was that a peripatetic hunting people must bow before the superior claim of cultivators of the earth. As Mourt's *Relation*, p. 148, formulates this principle: "It is lawful now to take a land which none useth, and make use of it" (*A Relation or Journall of the beginning and proceedings of the English Plantation settled at Plimoth in New England* [London, 1622], facsimile rpt., ed. Henry Martyn Dexter [Boston, 1865]). The Virginian Robert Gray advances several arguments: first, Indians range over the land like animals, and thus own none of it; second, they are willing to give up or sell the land whites want in any case; third, a Christian king can lawfully "make warre upon barbarous and savage people, and such as live under no lawfull or warrantable government" (*A Good Speed to Virginia* [London, 1609], facsimile rpt., ed. Wesley F. Craven [New York, 1937], sig. C3ᵛ C4ʳ, quote on C4ʳ).
5. See Wilcomb E. Washburn, *Red Man's Land: White Man's Law* (New York, 1971), p. 33: "Nothing is so frequently recorded in the earliest chronicles as the warmth of the reception accorded the first colonists."
6. Frederick Jackson Turner, "The First Official Frontier of the Massachusetts Bay," *The Frontier in American History* (New York, 1920), p. 46, states: "The Massachusetts frontiersman like his western successor hated the Indians"; cf. Lucy Lockwood Hazard, *The Frontier in American Literature* (New York, 1927), p. 12: "From the rifling of the grave of an Indian child by the Plymouth colonists, to the systematic extermination of the Pequot War, the journals of Puritan New England breathe the proverbial conviction that the only good Indian is a dead Indian."
7. Richard Slotkin, *Regeneration Through Violence* (Middletown, Conn., 1973), p. 23, refers to the captivity theme as the "Puritan myth of America."

8. Richard Van Der Beets, "The Indian Captivity Narrative as Ritual," *American Literature* 43 (1972), pp. 548-562, finds the enduring appeal of the captivity story to reside in its structure of ritual acts and patterns which embody fundamental truths of experience. Most significant is the archetypal heroic journey, which proceeds from Separation through Transformation to Return (p. 562).

9. Mather places a number of captivity stories within the context of a larger action, King Wiliiam's War, but the effect is little different from that of an isolated captivity episode, i.e., that the Indians had no humanly comprehensible motive for their actions against the whites, but were moved by devilish or bestial impulses.

10. In *Narratives of the Indian Wars*, p. 118. Further references will appear in the text. Mrs. Rowlandson's *Narrative* was the first American prose best seller, according to Frank Luther Mott, *Golden Multitudes* (New York, 1947), p. 20; he omits from consideration Bibles, cookbooks, and hymnals.

11. The Puritans generally believed that the plague which decimated the Massachusetts Indians some years before the colonists' arrival was divinely ordained to foster white settlement. As Cotton Mather writes: "The woods were almost cleared of those pernicious creatures, to make room for a *better growth*" (*Magnalia Christi Americana* [New York, 1967], vol. I, p. 51).

12. Roy Harvey Pearce, *Savagism and Civilization*, rev. ed. (Baltimore, 1967), p. 29, finds that both Eliot and Williams subscribed to a satanic influence in Indian life, although unlike the majority of Puritans they believed it could be combated.

13. Captain John Smith, *A True Relation* (London, 1608), in *Narratives of Early Virginia, 1606-1625*, ed. Lyon Gardiner Tyler (New York, 1930), p. 54; cf. the Puritans' contemptuous references to "king" Philip.

14. Captain John Smith, *A Map of Virginia: with a Description of the Countrey, the Commodities, People, Government and Religion* (Oxford, 1612), in Tyler, *Narratives of Early Virginia*, p. 113.

15. Robert Beverley, *The History and Present State of Virginia*, ed. Louis B. Wright (Chapel Hill, 1947), p. 233.

16. Ibid.

17. Ibid., p. 30. In the 1722 edition, this suggestion is withdrawn, but cf. Thomas Jefferson, "Advice to Indian Chiefs," (Dec. 21, 1808), *Letters and Addresses of Thomas Jefferson*, ed. William B. Parker and Jonas Viles (New York, 1905), p. 190: "You will mix with us by marriage, your blood will run in our veins, and will spread with us over this great island."

18. Smith, *A Map of Virginia*, p. 98, cites this figure as the Indian population within a sixty-mile radius of Jamestown. Byrd notes that the Indian town of Nottoway which he visited had a population of two hundred and comprised "the only Indians of any consequence now remaining within the limits of Virginia" (*The Prose Works of William Byrd*, ed. Louis B. Wright [Cambridge, Mass., 1966], p. 219).

19. Byrd, *History of the Dividing Line*, p. 22. His remarks were anticipated more than a century earlier by Robert Gray, sig. C2^r: "It is not the nature of men, but the education of men, which make them barbarous and uncivill, and therefore chaunge the education of men, and you shall see that their nature will be greatly rectified and corrected."

20. Bernard W. Sheehan, *Seeds of Extinction* (Chapel Hill, 1973), discusses the

intellectual origin of this view, its implementation, and its ultimate failure.

21. Thomas Jefferson, *Notes on the State of Virginia* (New York, 1801), p. 91.
22. Ibid., p. 97.
23. Pearce, *Savagism and Civilization*, p. 4.
24. Mott, *Golden Multitudes*, pp. 20-22: of the eight seventeenth-century American best sellers, two were captivity narratives: Mrs. Rowlandson's *Narrative* and Jonathan Dickinson's *Journal; or God's Protecting Providence* (1699). Another best selling captivity narrative followed early in the eighteenth century: John Williams's *Redeemed Captive* (1707).
25 "Savagism" is Pearce's term for the white idea that Indians had a coherent culture which was primitive and inferior to white civilization.
26. The frontier romance began to be popular in the 1820s and was successful during the 1830s and 1840s. While it continued to be produced and read during the 1850s, its popularity declined. At this time it also passed into the subliterature of the dime novel.
27. At the same time, the efforts made to escape the historical paradigm should not be overlooked. Wilcomb E. Washburn, *Red Man's Land: White Man's Law*, is one of many scholars who discuss the various governmental policies and programs directed toward the Jeffersonian ideal of cultural assimilation of the Indian.
28. Alexis De Tocqueville, *Democracy in America*, Henry Reeve text, rev. Francis Bowen and Phillips Bradley (New York, 1945), vol. I, p. 347.

PART 1

The White Fantasy World of the Frontier Romance

Man, my wooden head is splittin'—that's because
You're in my mental reservation.

John Lefeather, "HI, PALEFACE"

By the beginning of the nineteenth century, when a substantial amount of fiction using Indian characters began to appear, the initial shock of confrontation between two disparate cultures was long over in the settled regions which produced the nation's first authors. While the drama would be reenacted repeatedly on the moving frontier in the first half of the coming century, it would not deviate from the pattern imposed by the pilgrims upon the seaboard Indians. Only with the complete passing of autonomous Indian tribes in the generation after the Civil War would any change take place in either history or fiction.

For this reason, the body of fiction containing Indian characters and written between 1790 and 1860 constitutes a distinct and coherent genre which will be referred to in this study as the frontier romance. To quote Hugh Henry Brackenridge's Indian treaty-maker, it can be said of the contributions to this genre: "These things are now reduced to a system: and it is so well known to those who are engaged in the traffic, that we think nothing of it."[1] Conventions were quickly established and little questioned: a standard plotting device, stereotyped characters, and a racist-nationalistic philosophy of white-Indian relations are shared by almost all authors who use Indians in their fiction.

The prevailing attitude of the frontier romance is aptly expressed by Francis Parkman:

> For the most part, a civilized white man can discover very few points of sympathy between his own nature and that of an Indian. With every disposition to do justice to their good qualities, he must be conscious that an impassable gulf lies between him and his red brethren. Nay, so alien to himself do they appear, that, after breathing the air of the prairie for a few months or weeks, he begins to look upon them as a troublesome and dangerous species of wild beast.[2]

A few notable writers believed Indians to be "much more like ourselves than unlike,"[3] but those who wrote within the genre of the frontier romance exemplify Parkman's position. Whatever their good intentions, the "impassable gulf" intervened and negated them. Unable to perceive a common humanity shared by Indian and white, and thus bound by a concept of the Indian as both Other and Inferior, these writers could not achieve the insight into their Indian characters necessary for valid aesthetic creation. Like Benjamin West's portrait of Colonel Guy Johnson, their fiction points up the splendor of the prepossessing white man in the foreground and consigns the Indian to a shadowy and implicitly inferior background.[4] As literature, the frontier romance exemplifies the clash of aesthetic and nonaesthetic demands within a fictive construct and the problem of writing fiction about a radically different culture. As cultural document, it reflects the racism and nationalism characteristic of the society which produced it.

NOTES

1. Hugh Henry Brackenridge, *Modern Chivalry*, ed. Lewis Leary (New Haven, 1965), p. 74.
2. Francis Parkman, *The Oregon Trail* (Boston, 1891), pp. 267-268.
3. *The Journal of Henry D. Thoreau*, ed. Bradford Torrey and Francis H. Allen (Boston, 1906), vol. XI, p. 437.
4. The painting also illustrates other facets of the white-Indian relationship commonly depicted in frontier romances. Colonel Johnson's moccasins symbolize the white appropriation of aspects of the Indian way of life suitable for a wilderness existence. His prominently displayed rifle images white technological superiority.

1

Nationalism and the Frontier Romance

'Tis true, the European campaigns for the *numbers* of men appearing in them, compared with the little numbers that appear in these American actions, may tempt the reader to make a very diminutive business of our whole Indian war: but we who felt ourselves assaulted by unknown numbers of *devils in flesh* on every side of us, and knew that our minute numbers employ'd in the service against them, were proportionably more to *us* than mighty *legions* are to nations that have existed as many centuries as our colonies have years in the world, can scarce forbear taking the colours in the Sixth Book of Milton to describe our story: and speaking of our Indians in as high terms as Virgil of his *pismires: It nigrum campis agmen!*

Cotton Mather, MAGNALIA CHRISTI AMERICANA

1

Between the American Revolution and the emergence of the frontier romance as a recognizable genre in the 1820s, a number of demands for cultural emancipation from England were made.[1] An independent literature was especially wanted because, as Noah Webster wrote: "We shall always be in leading strings till we resort to original writers and original principles instead of taking upon trust what English writers please to give us."[2] What these "original principles" might be, or what elements of American life might be fashioned successfully into a national literature, were not at first clearly defined; what mattered in the earliest period of nationhood was to call for action. Thus, Samuel Woodworth's prefatory remarks to his venture into the frontier romance in 1816 anticipate approval simply on the grounds of being American: *"The Champions of Freedom* cannot fail of being patronised by Americans, even though dressed in homespun uniform, coarse and inelegant. It is of domestic manufacture, and cannot displease the eye of a patriot."* Still earlier, in the preface to *Edgar Huntly* (1801), Charles Brockden Brown had asserted a more substantive claim:

> that of calling forth the passions and engaging the sympathy of the reader by means hitherto unemployed by preceding authors. Puerile superstition and exploded manners, Gothic castles and chimeras, are the materials usually employed for this end. The incidents of Indian Hostility, and the perils of the Western wilderness, are far more suitable; and for a native of America to overlook these would admit of no apology.

At the time, however, neither Brown nor other writers of prose fiction were ready to utilize this frontier subject matter.

Before the 1790s, in effect before the American Revolution had been assimilated by writers, the captivity narratives provided a sufficient treatment of the conflict of cultures.[3] After the Revolution, the impulse of nationalism began to find expression in a demand for both American-authored imaginative literature, including fiction, and native themes. For all their simple virtues, captivity narratives were inadequate as vehicles for nationalism and as art: whatever the embellishments and exaggerations which came to be incorporated into these accounts during the latter half of the eighteenth century, they remained purportedly authentic chronicles of limited scope.[4]

2

As sentiment for a national literature increased, given impetus by a second victory over the British in the War of 1812, Indians naturally received further scrutiny as a possible subject for fiction. Theodore Dehon, in his Phi Beta Kappa address, "Upon the Importance of Literature to Our Country" (1807), proposed the

Indian as "the chief hope for an original American literature."[5]
William Tudor, Jr.'s Phi Beta Kappa address of 1815, which
appeared in the *North American Review*, compared Indians to
Homeric heroes at length: the original Indians, uncontaminated
by white association, "possessed so many traits in common with
some of the nations of antiquity, that they perhaps exhibit the
counterpart of what the Greeks were in the heroick ages, and
particularly the Spartans during the vigour of their institutions."[6]
In another issue of the *North American Review*, he advances as
worthy of literary treatment "the important part played by the
various Indian tribes, particularly the Six Nations, whose history
is abundantly interesting."[7]

What very likely translated the academic speculation into the
first wave of frontier romances was the availability of an
adaptable pattern in Scott's *Waverley* novels and the popularity of
Yamoyden, a long romantic poem about King Philip's War which
was published in 1820.[8] The separate success of historical
romance and Indian subject matter made the union of this form
and content irresistible. John G. Palfrey's enthusiastic review of
Yamoyden in the prestigious *North American Review* concludes by
particularly commending the white-Indian encounter to writers
of fiction: "Whoever in this country first attains the rank of a first
rate writer of fiction, we venture to predict, will lay his scene here.
The wide field is ripe for the harvest, and scarce a sickle has yet
touched it."[9] William Howard Gardiner's review of *The Spy*, which
also appeared in the *North American Review*, similarly suggests the
writing of romance built around Indian characters:

> We are confident that the savage warrior, who was not less
> beautiful and bold in his figurative diction, than in his
> attitude of death . . . patiently enduring cold, hunger, and
> watchfulness, while he crouched in the night-grass like the
> tiger expecting his prey, and finally springing on the un-
> suspicious victim with that war-whoop, which struck terror to
> the heart of the boldest planter of New England in her early
> day, is no mean instrument of the sublime and terrible of
> human agency.[10]

Obviously enamoured of the same savage menace that Gardiner

promotes, R. C. Sands, a year later, commends the American aborigine to the attention of native literature:

> If scenes of unparalleled torture and indefatigable endurance, persevering vengeance and unfailing friendship, hair-breadth escapes and sudden ambush; if the horrors of the gloomy forests and unexplored caverns, tenanted by the most terrible of banditti; if faith in wild predictions and entire submission of the soul to the power of ancient legends and visionary prophecies, are useful to the poet or romancer, here they may be found in abundance and endless variety.[11]

Even after frontier romances had inundated the country, literary figures continued to expatiate on the fitness of the Indian for romance: such well-known writers as John Greenleaf Whittier and N. P. Willis in the thirties and Edgar Allan Poe and William Gilmore Simms in the forties reiterated the Indians' literary virtues. Poe's review of Cooper's Indian romance *Wyandotté* praised its theme, life in the wilderness, as "one of intrinsic and universal interest, appealing to the heart of man in all phases."[12] Simms proclaimed that the fate of the Indian "may be wrought into forms as nobly statuesque as any that drew a nation's homage to the splintered summits of Olympus."[13] Elsewhere he recommends the stories of such Indians as Osceola, Tecumseh, and Logan as subjects which "in a community even partially civilized would have been worthy of all fame and honour in succeeding times."[14]

Not everyone agreed that Indians constituted a valuable resource for American literature. Most of the dissenters deemed it a narrow and quickly exhausted vein, one unsuited to the literary needs of an advanced people. At a time when little use of Indians had been made by fiction, John Bristed predicted that "a novel describing these miserable barbarians, their squaws, and papooses, would not be very interesting to the present race of American readers."[15] Seven years later a review of *Escalala*, a poem about Indians, opens with the flat assertion that "the character of the North American Indian affords but a barren theme for poetry."[16] The disparity between primitive and civilized which Bristed had considered detrimental to possible Indian fiction is also remarked by the *Escalala* reviewer:

> The Indian has a lofty and commanding spirit, but its deeply marked traits are few, stern, and uniform, never running into those delicate and innumerable shades, which are spread over the surface of civilised society, giving the fullest scope to poetic invention, and opening a store of incidents inexhaustible, and obedient to the call of fancy.[17]

After a substantial number of frontier romances had been written, reviewers still invoked the cultural gulf between reader and subject as a prime obstacle to its success. Apropos of Cooper's first two Leatherstocking novels, Granville Mellen wrote:

> It appears certain to us that there is a barrenness of the novelist's peculiar circumstance in the life of a savage . . . and it must necessarily be a troublesome tax upon the ingenuity to throw a moderate share of interest round a narrative founded upon events connected with these simple, silent creatures . . . . There is not enough in the character and life of these poor natives to furnish the staple of a novel.[18]

The focus of critical disdain for the literary Indian was centered in the paucity of interesting activities to be found in his primitive way of life and in the boredom which enforced repetition would presumably generate in civilized readers. As early as 1826, one writer complained that Indians were so limited as a subject that "almost every production into which they are introduced partakes more or less of the same character and abounds in incidents and sentiments that are similar, and evidently copies of one common original."[19]

In the same year a reviewer of *The Last of the Mohicans* queried: "How many novels can he [Cooper] afford to write? How many changes can he ring upon scalping, shooting, tomahawking, etc.?"[20] Constantly turning from his review of *The Red Rover* to consider Cooper's frontier romances, Mellen similarly objects: "Once done, it is, comparatively, done for ever; and our complaint is, that we are overdoing the matter."[21] Significantly, he concluded: "The Indians as a people, offer little or nothing that can be reasonably expected to excite the novelist, formed as his taste must be on a foreign standard."[22] Although he failed to see its implications, Mellen's observation was accurate: having no interest in Indians *per se*, novelists would only concern themselves with Indians in contact with whites; having little or no firsthand experience with Indians and many preconceptions about them, they would invariably create lifeless and narrowly conceived stereotypes in their works.

Critics who saw no literary potential in the Indian thus failed to perceive what supporters and writers of the frontier romance seemed to know instinctively: that the genre would not only be written by white authors for a white audience; it would also be about whites, and especially their superiority to Indians. Tudor, for example, enthusiastically commends the Indian to the novelist for "perilous and romantick adventures, figurative and eloquent harangues, strong contrasts and important interests,"[23] but the incidents he employs to illustrate these generalities are all white-Indian episodes which glorify whites. As the modern critic Benjamin T. Spencer states: "The Indian was to appear only as grist for the conqueror's mill, not as a sensitive being fit for tragic, epic, or lyric treatment in his own right."[24]

The unfriendly reviewer of *Escalala* had some inkling of this state of affairs when he noted that "seemingly aware of these difficulties [the barrenness of the Indian theme], the author of *Escalala* has employed the agency of civilised men, in filling up some of the most important parts of his poem."[25] By the time of Simms the formulation was more forthright: the native writer must "learn to dwell often upon the narratives of the brave fathers who first broke ground in the wilderness, who fought or treated with the red men."[26] As Harriet V. Cheney wrote in her early novel *A Peep at the Pilgrims* (1824):

> The Indians continued their hostilities, which were marked by the most atrocious cruelties that ever harrowed the feelings of humanity . . . . Nothing but that persevering energy and unwavering confidence in divine protection, which so remarkably characterized the venerable pilgrims of

New-England, could have enabled them to endure such complicated trials.

The title of Mrs. Cheney's book accurately indicates her subject, but many a work given the name of an Indian focuses largely upon the white characters. John Shecut's *Ish-Noo-Ju-Lut-Sche,* for example, is dedicated to the "honored and truly respected descendants of the venerated Knickerbockers, or primitive settlers of 'Der Nieu Niederlands' . . . designed to transmit to posterity the integrity, virtue, and patriotism of those illustrious personages."

Writers who failed to give the white side its due in the confrontation with Indians were taken to task by critics. Palfrey's landmark review of *Yamoyden* praises "the very happy use which the writers have made of their reading in the antiquities of the Indians,"[27] but faults the role assigned to whites in the poem: "But we doubt whether poetically, and we do not doubt whether historically speaking it was best to represent the settlers as entirely in the wrong, and the Indians as wholly in the right" (p. 485). Palfrey's own attitude is revealed by a disquisition on history which precedes the discussion of the poem. "We are glad," he begins, "that somebody has at last found out the unequalled fitness of our early history for the purposes of a work of fiction" (p. 480). This leads not to a consideration of *Yamoyden's* noble red men, the subject of the poem, but to a long paean on the white settlers:

> The men who stayed by their comfortable homes to quarrel with the church and behead the king, were but an inferior race to those more indignant if not more aggrieved, who left behind them all that belongs to the recollections of infancy and the fortunes of maturer life . . . to lay the foundations of a religious community in a region then far less known to them than the North Western Coast of our continent is now to us. . . . Wrong or right, every thing about these men was at least prominent and high-toned. (pp. 480-481)

The early colonists appear to be ideal types: "Consummate

gentlemen and statesmen, like Winthrop, . . . soldiers, intrepid and adventurous like Standish and Church" (p. 481). Opposed to these heroes are the Indians: "Phlegmatic but fierce, inconstant though unimpassioned, hard to excite and impossible to soothe, cold in friendship and insatiable in revenge" (p. 483). Elsewhere the debunker of Philip's greatness, Palfrey castigates the views of the authors of *Yamoyden* as more romantic than historical, more likely derived "from Mr. Irving's life of Philip . . . than from any graver authority" (p. 485).[28] Both the nature of his treatment of whites and Indians and the small amount of space he devotes to the latter in proportion to the former more clearly presage the frontier romance than anything *Yamoyden* itself does.

3

As Palfrey envisioned, the most obvious way in which American literature can serve as a vehicle for nationalism is in depicting the triumph of whites who were willing to become a new people and to wrest the land by violence from the native inhabitants and from those whites who held to their Old World identities. Thus, fiction which takes place during the French and Indian Wars shows the colonists defeating the French and their Indian allies; fiction of the Revolution shows them defeating the British and their Indian allies. When no foreign whites are involved in the action, the American settlers are victorious over Indians alone: Indians exist in the frontier romance primarily to be killed by whites.

At the beginning of *The Prairie Flower*, the work of one of the least reflective of frontier romancers, Emerson Bennett, one young man proposes to another that they go West to " 'hunt, fish, trap, shoot Indians, anything, everything, so we manage to escape ennui, and have plenty of adventure!' " The distinctively American rite of Indian-killing is not so openly acknowledged by James Kirke Paulding, who refers to an encounter with Indians as the initiation ritual into manhood:

Young men bordering on the frontiers were accustomed almost universally to commence the business of this world with a trading voyage among the savages of the borders. Previous to assuming the post and character of manhood, it was considered an almost indispensable obligation to undertake and complete some enterprise of this kind, replete with privations and dangers. (*The Dutchman's Fireside*)

The vague allusion at the end of the passage covers the possibility which is always actualized in the frontier romance: the proof of manhood not by the unglamorous activity of trading with the Indians but by killing them. More explicitly, a frontiersman tells an uninitiated stranger in Robert Montgomery Bird's *Nick of the Woods*: " 'When you kill an Injun yourself, I reckon . . . you will be willing to take all the honor that can come of it, without leaving it to be scrambled after by others.' " The patriotic aspect of Indian-killing is asserted by another frontiersman in the same novel: " 'I go for the doctrine that every able-bodied man should sarve his country and his neighbors, and fight their foes; and them that does is men and gentlemen, and them that don't is cowards and rascals, that's my idear.' " The large numbers of Indians killed in frontier romances indicate that such a credo was subscribed to by the writers in the genre.[29]

In spite of their endless avowals to do justice to the Indian, these authors could not put aside history, which showed the white man's triumph over the native inhabitants, or their own feelings of racial and cultural superiority. They saw themselves as the measure of man, and the Indians, by this standard, were sadly deficient. Most of the frontier romancers make some statement like the one which opens the anonymous *Christian Indian*: "It must always be a subject of regret to the true-hearted American, that the soil he now possesses was the price of plunder, and persecution, and bloodshed, to its original owners." But none were willing to place the Indians' claims to the continent above the white man's: the same book ends on a note of satisfaction that "cultivated fields and thronged city have replaced trackless deserts and barren moors. . . . We compare again and again the past and the present, and see in our own superior blessings, the realization, almost of all the glowing and bright anticipations of the early sage."[30]

From the earliest settlement, apologists had advanced some version of justification by cultivation to rationalize the expropriation of the Indian, an argument which continued to have great appeal in the nineteenth century. As William Henry Harrison demanded rhetorically: "Is one of the fairest portions of the globe to remain in a state of nature, the haunt of a few wretched savages, when it seems destined by the Creator to give support to a large population and to be the seat of civilization?"[31] At the end of the century Theodore Roosevelt answered: "The settler and pioneer have at bottom had justice on their side; this great continent could not have been kept as nothing but a game preserve for squalid savages."[32] Saved from starvation by Indian corn, the first colonists had reason to know that some Indians did cultivate the land, but even had this been true of all, the cultivation pronouncements made by Harrison and Roosevelt contained an equally potent underlying argument: the Indians were savages whose failure to cultivate was simply a convenient indicator of their great inferiority to the white man. When in the early 1770s colonists broke the crown law by settling on Indian lands, Governor Dunmore of Virginia observed: "Nor can they be easily brought to entertain any belief of the permanent obligation of Treaties made with those People, whom they consider as but little removed from the brute Creation."[33] More than a century later, in pondering why "the Phoenician factory . . . fostered the development of the Mediterranean civilization, while in America the trading post exploited the natives," Frederick Jackson Turner concluded: "The explanation of this difference is to be sought partly in race differences, partly in the greater gulf that separated the civilization of the European from the civilization of the American Indian as compared with that which parted the early Greeks and the Phoenicians."[34]

Living in an intensely nationalistic and progressive period, those members of the conquering race who elected to write frontier romances could hardly be expected to solve the historical dilemma, to find even a literary way of doing justice to the Indian. The noble savage might display virtues in a remote primitive milieu, but once he was juxtaposed to the white man, he had to be judged inferior.[35] As the authors of *Yamoyden* were reminded, sympathy for the Indian must be subordinated to a celebration of the American achievement.

The cultivation rationale, with its concomitant assumption of white superiority, quickly found its way into the frontier romance, not only through the dramatized successes of the white characters, but also through authorial comment.[36] At either the beginning or end of a work, or in both places, the writer is apt to compare past and present. Thus, M. C. Hodges's *The Mestico* concludes: "The restless, indolent, discontented Indians have been removed to their western reserve; and much of the fertile land that was wasting under their miserable tillage, now blooms under the industry of the whites." Making the same point, but less obtrusively, Mrs. Cheney has the hero of *A Peep at the Pilgrims* observe "where the wilderness of nature had yielded to the hand of cultivation, villages were arising, and the soil teemed with all the rich and varied bounties which could spring up to reward the labours of the husbandman." Characters, too, are apt to express this view. Earth, the frontiersman in James Strange French's *Elkswatawa*, defends his position to the more idealistic hero, Rolfe: " 'I believe I think as most of the whites do, and that is, that these lands are too good for them; they should be cultivated instead of lying waste for them to prowl over.' " Even the Indians are expected to appreciate the reasonableness of this argument in James McHenry's *The Wilderness*. To persuade them to free their captive, George Washington, the prophet Tonnaleuka tells the Indians: " 'The whole of this waste wilderness will yet bloom and flourish, in consequence of his great deeds and heroic virtues.' "

Another variation on the defense of white dispossession of the Indian by cultivation is Charles Fenno Hoffman's short story "Queen Meg." In the midst of a "long settled and highly cultivated district," a few boat hours from New York City, the author comes upon a household of squatter Indians: "A more wretched-looking set of objects I never saw." Evidently the matriarch of the family is of high Indian lineage: owing to "her confused ideas of what she deemed her natural rights," she haughtily rejects the idea of her progeny working as day laborers. Authorial disapproval comes down heavily on Queen Meg and her shiftless brood. Here is, in Hoffman's eyes, an excellent exemplification of why whites deserve the land: they settle and cultivate; the Indians squat and degenerate. Hawthorne or Melville might have found irony in the relative positions of Indians and whites, the transformation of rightful possessors into squatters and vice versa, but to Hoffman, Queen Meg's refusal to accept the change is merely ludicrous.

Karl Postl is more candid in exposing the reality behind the cultivation rationale. In his *Tokeah*, although Indians have been industriously cultivating the land, white hostility toward them is undiminished: "Already in those early times they began to look with an unfriendly eye upon the lawful possessors of these lands, whom they considered as a sort of nuisance that could not be too soon removed." Regardless of what use Indians make of it, whites want the land for themselves.

As James Hall admitted in his short story "The War Belt," the white acquisition of Indian land was never a historical issue:

> That the enterprising and intelligent population of the United States would spread out from the seaboard over the wilderness; that the savage must retire before civilized man . . . were propositions too evident to be concealed or denied. But it never was intended that the Indian should be driven from his hunting grounds by violence; and while a necessity, strong as the law of nature, decreed the expulsion of the mere hunter, and gave dominion to art, industry, and religion, it was always proposed that the savage should be removed by negotiation, and a just price given for the relinquishment of his possessory title.

However accurate Hall's assessment of white intentions to purchase the land, fictive and nationalistic purposes conjoined to require that the land be bought, as historically it often was, primarily by bloodshed. Beginning with the established captivity narrative sequence, author after author describes an unprovoked Indian attack which makes some whites captives. Departing from the authentic captivity narratives, they then show white retaliation: the captives must be restored and the civilized community freed from future threat. By the work's conclusion the Indians have been soundly defeated, and, as a result, the white characters will be able to "make the wilderness bloom."[37]

Because it placed the Indians totally in the wrong, such a formula was infinitely more satisfying than the land purchase policy. The Indians forfeited their right to the land by shedding the first blood; more compelling than their failure to cultivate or their other primitive characteristics, this gratuitous demonstration of innate wickedness justified not only the white claims to the continent but the extermination of the Indian. As David Brion Davis explains: "Writers had a certain justification for dwelling upon the ritual [of killing Indians], since it signified the free white man's possession of the rights and privileges of his civilization, a racial eucharist, granting secular freedom and wealth after the sacrifice of a red man's flesh and blood."[38] By slaying the Indian, European whites killed Cotton Mather's serpent in the New World garden, a rite of passage from which they emerged a new people.

4

Although the conventions of English literature which the frontier romance relied on dictated the aristocratic lineage of the white hero and heroine, these children of nobility invariably became permanent citizens of the New World. While large portions of Susannah Rowson's *Reuben and Rachel* are set in England, for example, the ending upholds an American residency in the most telling terms: those of property. Reuben is unable to inherit his English estate: "His dark complexion, the nature of his father's marriage to Oberea [an Indian] which in law would have been termed illegal, all militated against success." The hindrances of the Old World are not found in the new: in the novel's conclusion, Reuben takes possession of his father's Pennsylvania estate, marries, and settles down there. More openly didactic is the ending of *A Peep at the Pilgrims*: "Major Atherton, in the following year, revisited his native land, but the ties which once bound him to it were weakened by absence . . . . He disposed of his paternal inheritance, and returned to America, where his affections were entirely concentrated."[39] As it is described in the frontier romance, the Old World is a place where difficulties like the failure to obtain one's rightful inheritance or religious persecution are experienced. Several works use lovers who are separated in England and reunited in America.

Should a white villain be part of the plot, he is typically British, often aristocratic, and usually involved in anti-American activities. Such is the case in Gideon M. Hollister's *Mount Hope*, where the villain not only kidnaps the heroine but pursues the regicides Goffe and Whalley. In Catharine Maria Sedgwick's *Hope Leslie*, the evil Sir Philip similarly combines anti-Puritan policy with an attempted abduction of the heroine. In the more modern time of the War of 1812 the villain of Anna L. Snelling's *Kabaosa* is a British officer who has betrayed his Indian friend by seducing his wife. He plots against the American side in general, and in particular, with appropriate rant, against the white heroine: " 'When once I have her in my power, I'll make her rue this hour of insult.' " Needless to say, both the New World and the heroine are preserved from these intended British villainies.

A certain restraint and decorum are evident in intrawhite conflicts of this sort which are absent from the clash of whites and Indians. Although on opposing sides, whites share a common Western culture; they remain gentlemanly. In Eliza Lanesford Cushing's *Saratoga*, for example, the British partisan Major Courtland is gradually won over to a high opinion of the rebels by demonstrations of their fighting ability. For most of the novel's two volumes he withholds his approval of his daughter's American suitor, but after she has refused the preferred British aspirant, he acquiesces gracefully. Mutual respect for each other's country prevails between Major Courtland and the American Colonel Grahame.

On a larger scale the same kind of understanding obtains between the English and French in James Fenimore Cooper's *The Last of the Mohicans*. When Fort William Henry is forced to surrender, General Montcalm shows the English "unusual and unexpected generosity"; all is arranged in accordance with military honor. As the Munro sisters leave the fort, "the French officers, who had learned their rank, bowed often and low, forbearing, however, to intrude those attentions which they saw, with peculiar tact, might not be agreeable." In contrast to this deference, the Indian allies of the French treacherously attack the English:

> More than two thousand raving savages broke from the forest at the signal, and threw themselves across the fatal plain with instinctive alacrity. We shall not dwell on the revolting horrors that succeeded. Death was everywhere, and in his most terrific and disgusting aspects. Resistance only served to inflame the murderers, who inflicted their furious blows long after their victims were beyond the power of their resentment. The flow of blood might be likened to the outbreaking of a torrent; and, as the natives became heated and maddened by the sight, many among them even kneeled to the earth, and drank freely, exultingly, hellishly, of the crimson tide.

Groups of whites in the frontier romance are never guilty of such wanton and seemingly irrational atrocities. At times they may be forced to take harsh measures against the Indians, like the burning alive of hundreds of Pequots at Mystic, but these are depicted as rational and necessary acts, never as gratuitous barbarism.

Undoubtedly, part of the overembellishment in battle descriptions like Cooper's can be attributed to the defensiveness which American authors often displayed about the worth of their native materials. It might be true, as Palfrey asserted, that "compared with some of ours, Scottish rivers are but brooks, and Scottish forests mere thickets" (p.484),[40] but scenery was of little help. The writer needed huge deeds more than huge rivers. For the settler to reap the maximum glory, he had to overcome a foe of the first magnitude: unable to compete with the armies of Europe in size or magnificence, Indians had to excel in gruesome accomplishment—hence Cooper's hellish blood drinkers. In *Tom Hanson, the Avenger*, Samuel Young defiantly challenges the Old World to equal the horror of Indian warfare:

> Talk, ye philanthropists, of barbarity in the Dark Ages: tell of

the tyranny of superstition, of the horrors of civil wars: tell of France and her bloody scenes, when frantic with revolutionary frenzy. Yea, summon more, and let all fail in rendering a comparison to those terrible scenes of bloodshed and havoc perpetrated in the New World, amid a wilderness infested with devils in human shape.

Taking a different tack, Mrs. Cheney points out somewhat apologetically that the battle of Mystic was disproportionately significant to the small numbers involved in the fighting:

> This memorable, but almost forgotten contest,—however trifling it may appear in comparison with the more brilliant conquests of Europe, which have so often convulsed her fairest kingdoms and deluged her fields with the blood of thousands of victims to her ambition or revenge,—was notwithstanding productive of the most important consequences, and strikingly exhibits the firmness and courage of the early settlers of New-England. (*A Peep at the Pilgrims*)

Where whites are victorious, the author stresses their valor, although "the laurels of the conqueror were unhappily stained with the blood of the innocent and defenceless."

Even should an author regard an action like the attack on Mystic as white cruelty, he could scarcely reject the major assumption that the development of the American continent for white civilization was a desideratum. Daniel Thompson's *The Doomed Chief*, a romance set in the time of King Philip's War, is sympathetic to the Indians and strongly censorious of the Puritans. The white characters who hate Indians are at worst scheming hypocrites, at best honest tools of the unscrupulous villains. In contrast, the hero is a vigorous partisan of Philip's nobility. In the trial of the three Indians, which led to the outbreak of war, Thompson sums up the Puritan defects:

> Great was the displeasure of the court functionaries and their supporters, at Williams' triumphant vindication of King Philip, the great Diabolus of their prejudice, fear and

hatred; at his fearless unmasking of their disguised policy for
the subjugation of the Indians, and especially at his ungra-
cious exposure of the weakness of their testimony against the
already death-doomed prisoners.

Their corrupt system of justice, secret machinations against an
Indian policy established by treaty, and warped feeling make the
Puritans singularly unattractive, but immediately after this harsh
indictment, Thompson is forced to partially recant: in spite of
their failings, the Puritans contributed to "the still more
beneficent fabric of our present American liberty." And in spite
of the praises heaped upon the Indians, they become the familiar
"infernal scamps" and "murderous hounds," pursued by the
hero, among others, when the war gets under way. The best that
Thompson can do for his Indians is to allow them to die as they
want on their home ground rather than being sold into slavery.

An analogous situation exists in *Mount Hope*, which treats the
same historical events as *The Doomed Chief*. Its author, Gideon M.
Hollister, is a partisan of the noble savage as long as he is not in
direct conflict with the white man. Although he professes
"sympathies . . . almost equally divided" between the two sides, in
battle he portrays the standard savage of the captivity narrative
tradition, a barbaric scalper and mutilator of the wounded who is
no match for the intrepid white sharpshooters. The Indians'
nobility ultimately resides in their death, and here Hollister is
generous: "The records of Spartan and Roman fame do not
contain a sentiment more worthy of a hero when passing to the
land where his religion has taught him that valour shall be
rewarded, than the last word of the son of Miantunnamoh."

However reluctantly, writers of the frontier romance learned
the lesson which Palfrey sought to impart in his review of
Yamoyden. Should they espouse the Indian cause too ardently,
they faced the consequences predicted by Irving in his discussion
of the prospects of the Indian in American literature:

Should he [the poet] venture upon the dark story of their
wrongs and wretchedness; should he tell how they were
invaded, corrupted, despoiled; driven from their native

abodes and the sepulchres of their fathers; hunted like wild
beasts about the earth; and sent down with violence and
butchery to the grave; posterity will either turn with horror
and incredulity from the tale, or blush with indignation at the
inhumanity of their forefathers.[41]

Horror and incredulity, or the blush of shame, would have been
unpleasant reactions to elicit from a reading public. Nor could
they comfortably coexist with a number of ideas sacred to
nineteenth-century Americans: the inevitability of an advanced
people supplanting a primitive one,[42] the appropriateness of a
Christian supplanting a heathen society, and the greatness of the
country's pioneer forebears. If writers believed, like Thompson,
that white dealing with the Indians constituted a "damning
record . . . of turpitude and wrong," they also had to believe that
the best of all possible choices had been made. As James Kirke
Paulding piously appraised the situation: "The red man is gone,
and the white man is in his place. Such are the mutations of the
world! Shall we lament them? No. It is the will and the work of
Him that made all, governs all, disposes all; and it is all for the
best." Mrs. Snelling, in contrast, entertains the shadow of a doubt:
"It is *almost* with feelings of self-reproach that we look back upon
the past" [emphasis added]. More than counterbalancing the
destruction of the Indians was the creation of the mighty nation
of which Thompson and his literary confreres were part.

5

Although the desirability of white dispossession of the Indian
and the necessity of doing so violently were assumptions shared
by most writers of the frontier romance, it did not follow that they
should be utterly heedless of the Indian's passing. Sympathy for
the foreign powers expelled from the North American continent
was uncalled for; the French, Dutch, Spanish, and British had
nation-states in Europe to retreat to. Indians, on the other hand,
were only able to leave America feet first; already virtually
exterminated along the Eastern seaboard, they seemed in the first

half of the nineteenth century to face rapid and complete extinction. As Cooper wrote in *The Redskins*:

> We white men are so occupied with ourselves, and our own passing concerns, look on all other races of human beings as so much our inferiors, that it is seldom we have time or inclination to reflect on the consequences of our own acts. Like the wheel that rolls along the highway, however, many is the inferior creature that we heedlessly crush in our path. Thus has it been with the red-man, and . . . thus will it continue to be.

Writers of the frontier romance accepted the process as inevitable; what whites could do, Cooper vaguely suggests, is pause for a moment and contemplate what they had done. It was thus a minor motif of nationalism in the frontier romance to have, in James Hall's words, "sympathy for the fallen fortune of those who once flourished and are now no more."

As a chapter in the continent's past, the aboriginal inhabitants warranted preservation in literature (if not in actuality); indeed, one argument advanced by critics who called for the literary treatment of the Indian was the importance of memorializing him:

> Gradually receding before the tread of civilization, and taking from it only the principle of destruction, they seem to be fast wasting to utter dissolution, and we shall one day look upon their history, with such emotions of curiosity and wonder, as those with which we now survey the immense mounds and heaps of ruin in the interior of our continent.[43]

Given the repeated failure of attempts to halt the rapid degeneration of Indians in contact with whites, writers of the frontier romance believed that Indians would soon exist only in their pages: "The memory of the race is destined to be saved, if saved at all, only by a miracle. Already the flame flickers in its socket;—its fading rays linger only on the pages of romantic fiction. The night will come, and the sun will go down upon the Indian forever" (*Miriam Coffin*).[44]

The flourishing cities and fields which were ritualistically invoked at the end of the tale presupposed a disappearing wilderness, and along with it, the vanishing Indian figure. At times the new and more advanced literally replaces the old and primitive; as Mrs. Cheney notes: "The houses of the European planters arose on the ashes of their humble wigwams." In keeping with the white man's superior ability to change the natural environment, and perhaps to emphasize the finality of the Indians' tragedy, authors often remarked that Indians left no trace of their one-time presence. As Joseph C. Hart writes about Nantucket: "Nothing now remains to indicate their locality [the Indian towns], but deep beds of ashes, mixed with seashells, which unerringly point out the hearths of the wigwams of the Indian." John Davis's *The First Settlers of Virginia* concludes in a more philosophical vein: "No vestige is left behind of a powerful nation, who once unconscious of the existence of another people, dreamt not of invasions from foreign enemies, or inroads from colonists, but believed their strength invincible, and their race eternal."[45]

If the historical Indians of precolonial times believed their race eternal, those of the frontier romance do not. Rather than making statements in their own person, authors sometimes elect to have Indian characters themselves comment upon their declining fortunes. Joseph Brant, for example, refers to himself in Charles Fenno Hoffman's *Greyslaer* as one of nature's "doomed children that must soon pass away." In another Revolutionary War novel in which Brant appears, the doom is already accomplished. An Indian making a treaty with the Tories asks rhetorically:

"Where are now those dwellings of the brave? They have vanished like the blossoms that are beautiful when fanned by the gale of spring, but that wither and fade away when the fierce summer bursts upon them with the relentless scorching of his beams. So have our people faded before the wrath of the children of your father."

Indians are apt to be prescient in foreseeing the outcome of their encounter with the white man. In Davis's *The First Settlers of Virginia*, an Indian attributes his tribe's attack on the exploratory expedition of Captain John Smith to a suspicion that the English "were a people come from under the world to take their world from them."

After *The Last of the Mohicans*, a number of authors embodied the elegiac theme in a "last red man" character, usually a chief who is the last of his tribe or line.[46] In an anonymous tale, "The First and Last Sacrifice," a dying warrior laments: " 'I had a father, I had a mother; I had a wife, I had children. I have no father, I have no mother; I have no wife, I have no children. I am the last of my race. I have no kindred.' " Some of these lonely figures think to journey into the wilderness beyond the reach of the white man, but by the time most frontier romances were written, it was apparent that no western removal could permanently appease the white man's desire for land. As Cooper's Trackless describes the Indian's situation in *The Redskins*: " 'The red-man keeps on his trail, and the pale-face is never far behind. . . . When that other lake is seen, the red-man must stop, and die in the open fields, where rum, and tobacco, and bread are plenty, or march on into the great salt lake of the west and be drowned.' " The dying out of the race is the end which Uncas also envisions in the anonymous romance *The Witch of New England*: " 'A little longer and the whitemen will cease to persecute us,—for we shall have ceased to exist and the great names of our fathers will have no tongue to repeat them.' "

Generally, a sympathetic understanding of the Indian's untenable position in the unequal struggle with the white man is found in the hero of a full-length frontier romance.[47] The bringer of civilized values and humane feelings into the wilderness milieu, he can see the conflict more objectively than the hate-ridden frontiersmen. Nevertheless, action and attitude are often at variance. When fighting occurs, the hero must perform bravely on the right side, but he refuses to commit, and is often repulsed by, the excesses of wanton killing and scalping which characterize the frontiersman's behavior. This contrast in white attitudes is brought out in a number of hero and frontiersman couples: Rolfe and Earth in *Kabaosa,* Sumner and Luke in *Elkswatawa,* Herrick and Adherbal in *The Hawk Chief,* and Greyslaer and Balt in *Greyslaer.* While the old, experienced hunter pleads frontier necessity, the novice-hero displays a conscience about the Indian which appears to be a luxury in the wilderness environment.

At times, set debates about Indian character take place in the frontier romance in which the hero defends the aborigine as a noble savage. Edward Bradley, in *The Witch of New England,* extols the character of the American Indian to a skeptical friend: " 'He is brave, hospitable, a faithful friend and kind husband according to the habits of his people. . . . The catalogue of his virtues far out-vies the list of his vices.' " Colonel Grahame, the hero of *Saratoga,* is equally certain that "even in their savage state, they possess many virtues, and those the noblest that can dignify humanity." Most eloquent of all is that atypical frontiersman Natty Bumppo, who praises and sympathizes with the Indians of his choice throughout the *Leatherstocking Tales.*

6

Most frontier romances were produced between the War of 1812 and the Civil War, a period of high nationalistic consciousness. Secure in having twice defeated the British, the young nation saw a glorious future for itself. As G. Harrison Orians describes the period: "The eighteenth century with its chain-of-being and its concept of a fixed universe had partly given way before a vision of a world whose limits were constantly expanding and whose denizens had a passion for physical progress."[48] Indians, with their stubborn adherence to a primitive way of life, could have no place in the progressive and materialistic American world of the nineteenth century; whether or not they actually became extinct, as the writers of the frontier romance expected, their meaning for white Americans was clearly linked to the country's past, to the transient frontier situation. In this context they played a vital part: like the ancient dragon guarding the treasure, Indians were the evil enemy who must be slain before whites could possess the land. As the painted devils and formidable foes of white settlement whose image had already been widely disseminated by the popular captivity narratives, Indians lived on into fiction. By overcoming them, whites demonstrated those superior qualities which writers never grew tired of praising; moreover, they suffered hideous tortures, scalpings, and massacres, which consecrated their cause. Through the loss of their own blood and the shedding of the Indians', "the brave pioneers who led the van of civilisation" felt that they had paid the price for their new world inheritance.[49] Having established their right by conquering the original inhabitants, Americans could then eject the strongest foreign claimant—the mother country.

Opposed to the success story which dominates the pages of the frontier romance is the fate of the defeated and dispossessed. As civilized life replaced frontier survival conditions, the brutal aspects of white conquest assumed greater prominence. The victor could not repudiate the victory, nor genuinely repent what he yet enjoyed, but he could express an appreciation of the Indian's life and character—as exhibited apart from white contact—and a regret that the white man's inevitable triumph had so utterly destroyed him. A concern with the tragedy of the Indians was a legitimate manifestation of nationalism, for from that tragedy, what promised to be the greatest example of Western civilization took its being.

NOTES

1. Because of the large number of frontier romances referred to, dates of individual works will be given in the text and in explanatory notes only when chronology is important to the discussion at hand. For a chronological overview of the frontier romance, the reader is referred to Appendix A. Most of this forgotten fiction is now out of print and generally inaccessible; therefore, page numbers for quotations will not be given. To avoid mechanical repetition, authors are not always indicated when frontier romances are cited. Appendix B lists these works alphabetically by title and gives their authors.
2. Noah Webster, Letter to Joel Barlow, quoted in Benjamin T. Spencer, *The Quest for Nationality* (Syracuse, 1957), p. 28. Spencer, pp. 25-72, documents the exhortations for cultural autonomy which were made during the period of 1783-1814.

3. Philips D. Carleton, "The Indian Captivity," *American Literature* 25 (1943-1944), p. 169, asserts that "their painful realism, their simple unaffected prose, their revelation of a pioneer people [exemplify] the virtues of true literature."

4. Roy Harvey Pearce, "The Significance of the Captivity Narrative," *American Literature* 19 (1946-1947), p. 13, has listed a number of supposedly authentic captivity accounts which are, in fact, fakes; undoubtedly, others contain truth and fiction in varying proportions impossible to determine today. Nevertheless, the generic distinction between captivity narrative and frontier romance is a valid one. Pearce discusses the evolution of the captivity narrative from the early simple account of an unlettered author-victim into the partially or totally fictive product of a professional writer. Even in the last stages of the process, however, the captivity narrative is still committed to an appearance of authenticity, with all its limitations.

5. Theodore Dehon, quoted in Fred Lewis Pattee, *The First Century of American Literature* (New York, 1935), p. 353.

6. William Tudor, Jr., "An Address delivered to the Phi Beta Kappa Society, at their anniversary meeting in Cambridge," *North American Review* 2 (1815), p. 19.

7. Tudor, Review of *Moral Pieces in Prose and Verse* by Lydia Huntley, *North American Review* 1 (1815), p. 120.

8. Albert Keiser, *The Indian in American Literature* (New York, 1933), p. 43, writes: "Historically *Yamoden* [*sic*] proved to be of the greatest importance, since its popularity augured well for those desirous of utilizing material from what seemed to be a rich mint."

9. *North American Review* 12 (1821), pp. 484-485.

10. *North American Review* 15 (1822), p. 258.

11. *The Atlantic Magazine* (1823), p. 133, quoted in G. Harrison Orians, "The Romantic Ferment after *Waverley*," *American Literature* 3 (1931-1932), p. 419.

12. *The Complete Works of Edgar Allan Poe* (Boston, 1908), vol VIII, p. 204.

13. William Gilmore Simms, "The Epochs and Events of American History, as suited to the Purposes of Art in Fiction," *Views and Reviews in American Literature History and Fiction, First Series*, ed. C. Hugh Holman (Cambridge, Mass., 1962) p. 83.

14. Simms, "Indian Literature and Art," ibid., p. 142.

15. John Bristed, *Resources of the United States of America* (New York, 1818), pp. 355-356.

16. *North American Review* 20 (1825), p. 210.

17. Ibid., p. 211.

18. Granville Mellen, Review of *The Red Rover, North American Review* 27 (1828), p. 141.

19. *The American Athenaeum* 1 (1826), p. 441, quoted in Orians, "The Romantic Fermant After *Waverley*," p. 425; it did not occur to this critic to blame lack of invention on the writers rather than on the Indians.

20. *United States Literary Gazette* (1826), quoted in Pattee, *The First Century of American Literature*, p. 357.

21. Mellen, *North American Review* 27, p. 143.

22. Ibid., p. 141; Spencer, *The Quest for Nationality*, p. 104, remarks: "Though he [the American writer] knew that the red men were his distinctive literary possession, he could scarcely give them an indigenous focus which would at

once do justice to the cultures of the conquered and the conquerors."

23. Tudor, "An Address delivered to the Phi Beta Kappa Society," pp. 28-29.

24. Spencer, *The Quest for Nationality*, p. 52.

25. *North American Review* 20, p. 212.

26. Simms, "Americanism in Literature," *Views and Reviews*, pp. 16-17.

27. Palfrey, *North American Review* 12, p. 477; subsequent references will appear in the text.

28. In his *History of New England During the Stuart Dynasty* (Boston, 1865), vol. III, p. 223, Palfrey describes Philip as "a squalid savage, whose palace was a sty, whose royal robe was a bearskin or a coarse blanket, alive with vermin. . . . To royalty belong associations of dignity and magnificence . . . the Indian *King Philip* is a mythical character." Washington Irving had described Philip as possessing "heroic qualities and bold achievements that would have graced a civilized warrior and have rendered him the theme of the poet and the historian" ("Philip of Pokanoket, an Indian Memoir," *The Sketch Book of Geoffrey Crayon, Gentleman* [London, 1821], vol. II, pp. 214-215).

29. Orville J. Victor, editor of Beadle's popular dime novel series, related the company response to the success of a rival firm: " 'What did we do then? Oh, we had to kill a few more Indians than we used to' " (quoted in Edmund Pearson, *Dime Novels* [Boston, 1929], p. 99).

30. Although deserts and moors seem to be singularly inappropriate terms for the wilderness of the Atlantic seaboard, "desert" occurs frequently in this period in the now obsolete sense of "any wild uninhabited region, including forest-land" (*OED* [Oxford, 1961], vol. III, p. 240).

31. William Henry Harrison, quoted in William T. Hagan, *American Indians* (Chicago, 1961), p. 69.

32. Theodore Roosevelt, *The Winning of the West* (New York, 1889-1896), vol. I, p. 90.

33. Quoted in Hagan, *American Indians*, p. 27.

34. Frederick Jackson Turner, *The Character and Influence of the Indian Trade in Wisconsin* (Baltimore, 1891), p. 9.

35. This is not, of course, the case in other kinds of writings about the noble savage; Orians, "The Rise of Romanticism, 1805-1855," p. 212, n. 73, cites the outlander essays of Montesquieu, Goldsmith, and Freneau as works in which "the savage was frequently held up to shame the civilized readers of an effete age" (*Transitions in American Literary History*, ed. Harry Hayden Clark [New York, 1967]). P. W. Sproat's *The Savage Beauty* (1822), subtitled *A Satirical Allegorical Novel*, belongs in this category, as does much of the early Melville (see Chapter Seven).

36. A counterdesire to preserve the wilderness is embodied in some white frontiersmen, notably Natty Bumppo. In *The Prairie*, he predicts that "an accursed band of choppers and loggers will be following . . . to humble the wilderness . . . and then the land will be a peopled desert from the shores of the main sea to the foot of the Rocky Mountains; filled with all the abominations and craft of man, and stript of the comforts and loveliness it received from the hands of the Lord." The frontiersman Adherbal has no desire to live another hundred years because "the settlers will cover this ground before that, and the deer will be gone, and these prairies will be cornfields" (John T. Irving, Jr., *The Hawk Chief*). Citing Parkman's observation that civilized society extirpates its own predecessors, Warren S. Walker

notes that both frontiersmen and Indians had to fall before the advancing wave of civilization ("The Frontiersman as Recluse and Redeemer," *New York Folklore Quarterly* 16, [1960], p. 114).

37. It seems ironic that "making the wilderness bloom" should become the customary expression in the frontier romance for the substitution of human communities for nature.

38. David Brion Davis, "The Deerslayer, a Democratic Knight of the Wilderness: Cooper, 1841," *Twelve Original Essays on Great American Novels*, ed. Charles Shapiro (Detroit, 1958), p. 16.

39. The only instance in the frontier romance where the Old World is preferred is Cooper's *Wyandotté*, in which the hero and heroine, both born in America, accept an English inheritance and become Sir Robert and Lady Willoughby. Sir William Drummond Stewart's *Altowan* has a similar denouement, but it was written by an Englishman, and Roallen, the character who returns to become a lord, was merely travelling through the United States—he is English by birth. Altowan, half Indian and half British noble, does not survive his transplantation to the Old World.

40. Cf. Tudor, Review of *Moral Pieces in Prose*, p. 120: "Let it be remembered how much the genius of Scott has struck out from his Scottish highland chiefs and the border warfare with England; where both men and events are almost beneath the dignity of history."

41. Washington Irving, "Traits of Indian Character," *The Sketch Book*, vol. II, p. 182.

42. A contemporary formulation of this view is found in Henry Rowe Schoolcraft, *Algic Researches* (New York, 1839), vol. I, p. 34: "It must needs have happened, that the party which increased the fastest in numbers, wanted most land, and had most knowledge (to say nothing of the influence of temperance and virtue), should triumph, and those who failed in these requisites, decline."

43. Gardiner, Review of *The Spy*, p. 257; Edward H. Spicer, *A Short History of the Indians of the United States* (New York, 1969), p. 3, remarks in this period "a prevailing illusion that Indian societies are vanishing, that one after another each Indian group is taking the road to disappearance."

44. Writers frequently use imagery of light and darkness to describe the relative positions of the two races: "Like the wild plants of their deserts they [Indians] thrive best in the dark and silent shades; shrink from the withering hand of cultivation and perish beneath the genial heat and influence of the sun" (*The Witch of New England*); Magawisca comments in *Hope Leslie*: "The sunbeam and the shadow cannot mingle"; cf. *Logan*: "The sun of their [Indian] glory hath set in darkness."

45. For Mrs. Sedgwick, however, the absence of Indian remains seems to be a reason for *not* lamenting the vanishing peoples. She writes in *Hope Leslie*: "It is not permitted to reasonable, instructed man to admire or regret tribes of human beings who lived and died, leaving scarcely a more enduring memorial than the forsaken nest that vanishes before one winter's storms."

46. The popularity of such a figure can be attributed to both fictive and historical sources: the historical Indian chief Logan, whose speech lamenting his lack of surviving issue was widely known, and the influence of Ossian. Cf. Orians, "The Rise of Romanticism," p. 215: "MacPherson's brooding heroes sitting in their foggy gloom were cousins german to Indian chieftains lamenting the

destiny of their race or, at the ruins of a cherished landmark, dolefully chanting of old wrongs and former griefs."

47. It is also evident in Natty Bumppo and Hurry Harry in *The Deerslayer*, although Natty is neither the conventional hero nor frontiersman. As the established frontiersman in the other *Leatherstocking Tales*, he exhibits a humanity notably absent from the stock frontiersman of the frontier romance.

48. Orians, "The Rise of Romanticism," p. 190.

49. James Hall, *Sketches of History, Life, and Manners in the West* (Philadelphia, 1835), vol. I. p. 208.

2

The Fictive Design:
Beyond the Captivity
Narrative

I may say, that as none knows what it is to fight and pursue such an enemy as this, but they that have fought and pursued them: so none can imagine what it is to be captivated, and enslaved to such atheisticall, proud, wild, cruel, barbarous, bruitish (in one word) diabolicall creatures as these.

NARRATIVE OF THE CAPTIVITY OF MRS. MARY ROWLANDSON

1

Although the captivity narrative continued to be published successfully during the first three quarters of the nineteenth century, by 1800, according to Roy Harvey Pearce, it "had all but completed its decline and fall."[1] Its vitality passed at this time into overt fiction in which the horrors and travails of the frontier experience were combined with a complicated romantic plot of English origin. In this amalgam, a set of foreign and artificial conventions was superimposed on the basically real and indigenous captivity events. D. H. Lawrence describes it as "the old world holding its own on the edge of the wild."[2] The mixture is what I have called the frontier romance, a genre which began in the

1790s, increasingly gathered momentum during the early decades of the nineteenth century, and declined during the decade preceding the Civil War. Influenced by the eighteenth-century novel and by Sir Walter Scott, the frontier romance exhibits the major characteristics of the English historical romance: against the backdrop of a significant historical moment, a genteel hero and heroine experience adventures which temporarily separate them before the resolution dispels whatever obstacles to their union existed.

The genre promulgated a more complex attitude about white-Indian relations than the captivity narrative, placing the basic captivity experience within the larger context of the struggle for possession of the continent. Since even the last-gasp efforts of Tecumseh were behind all but a few of the writers, the elemental battle for white survival against the Indian no longer demanded the single-minded focus of the captivity genre. Observing the irresistible white progress westward, most writers assumed that the Indian was declining into extinction and felt free enough from Indian threats to give some attention to the greater issues of which captivity was only one manifestation. Armed with an idea of white superiority vindicated by history, but able at the same time to understand the Indians' resistance to white conquest, the authors of the frontier romance felt themselves able to portray a historical truth which went beyond the individual experiences of captivity narratives. In doing so they could celebrate their race and satisfy the nationalistic demand for art created out of native materials.

2

In spite of these larger purposes which were brought to the writing of the frontier romance, the captivity persists into the new genre as the central plot episode. In *Kabaosa* the comment of the old frontiersman Luke to the young hero reveals just such an understanding of what a typical plot would unfold: " 'This is rather a dull beginning of our campaign. You have neither

taken an Indian chief prisoner, nor I rescued a captive maiden!' "
Even such a terse formulation, however, betrays certain
departures from the events of a captivity narrative. Most apparent is the shift in focus from the captive to the rescuer. In the
earlier genre there was seldom opportunity for a heroic rescue:
because Indians with captives immediately retreated into the
wilderness, travelling rapidly, they were generally successful in
evading any whites who might have pursued them. The nearest
and dearest to the captives, moreover, if not themselves captured,
were seldom in any condition for heroics, having been killed or
wounded in the Indian raid, or, at best, left in a state of shock
which precluded immediate action. The opposite is true in the
frontier romance: whites eagerly give pursuit and perform feats
of endurance and woodsmanship in order to keep on the trail of
the wily enemy. They are thus in a position not only to free
captives, but, as Luke remarked, to capture "Indian chiefs."
Chiefs seldom play a part in captivity narratives, but, true to the
aristocratic nature of romance, fictive Indians who have
prominent roles are almost always chiefs, or, in the case of
women, wives and daughters of the tribal leaders. This high
status and the exceptional qualities it entails make the Indians either worthy opponents or friends of the white characters.

Real captives were usually ransomed directly from the Indians
or from their French allies; occasionally, they escaped on their
own initiative. There were, of course, some "captive maidens" in
authentic captivity narratives, but the large majority of extant
accounts relate the experiences of men and married women.
Those nubile girls who did fall into Indian hands were not able to
make romantic capital out of their predicament.[3] In the frontier
romance, in contrast, no captive maiden is without a friend—
either her approved lover or a disinterested knight of the
wilderness—who zealously works to bring about her release. Most
real captives did not owe their freedom to this kind of personal
intercession, but to the negotiations to redeem captives undertaken by some official group; they attributed their salvation to
divine mercy rather than to individual initiative. In the frontier
romance, heroes and frontiersmen function as Providence did in

the captivity narratives: a direct triumph of God over the savages is replaced by a scheme of things in which man, acting with God's approval, receives the credit.

The major differences between authentic and fictive captivities can be subsumed under plot. Because the frontier romance added a plot to the simple sequence of events in a captivity narrative, a number of divergences between the two treatments occurred. The standard pattern of a captivity took the victim from an Indian raid during which capture took place, through a wilderness trek, to some sort of permanent resting place, either at an Indian village or with the French. Most of the narrative concerned the journey period and the time spent in the Indian camp. A brief description of rescue, almost always a negotiated one, and the return home concluded the story. Although the victim might have begun the experience with friends, relatives, or children, the Indian practice of distributing captives usually separated them and prevented concerted action. In the frontier romance all of these particulars change. More often than not, the point of view is focused upon approaching white rescuers rather than on captives; replacing the emphasis on time spent among the Indians, rescue becomes the central element in the fictionalized captivity sequence. And instead of the release of prisoners being a settlement mutually agreed upon between the Indians and whites, it is transformed into the triumph of white intrepidity and courage in robbing the Indians of their prey.

Plotting also demanded more personalized relationships among the characters than captivity narratives afforded. Occasionally, fictive Indians abduct particular persons, almost always young heroines, for thinly veiled sexual purposes; but if the heroine is abducted by chance, she soon excites an Indian's lust nevertheless. Interested whites are always on hand to give chase and contest the Indian's claim: the heroine is the passive center of plot maneuvers by Indian and white characters who vie for her possession. In a full-blown captivity plot there are apt to be five contending males: the young white hero, his older frontiersman ally, and a good Indian friend, all against a bad Indian and a white villain.[4] At times a good Indian maiden also takes an active part in the rescue operations. The number of characters committed to freeing the heroine gives a false impression of numerical superiority, however. The rescuers tend to be alone; the bad characters are supported by whole tribes or parties of "howling savages" who are not individualized.

R. W. B. Lewis's description of *The Last of the Mohicans* can be applied to the whole genre of the frontier romance: "The plot is little more than a medley of captures and rescues, scalpings and shootings, tactics and countertactics."[5] To provide sufficient interaction for the opposing sides, writers introduced more captivity episodes without treating any in the depth characteristic of their narrative predecessors. The high points—threats, torture, and other examples of fiendish Indian behavior—continued to be exploited, but the everyday detail which captivity narratives contain was eliminated. By increasing the number of incidents, authors repeated the excitement and suspense inherent in Indian seizure and multiplied instances of white ingenuity in escaping or rescuing others. The greater number allowed for variety in all these particulars and in the characters involved: the heroine was likely to change hands several times during the course of a typical two-volume novel, the hero himself could be captured, or the frontiersman, or the good Indian. It was only necessary that some one person on the side of good be free at any given time to effect the rescue of the others. Those expedient contrivances whereby bad Indians inexplicably release their prisoners indicate that writers who plotted carelessly were often sorely beset to arrange the mandatory liberation of their white characters.[6]

3

To the mainstay of captivity episodes a number of conventions from English fiction were simply and often incongruously transposed to an American frontier setting. As De Tocqueville observed:

Not only do the Americans constantly draw upon the treasures of English literature, but it may be said with truth that they find the literature of England growing on their own soil. The larger part of that small number of men in the United States who are engaged in the composition of literary works are English in substance and still more so in form. Thus they transport into the midst of democracy the ideas and literary fashions that are current among the aristocratic nation they have taken for their model.[7]

In one sense these accretions are infelicitous borrowings of a fledgling literature; in another they comprise a serious attempt on the part of consciously American writers to blend disparate elements—drawing room and wilderness, British noble and American frontiersman, tradition and innovation—into a new entity. The New World had made Americans out of British gentlemen; it might be expected to transmute literary materials in the same manner.

In developing a new literature, authors joined distinctive American experiences to conventional plotting devices of romance and often added a historical context suggestive of Scott. Thus, in a wilderness millieu populated by Indians and exotic flora and fauna in which a struggle between contending nations of whites and Indians is in progress, heroes and heroines of gentle birth live a series of adventures little different from their counterparts in English literature. Mysteries of birth, unhappy secrets, and misdirected or stolen letters all function in the fictive New World as successfully as in the Old, nor is the plot staple of Indian captivity necessarily different from the situations of well-known English heroines. Literal captivity of a heroine by Indians, Sophia's imprisonment by an unfeeling parent in *Tom Jones*, Clarissa's enforced brothel stay, Pamela's beseigement by Squire B., and even Elizabeth's difficulties as part of the poorly managed Bennett family in *Pride and Prejudice*, all serve the same plot end: the placing of the heroine in a position of peril. In all these cases a damsel in distress needs rescuing from either a literal or a metaphoric imprisonment. Most important of the literary borrowings of the frontier romance is that central issue of romance, the question of identity. In the American context, the mystery of the hero's birth is often resolved in a way similar to earlier treatments: the wish fulfillment of discovering aristocratic lineage, always, of course, accompanied by wealth.

Given the fusion of the romantic plot apparatus of the English novel and the indigenous captivity narrative, the ending of a frontier romance had to release the captives from the Indians and unite the hero with the heroine in marriage. Departures from the happy ending formula are always accounted for by some unusual circumstance. In *The Last of the Mohicans,* in which Hawkeye often refers to himself proudly as a man "without a cross," i.e., without race mixture, Cora's small taint of Negro blood deprives her of the full measure of white heroinehood. Her sister, as coheroine, can play the conventional role and marry the hero. The past indiscretion of Judith Hutter alluded to in *The Deerslayer* disqualifies her from marrying the combination frontiersman-hero Natty Bumppo. The identity confusion resulting from mixed blood seems to be the barrier to Jessy's happiness in *The Shoshonee Valley,* while for Elluwia, the only important woman in *Tadeuskund,* identification with the Indians by whom she was adopted as a child is too strong to be reversed by the knowledge of her real parentage. She prefers to join her adoptive father Tadeuskund in the spirit world rather than be reborn as a white heroine. The only other white heroines to end tragically also have disabilities which bar the usual denouement: the hopeless insanity of Miss Argal in *Lord Fairfax* dooms her romance with the hero, as does the married status of the heroine of *The Cassique of Kiawah.*

With these few exceptions, frontier romances conclude by marrying the white hero and heroine and paying the conventional epilogue visit to the thriving household in later years. With no exceptions the bad Indians are thoroughly vanquished, the prominent figures among them almost always killed.[8] More scope is allowed in the disposition of good Indian helpers, but, given the white settlement of the entire continent which authors envisioned, they represent a dead end. If good Indians do not die sooner during attempts to rescue whites, they die later, or, more accurately, they die out because they have no heirs. At best, their meritorious service to whites can buy them a few more years of life than fictive bad Indians enjoy, but it cannot buy race survival.

Whatever the manner in which good Indians die, the meaning of their deaths remains the same; white settlement and the inevitable expropriation of the Indian could not be circumvented by even exemplary conduct on the part of the Indian. In *Tokeah,* for example, the Creek Tokeah had peaceably obeyed the white men in giving up his tribe's land in Georgia and removing to the Mississippi. Here his daughter is killed in a fight between the Indians and the pirate Lafitte, and white settlement pressure again demands a move further west. Ready to comply once more, Tokeah wishes only to transport his parents' bones to the new location, but on his journey back to Georgia he finds the graves defiled by white encroachment. During his subsequent travels west, the old chief is killed by hostile Indians, but obviously his spirit, like his only child, had already been killed by the whites.

The chief Eoneguski in *Eoneguski* is also killed in spirit by the whites he has always befriended. While he is away fighting for the United States in the War of 1812, a white man steals both Eoneguski's fiancee and his chieftancy; the false chief then proceeds to make unscrupulous deals with other whites to divest the tribe of their land. Thwarted in both his personal and public life, the celibate Eoneguski becomes a courthouse fixture in the white man's town, deprived of any purpose for living but pointed out by whites as a "good Indian."

Even more unenviable is the fate of Benjamin Tashima, chief of the dwindling tribe of Nantucket Indians in *Miriam Coffin*. Tashima is not only friendly to whites like all good Indians, but he also does his best to instill white culture in his people. In the model community which he has organized, everyone plays a white role: the women are engaged in domestic pursuits inside their neat cottages, the men labor in well-ordered garden plots, and the children go to school. The Indians' success is encapsulated in the "sheets of incomparable whiteness" which a group of white visitors touring the Indian village exclaim over. Referring to Tashima's death, which has apparently been hastened by a white man's seduction and abandonment of his daughter, the author makes a pointed comparison of the chief to other well-known Indians:

> The example of such a man—such an Indian, if you please—is worth more to posterity,—and,—the phil-anthropist will say,—should be dearer to it, than all the savage glories of a thousand Philips or Tecumthes, whose claims to admiration rest upon countless deeds of blood and

rapine, and a very questionable valour displayed in the slaughter of women and children. May God forgive the uncharitableness!—but of such a race of miscreants we are almost ready to say—"Perdition catch their souls!"—as, like the ghosts of Banquo's line, the red visions of their cruelties rise up before us:—But to the manes of such a truly godlike Indian as Benjamin Tashima, we would say with fervour— "REQUIESCAT IN PACE!"

The same words pronounced by Poe's Montresor over his walled-up enemy are scarcely more ironic than this benediction for the "truly godlike Indian." The price of such white approbation and apotheosis is complete extinction: the renunciation of Indianness in life and death without surviving progeny.

In contrast to such a definition of a good Indian, the integrity of a Philip or a Tecumseh and the respect whites accord them as noble enemies seem preferable. Rather than living into old age like Indian John in *The Pioneers*, painfully aware of his own degeneration and of white supremacy, how much better to die uncompromised like Queen Wetamoo in *The Doomed Chief*: "With a quickness of the outstarting antelope, she leaped, with a wild cry of exultation, out wide from the fearful brink, and then descended, like a bow-driven arrow, to her watery grave below." Perhaps as the only allowable expiation, authors of the frontier romance almost always grant a dignified and even triumphant death to these stubborn foes of the white man.

4

The uncertain welding of plot elements in the frontier romance before it became securely established in the 1820s can be seen in the early examples of the genre. Not surprisingly, the very first work, Ann Eliza Bleecker's *History of Maria Kittle* (1793)[9] is simply a fictionalized captivity narrative with some embellishment but no trappings of romance or history. The cast of characters which would later populate the frontier romance is missing; Maria herself is not the fair virgin of romance, but a sturdy pioneer wife whose personal experience, lacking plot machinations or a larger context, is the classic story of captivity and release. Nevertheless, signs that the captivity was starting a fictive life do appear. Rather than beginning abruptly with the Indian attack, the author sets the scene with several chapters devoted to the amicable relations between the Indians and the Kittle household. As a result, when trouble breaks out in the neighborhood, the Kittles are uncertain about their danger from the Indians until too late. In the description of the inevitable raid, contrary to authentic captivity practice, sensationalistic detail is prominent:

> An Indian, hideously painted, strode ferociously up to Comelia . . . and cleft her white forehead deeply with his tomahawk. Her fine azure eyes just opened, and then suddenly closing forever, she tumbled lifeless at his feet. His sanguinary soul was not yet satisfied with blood: he deformed her lovely body with deep gashes; and, tearing her unborn babe away, dashed it to pieces against the stone wall; with many additional circumstances of infernal cruelty.

And instead of being stunned and unprotesting like a real captive, Maria is able to rage with Matherian eloquence:

> "O barbarians!" she exclaimed, "surpassing devils in wickedness! so may a tenfold night of misery enwrap your black souls, as you have deprived the babe of my bosom, the comfort of my cares, my blessed cherub, of light and life—O hell! are not thy flames impatient to cleave the center and engulph [sic] these wretches in thy ever burning waves? are there no thunders from the Heaven—no avenging Angel —no God to take notice of such Heaven defying cruelties?"

Details of the captivity experience are meager when compared to an authentic account, and the few brief scenes, with the exception of the raid, are not vividly realized.

An even more noticeable departure from the typical captivity narrative is the amount of space devoted to Maria's stay in Montreal.[10] Although she is still a captive, she is no longer held by

Indians; placed among sympathetic whites who treat her humanely, Maria is now within the purlieus of civilization. Here she tells her story to a circle of genteel ladies, whose response might be intended to guide the reader's: when Maria and another captive finish reciting their woes, one French lady remarks: " 'My heart is now sweetly tuned to melancholy. I love to indulge these divine sensibilities, which your affecting histories are so capable of inspiring.' " The author continues: "After some time spent in tears, and pleasing melancholy, tea was brought in." As envisioned by Mrs. Bleecker, the captivity is in the tradition of affective literature, designed to provoke terror at the cruelty of the Indians and pity for the sufferings of the white victim. After the therapeutic expression of sensibility, the ritual of tea restores order.

Susannah Rowson's *Reuben and Rachel* (1798) joins captivity episodes to romance, a combination which would later become the established formula of the frontier romance. Already successful as a writer of sentimental novels in the Richardsonian vein, Mrs. Rowson naturally built her complicated tale around genteel heroes and heroines whose series of adventures includes Indian captivity. In the first movement of the plot, the children Rachel and William Dudley are captured by Indians in seventeenth-century New Hampshire. There is little scope for racial conflict, however, because these are good Indians, completely amenable to white enlightenment. William easily civilizes the chief, Otooganoo: "From the effects of his instructions [William's], his protector had made rapid advances towards civilization, had entirely lost his natural ferocity, and attained such a degree of rational information as made him a pleasant companion." Both William and Rachel welcome Indian lovers without a sense of race barrier: William marries the chief's daughter and has a son, Reuben; when Otooganoo dies, William is elected chief, as regent for his son, by unanimous voice. Rachel fails to marry her Indian warrior because he is killed in battle, but she remains true to his memory. No bad Indians or villains of any sort appear in this first episode, but the romantic involvement of whites and Indians is the beginning of a convention for the frontier romance.

More significantly, in the second volume of the novel, Reuben, the grandson of William, is loved by the Indian girl Eumea.[11] Setting the pattern for the Indian heroine, Eumea saves Reuben from death and unselfishly devotes herself to him: " 'I will be your handmaid, and love and serve you to the last hour of my life.' " In spite of the ready acceptance of Indian love by his grandfather and great-aunt, Reuben, like most white heroes of later frontier romances, is curiously unperceptive about Eumea's feelings. When he marries an English girl, Eumea becomes insane and drowns herself. Of the two possibilities for white-Indian love presented in *Reuben and Rachel,* authors invariably chose the second or unsuccessful relationship.

A dozen years passed before another significant plot addition to the frontier romance was made: the joining of the captivity episode to the love story of the hero and heroine, a union first effected in Jesse Holman's *The Prisoners of Niagara* (1810).[12] Although he lacks Charles Brockden Brown's ability to evoke horror, Holman uses Indians in much the same way that Brown did earlier in *Edgar Huntly* (1801), as trappings of wilderness gothic. The terrifying bad Indian of the captivity tradition is useful to Holman in a number of ways: to separate the hero Evermont from his real parents, to deprive him of his first protector, to kill his foster father, and, above all, to furnish occasions for heroic exploits on his part. As an adolescent, Evermont acquits himself well in saving his two foster sisters from attacking Indians:

"I plunged my dirk, to the hilt, in the back of the hindmost. The other turned round to learn what had happened to his brother, and I buried the bleeding weapon in his heart. They both fell down the rocks—I seized their guns, and sprang into the grotto, as a shower of balls rained on the rocks around me."

In young manhood, Evermont joins a group of Indian fighters who have the usual success of whites against Indians: "The Indians, being unaccustomed to such an impetuous attack, retreated in the utmost disorder."

The high point of Evermont's feats against Indians comes

when he decides to rescue an unknown female captive who proves to be his own beloved Zerelda.[13] In what could pass for a parody of Brown's best gothic manner, Holman describes the situation through Zerelda's eyes:

> Torn from her friends and family by the fearful heart-chilling savages, under the most alarming circumstances—What were her sensations when she first beheld herself in their grasp? It was the grasp of a Torpedo, and shot the benumbing effluvia of death through her soul. How did her tender heart, the seat of every generous virtue, toss itself in her bosom with a frightful quivering? Their painted visages, their eyes scowling the dark fire of revenge, their yell of hideous horror, were as tremendous to her shrinking senses, as the sight of death stalking in grinning fury amidst the myriad train of his ghastly apparitions.[14]

Oddly enough, after this depiction, Zerelda's danger comes not from the Indians, but from a white fellow prisoner who attempts to rape her. Evermont's rescue of the heroine is more immediately from this villain than from the Indians, possessors, in the author's words, of "the virtue of chastity in a higher degree than any modern civilized nation." In spite of this failure to integrate the captor Indians' role with their description, Holman did begin the practice of the hero's rescue of the heroine from captivity as the important plot episode in the frontier romance. *The Prisoners of Niagara* contains in addition several traditional romantic devices which often crop up in succeeding frontier romances: a pervasive mystery of identity, surrounding not only the hero but most other characters as well; the reappearance of people thought dead; and the use of letters which mislead through genuine error, ambiguity, or bad faith.

A further contribution to the classic plot of the frontier romance, the bringing together of good and bad Indians in the same work, was made in Samuel Woodworth's *The Champions of Freedom* (1816). Earlier authors had settled for the inimical figure of horror from the captivity narrative or the readily civilized noble savage. Before *The Champions of Freedom*, there had been no attempt to complicate the plot by maneuvering Indian enemies and allies in the same story. Woodworth's efforts in this direction are minimal: he presents both sorts of Indians and links them to the larger context of the War of 1812, but there is little dramatized interaction between the two groups and only one Indian character who is at all individualized. This is the good Indian Logan, who thanks the hero, George Washington Willoughby, for saving his son from drowning. The author subsequently reports that the young Logan died in battle, happy to give his life for the American cause. The enemy Indians are stereotyped as "merciless monsters" and "barbarous wretches"; when they raid the Willoughby estate, good Indians aid the whites in repulsing them. Woodworth visualizes the conflict of Indians for and against whites as the clash of undifferentiated masses: later writers of the frontier romance find more possibilities in pitting individual good and bad Indians against each other.

Although most of the pattern elements of the frontier romance were present inchoately by 1810, the genre did not recommend itself to a large number of writers or readers until the 1820s. Then, within a brief period, 1823-1824, eight works of fiction using similar plots and conventions were published.[15] From this time until the disappearance of the genre in the 1850s, the conventions of fiction which portrayed Indians and whites in a frontier setting were fixed. Some of these romances exhibit the plot elements already discussed in embryonic form only, but the existence of most elements in all eight suggests the presence of certain common assumptions. Thus, six of the eight contain both good and bad Indians; *The Pioneers,* Cooper's first *Leatherstocking Tale* and the first frontier romance best seller, has only the good, albeit mildly degenerate, Indian John. *The Pioneers* deviates in a further way: like *Hobomok,* but unlike the other six, it has no captivity episode.[16] All have the romantic plot to some degree; after the captivity of one or both, the white hero and heroine are restored to white society and united in marriage. In several cases this union entails the disappointment of a good Indian.

Excluding the atypical *Hobomok* and *The Pioneers,* the other works integrate plot elements which had been unconnected in earlier romances. Instead of the narrowly conceived captivity episode of *Maria Kittle*, the disjunction of captivity and romance in *Reuben and Rachel*, or the failure to involve individual Indian characters in *The Champions of Freedom* and *The Prisoners of Niagara*, the eight combine the activities of good and bad Indians vis-à-vis whites, the romance of the hero and heroine, and the captivity into a whole action. After this, no significant component was added to the genre; a larger cast of characters and more captivity episodes could increase the complexity of the fictive design, but the essential structure remained unchanged in the ensuing decades.

5

Written only a few years after the emergence of the frontier romance as a definable genre, Cooper's *The Last of the Mohicans* (1826) provides an excellent paradigm of the multiple captivity plot in which several captivity episodes give the major characters numerous chances to test and best one another. More complexity also results from the doubling of the good Indian and the splitting of the conventional heroine. In terms of character, the addition of Uncas merely provides a younger and more active version of Natty's good Indian companion Chingachgook. The very different Munro sisters each have some aspects of the usual heroine of the frontier romance, a girl who is genteel and helpless but with enough resolution to repulse the villain proudly. In the face of Magua's proposal, the dark-haired Cora is able to maintain "a secret ascendancy over the fierce native, by the collected and feminine dignity of her presence." Alice, the fair sister, has the standard heroine's fragility, but to the point of hysteria.

The first captivity occurs when the treacherous guide Magua leads the sisters, the hero Duncan Heyward, and the comic character David Gamut to a band of enemy Indians, his own Huron tribe. The frontiersman Hawkeye and his two good Indian friends save themselves in order to effect a rescue of the others at some more opportune moment. Several of the familiar occurrences of a captivity narrative form part of this episode.

Taken in a surprise Indian attack, the captives immediately begin a difficult trip: "mile after mile was . . . passed through the boundless woods, in this painful manner, without any prospect of a termination to their journey." Once the party halts, the familiar torture scene gets under way. The Indians prepare stakes, burning pine splinters and bent saplings for their assorted victims, and the enraged Magua hurls his tomahawk at Alice's head. Just as the whites are about to be killed in the melee which this action provokes, the rescuers arrive:

> Duncan already saw the knife gleaming in the air, when a whistling sound swept past him, and was rather accompanied, than followed, by the sharp crack of a rifle. He felt his breast relieved from the load it had endured; he saw the savage expression of his adversary's countenance change to a look of vacant wildness when the Indian fell dead on the faded leaves by his side.

The well-timed rescue sharply separates the fictive episode from a captivity narrative, but it is only the climax of a series of departures from the earlier genre.

In the interest of a more tightly knit plot structure, the whole episode is personalized in a manner which is entirely different from the captivity narrative and from early examples of the frontier romance. When first hurried into the wilderness in a state of shocked amazement, a real captive dumbly accepted the course of events with little speculation about the immediate future. Cooper's captives, in contrast, have just dispatched potential rescuers when they are seized. With this in mind, all but Alice are remarkably self-possessed: Cora attempts to leave clues along the trail; Duncan tries to bribe Magua from his purpose. Unlike the undifferentiated persecutors of the captivity narrative, Magua has a typically fictive motive for seeking out these particular victims: in retaliation for being "whipped like a dog" by Colonel Munro, he presents Cora with the choice of becoming his squaw or dying.

Owing to the separation of captives and the necessity for several kinds of rescue gambits, the second captivity is more complicated. First, Magua recaptures the Munro sisters and Gamut when Fort William Henry surrenders; the good Indians and whites quickly give chase. In a separate wilderness incident Uncas is taken prisoner, forced to run the gauntlet, and condemned to death. Help is at hand, however. Disguised as a French juggler, Heyward penetrates the Huron camp, where he is joined by Hawkeye in the garb of a medicine man. In separate adventures the two outwit the Hurons and free Alice and Uncas, but the rescue of Cora initiates another phase of the episode.

The Delawares, who accord safety to Uncas and his friends when he makes his identity known, are pledged to give up Cora to Magua. Nowhere is the fictive captivity's structure of move and countermove more artificially contrived than in the third time that Cora becomes a captive. She is simply handed over to Magua, who is given a head start and told that pursuit will begin at a certain time. Having assembled a group of whites and Indians, Cooper seems to be confessing that there is nothing he can do with them except set the chase in motion once again. Because he has split his heroine figure, he has the freedom to sacrifice Cora without violating the basic requirements of the frontier romance. Alice is saved to marry Heyward, but Cora and the two Indians who desire her all die. The happy ending, defined as the marriage of white hero and heroine, is qualified in *The Last of the Mohicans*, but not negated.

6

In addition to multiplying captivity episodes and linking them to a romantic plot, authors of the frontier romance often place them in a historical context. The immense popularity of Scott in the United States and the absence of historical conflict from pre-*Waverley* Indian fiction indicates that the English writer was the inspiration for this aspect of the genre.[17] Even had Scott's American imitators possessed his genius and erudition, however, it would not have been possible simply to transfer his concerns and method to a New World setting. As numerous American authors lamented, America lacked sufficient history, nor did what little history it had accumulated by the early nineteenth century seem to furnish the appropriate materials for historical romance.[18] As William Howard Gardiner complained:

> Here are no "gorgeous palaces and cloud capped towers;" no monuments of Gothic pride, mouldering in solitary grandeur; no mysterious hiding places to cover deeds of darkness from the light of the broad sun; no cloistered walls, which the sound of woe can never pierce; no ravages of desolating conquests; no traces of the slow and wasteful hand of time. You look over the face of a fair country, and it tells you no tale of days that are gone by. You see cultivated farms, and neat villages, and populous towns, full of health, and labor, and happiness.[19]

Neither Scott's chivalric spectacle nor his stratified society could be reproduced on this side of the Atlantic.

The element of unfamiliarity which romance required had to be found not in the pageantry and legends of bygone human epochs but in the scenic grandeur and primitive inhabitants of a virgin land. The political conflicts of English history—Jacobite and Hanoverian, Cavalier and Puritan—had to be replaced by the struggle of opposing colonial groups: English versus other nationalities of settlers, each with supporting Indians, or by the stark racial and cultural confrontation of whites and Indians. And where Scott might range over more than a thousand years of history for his "favourable opportunities of contrast," American authors were reduced to an uncomfortable proximity to their country's past: a mere two centuries separated them from its beginnings and less than a lifetime from the date of its national independence.[20] Little wonder that Cooper glumly wrote: "This country probably presents as barren a field to the writer of fiction . . . as any other on earth, we are not certain that we might not say the most barren."[21]

In spite of these difficulties, the influence of Scott was soon felt. The Revolutionary War became a popular subject for nineteenth-century literature in general, although other historical epochs were more suited to the frontier romance. A handful of works is found at the two extremes which Scott referred to as naturally interesting to the reader, antiquity and contemporary times: the earliest colonial history of Massachusetts and Virginia, and the still recent western uprising of Tecumseh. But most frontier romances are set during the immediate past when the contest for supremacy on the North American continent was bitterly fought out. Depending upon the author's view, Indians are depicted as creatures of the French, attacking English settlers according to the master's instructions, or as an independent power, fighting in their own behalf for the land. In keeping with Scott's practice, historical figures, usually military commanders, are sometimes brought in as peripheral characters; more frequently, they are merely mentioned without playing any part in the work.

The earliest use of historical events in the frontier romance, Samuel Woodworth's *The Champions of Freedom* (1816), is an apt illustration of Scott's criticism of his imitators for "a dragging-in [of] historical details by head and shoulders, so that the interest of the main piece is lost in minute description of events which do not affect its progress."[22] The important events of the War of 1812 are presented in journal form, mere lumps of chronicle matter in which the novel's characters are not involved at all. After Woodworth's unskillful separation of the two, writers did attempt to integrate the real and the fictive, but often without much more than a passing nod in the direction of history. A much vaguer historical ambience than Scott typically created, one which simply posited a frontier situation, was more suitable to the demands of the frontier romance.

Many open with a statement that the story recounted takes place during the Revolutionary War or some other identifiable time, but the work itself then continues without any recognizable indication of the supposed historical period. The opening remarks serve rather as the explanation for any white-Indian conflict which the author finds useful than for the building of a rich historical texture in the *Waverley* manner. In Charles Fenno Hoffman's *Greyslaer*, after the Revolutionary War period is established at the beginning, Joseph Brant is seen conferring with a British officer. This is all the deference Hoffman pays to history; although Indian raids are assumed to be motivated by the war, Brant and the British do nothing further in the novel. The French and Indian wars are similarly used in *Ish-Noo-Ju-Lut-Sche* as the rationale for Indian hostilities in New York, but no historical characters or encounters between the opposing sides are incorporated into the romance.

It could not be said that writers of the frontier romance found, as Bernbaum wrote of Scott, that "the entire complex of a nation's life, the correlation of its diverse social forces, and the intermingling of its classes from king to commoner, were more interesting than the personal fortunes of a pair of lovers."[23] The fate of the hero and heroine is the business to which these authors devote the most time and space and to which other matters are clearly secondary. Typically, a famous battle is primarily important for its effect on the main character. In *Elkswatawa*, for example, the Indians' preoccupation with battle preparations gives the captive white heroine a chance to escape. After his defeat at Tippecanoe, the Prophet seeks a scapegoat: blaming the heroine's loss for the Indian troubles, he orders the good Indian women who had helped her put to death. In two novels set in the time of King Philip's War, *The Doomed Chief* and *Mount Hope*, the most important outcome of decisive historical battles is to reunite the hero and heroine and free one or both of them from Indian captivity.

By the union of the white American couple at the conclusion, and by the death or defeat of the Indians and foreign whites, the frontier romance conveyed a historical truth which transcended the particulars of specific battles and wars: the ongoing possession of the North American continent by whites who had overcome the native inhabitants, and who had, by also expelling foreign whites, insisted upon a new national identity.

NOTES

1. Roy Harvey Pearce, "The Significance of the Captivity Narrative," *American Literature* 19 (1946-1947), p. 13.
2. D. H. Lawrence, *Studies in Classic American Literature* (New York, 1930), p. 80.
3. At least not the sort favored by the frontier romance; the famous eighteenth-century captive, Mary Jemison, whose story became a best seller in 1824,

married two Indians in succession and preferred to remain with the Indians all her life.

4. As applied to Indians in this study, the terms "good" and "bad" refer only to whether Indians are friendly or inimical to whites. See Chapter Three for a detailed discussion of these two stereotypes.

5. R. W. B. Lewis, *The American Adam* (Chicago, 1955), p. 104.

6. The unknown author of *The Witch of New England* (1824) encounters this problem when his hero is being tortured: "The air of stern dignity or contempt which had, at last, fixed itself on the features of young Bradley, seemed to make a sudden and forcible impression upon the savage. As if impelled by some novel but powerful impulse, he rushed through the flames that were now approaching rapidly towards the stake; scattered the faggots; cut the bands of the prisoner and drew him from his perilous situation."

7. Alexis De Tocqueville, *Democracy in America*, Henry Reeve text, rev. Francis Bowen and Phillips Bradley (New York, 1945), vol. II, pp. 55-56.

8. In *Elkswatawa*, the villainous Prophet flees to Canada, but in over sixty full-length frontier romances this is the only instance of a bad Indian escaping retribution.

9. According to Arthur Hobson Quinn, *American Fiction* (New York, 1936), p. 5, n. 1, the *History* was written in 1781 and first printed in the *New York Magazine* or *Literary Repository* (1790-1791), vols. I and II. Limiting my study to fiction first published in the United States rules out *The Emigrants* (London, 1793), purportedly written by the American author Gilbert Imlay, but more likely by Mary Wollstonecraft; see Robert R. Hare's introduction to *The Emigrants* (Dublin, 1794), facsimile rpt. (Gainesville, 1964).

10. Out of a total of 68 pages, 15 set the scene before the raid and 25 cover Maria's stay in Montreal after the period of Indian captivity has ended. Thus, little more than a third of the book is devoted to the standard captivity experience.

11. Eumea is actually a half-breed, but after this is first mentioned her white blood seems to be forgotten. Her experience, in any case, is paradigmatic of the role played by the good Indian maiden in many later frontier romances.

12. As Lillie Deming Loshe notes, the earlier novel *Edgar Huntly* (1801) conspicuously fails to make this connection: "In any modern work of the kind the fair captive would have been the heaven-sent bride of the hero, but the heartless Brown does not give her another page" (*The Early American Novel* [New York, 1907], p. 72). *The Emigrants* (1793) contains a captivity episode in which the hero rescues the heroine, but the incident is briefly reported and undeveloped.

13. Holman is fond of romantically named heroines; in addition to Zerelda, the novel contains Emerine, Emerald, Armilda, and Amacette.

14. Cf. Imlay's *The Emigrants*: "Unfortunate Caroline! How will her sensible heart palpitate in the agonizing dereliction [captivity]? How will her tender limbs support the fatigue of being hurried through briary thickets? How will her lovely frame be able to rest, without other covering than the cloud deformed canopy of the heavens? What will be the sensation of Arl-ton when he hears of the fate of Caroline."

15. 1823: James Fenimore Cooper, *The Pioneers*; James McHenry, *The Spectre of the Forest* and *The Wilderness*; James Kirke Paulding, *Koningsmarke*. 1824: Harriet V. Cheney, *A Peep at the Pilgrims*; Lydia Maria Child, *Hobomok*; Eliza Lanesford Cushing, *Saratoga*; anon., *The Witch of New England*.

Several other novels published before this time do not merit attention in terms of the development of the genre of the frontier romance: Charles Brockden Brown's *Edgar Huntly* (1801) briefly employs the stock captivity bad Indian; the anonymously written *St. Herbert* (1813) contains a few pages devoted to a philosophical Indian; John Davis's *First Settlers of Virginia* (1802) is barely fictionalized history, while his *Walter Kennedy* (1805) is a travel adventure with no plot; John Neal's *Keep Cool* (1817) has a short Indian episode unconnected to the novel's involved romantic plot, and his *Logan* (1822) has some of the elements of the frontier romance found in other works but is so incoherently plotted as to defy discussion. Fred Lewis Pattee's description of this author is definitive: "To read any of Neal's work with its slap-dash incoherence, its amazing digressions, its sheer ignorance, its almost total lack of critical power or stylistic beauty is like a journey through chaos" (*The First Century of American Literature* [New York, 1935], p. 282).

(*The First Century of American Literature* [New York, 1935], p. 282).
16. Cooper's later frontier romances fully exploit the good-bad Indian dichotomy and the captivity episode.
17. G. Harrison Orians introduces his extensive list of nineteenth-century comments about Scott's popularity in America with the remark that "literally thousands of testimonies" exist on the subject ("The Rise of Romanticism, 1805-1855," *Transitions in American Literary History,* ed. Harry Hayden Clark [New York, 1967], pp. 200-201, n. 56).
18. Benjamin T. Spencer, *The Quest for Nationality* (Syracuse, 1957), pp. 83-84, 95-96, describes an opposing school which regarded the absence of stock gothic properties as an asset to American literature. Cornelius Mathews is a representative champion of this school: "Humanity and nature are all with which the heart wishes to deal, and we have them here in their naked outlines and grandeur. There is enough here for author and reader if they be of strong minds and true hearts. A green forest or a swelling mound is to them as glorious as a Grecian temple; and they are so simple as to be well nigh as much affected by the sight of a proud old oak in decay near at home, as by the story of a baronial castle tottering to its fall three thousand miles off" (Preface to *Behemoth* [New York, 1839], p. v.).
19. William Howard Gardiner, Review of *The Spy, North American Review* 15 (1822), pp. 252-253; cf. Nathaniel Hawthorne's formulation of the problem in the preface to *The Marble Faun, The Complete Writings of Nathaniel Hawthorne* (Boston, 1900), vol IX, p. xxiv: "No author, without a trial, can conceive of the difficulty of writing a Romance about a country where there is no shadow, no antiquity, no mystery, no picturesque and gloomy wrong, nor anything but a common-place prosperity, in broad and simple day-light, as is happily the case with my dear native land. It will be very long, I trust, before romance-writers may find congenial and easily handled themes either in the annals of our stalwart Republic or in any characteristic and probable events of our individual lives. Romance and poetry, like ivy, lichens, and wall-flowers, need Ruin to make them grow."
20. Sir Walter Scott, *Waverley* (Philadelphia, 1873), p. 40. Scott refers to various disadvantages in setting *Waverley* only sixty years before the present, a period which he describes as lacking both the charm of antiquity and the relevance of contemporary times: "A tale of manners, to be interesting, must either refer

to antiquity so great as to have become venerable, or it must bear a vivid reflection of those scenes which are passing daily before our eyes, and are interesting from their novelty."

21. Cooper, *Home As Found* (Philadelphia, 1838), vol. I, p. iv. Although his practice bespoke success, Cooper occasionally voiced discouragement over the problems of creating an American literature; cf. *Notions of the Americans* (Philadelphia, 1841), vol. II, p. 108: "There is scarcely an ore which contributes to the wealth of the author, that is found, here, in veins as rich as in Europe. There are no annals for the historian; no follies (beyond the most vulgar and commonplace) for the satirist; no manners for the dramatist; no obscure fictions for the writer of romance; no gross and hardy offences against decorum for the moralist; nor any rich artificial auxiliaries of poetry."

22. *The Journal of Sir Walter Scott* (New York, 1891), vol. I, p. 275.

23. Ernest Bernbaum, *Guide Through the Romantic Movement*, 2nd ed. (New York, 1949), p. 146.

3

The White Man's Indian: A Range of Stereotypes

He is noble. He is true and loyal; not even imminent death can shake his peerless faithfulness. His heart is a well-spring of truth, and of generous impulses, and of knightly magnanimity. With him gratitude is religion; do him a kindness, and at the end of a lifetime he has not forgotten it.

**

He is ignoble—base and treacherous, and hateful in every way. Not even imminent death can startle him into a spasm of virtue. . . . His heart is a cesspool of falsehood, of treachery, and of low and devilish instincts. With him, gratitude is an unknown emotion; and when one does him a kindness, it is safest to keep the face toward him, lest the reward be an arrow in the back.

Mark Twain, "THE NOBLE RED MAN"

1

That the cluster of traits which are repeatedly used to characterize Indians in the pre-Civil War frontier romance constitute stereotypes may be inferred from some of the established

71

ethnographic data on the Indian. When colonists first arrived, the North American continent contained over six hundred different Indian societies speaking over two hundred languages and employing two thousand tribal designations.[1] Even a classification of North American Indian societies by cultural traits produces ten major areas comprising many subgroupings.[2] Given the diversity of physical environment, culture, and language, it seems hardly possible that all Indians—who recognized significant differences among themselves—should conform to the narrow range of attitudes and behavior ascribed to them in the frontier romance. For almost any aspect of manner or character attributed to fictive Indians it is no difficult task to find whole tribes which behave differently. Nor is it hard to discover nineteenth-century protests that fiction sterotyped the Indian. Washington Irving states: "As far as I can judge, the Indian of poetical fiction is like the shepherd of pastoral romance, a mere personification of imaginary attributes." His nephew, John T. Irving, Jr., complains that "writers have represented the Indians according to a conventional and artificial model"; James Hall similarly notes the "many popular errors about Indians" in his nonfictional book about the West, and William T. Snelling devotes a long preface to correcting the "typical novel presentation" of the aborigine in the light of his own experience living among Indians.[3] These four authors are among the few who had actual frontier experience; typically, a frontier romancer was Eastern, educated, and often from a prominent family. As A. Irving Hallowell observes: "Generally speaking, there was no inclination on the part of eastern novelists, dramatists, or poets who selected Indian themes to become acquainted with living Indians of the contemporary frontier as a background for their productions."[4]

In fiction, the Indian was subjected to a process which Walter Lippmann describes in his discussion of stereotyping:

For the most part we do not first see and then define, we define first and then see. In the great blooming, buzzing confusion of the outer world we pick out what our culture has already defined for us, and we tend to perceive that which we have picked out in the form stereotyped for us by our culture.[5]

When writers of the frontier romance began to use Indian characters, they did not see and define, but merely appropriated the stereotype of the bad Indian already delineated in the captivity narrative. Individual bad Indians might be singled out for prominent roles, but they remained pattern figures nevertheless, representative of the whole inimical race which threatened white settlers and settlement.

As Lippmann goes on to say, there are reasons why stereotyping is favored over disinterested observation:

> A pattern of stereotypes is not neutral. . . . It is the guarantee of our self-respect; it is the projection upon the world of our own sense of our own value, our own position and our own rights. The stereotypes are, therefore, highly charged with the feelings that are attached to them. They are the fortress of our tradition, and behind its defenses we can continue to feel ourselves safe in the position we occupy.[6]

Against the evil captor, pioneer heroism could be asserted in a number of ways; rescuing captives, defending homesteads, making war on the aggressors, and generally outperforming the Indian in his own wilderness skills illustrated and confirmed the superiority of white civilization.

Had it been possible to confine the Indian to the villainous captor role, doubts like those of the soldiers of the colonial army in King Philip's War who "seriously inquired, whether burning their enemies alive could be consistent with humanity, and the benevolent principles of the Gospel"[7] need never have arisen. The habitual murderers and mutilators of women and children who were instigated by the devil might fittingly be consigned to the flames, as witches were in the same colony some sixteen years later. But even within the Puritan experience, and aside from Apostle Eliot's "preying Indians,"[8] there was an impressive case for another kind of Indian. Just as the captivities seem blind to any acts of kindness of captor to victim, so the Puritan chronicles report without seeming to register the help of friendly Indians in all of the major white-Indian conflicts. Philip was betrayed and shot by one of his own Wampanoags, and the Narragansett sachem Canonchet was killed in the following manner:

> And that all might share in the Glory of destroying so great a Prince, and come under the Obligation of Fidelity each to other, the Pequods shot him, the Mohegins cut off his Head and quartered his Body, and the Ninnicrofts Men made the Fire and burned his Quarters; and as a Token of their Love and Fidelity to the English, presented his Head to the Council at Hartford.[9]

By the time another century of American history had been made, reasonable minds were able to perceive that much Indian trouble had been masterminded by the groups of whites—French, Spanish, Dutch, English, and Americans—who struggled to dominate the continent. For the rest, in Benjamin Franklin's dispassionate judgment: "During the Course of a long Life in which I have made Observations on public Affairs, it has appear'd to me that almost every War between the Indians and Whites has been occasion'd by some Injustice of the latter toward the former."[10] The men of the late eighteenth century had both history and scholarship enough to see the Indian as a primitive human who had been sadly wronged, but whose status as victim could not be changed.[11]

To recognize humanity but withhold its natural rights—life, liberty, and the pursuit of happiness being one popular formulation—created a dilemma for fiction as well as an Indian problem for the American government. Out of the historical existence of faithful Indian allies, worked upon by feelings of pity and guilt, the more varied, contradictory, and interesting stereotype of the good Indian emerges. While the bad stereotype justified dispossession and extermination of the Indian, the good counterimage was truly the *beau idéal* which critics complained of, the Indian conceived in white guilt who embodied a wishful notion of what a "civilized" Indian might have been: a friend and companion of white men.[12]

2

"Red Gifts": The Core of Indianness

Before describing the three Indian stereotypes of the pre-Civil War frontier romance, it is worthwhile to note that some characteristics were shared by all images of the Indian. These are not merely a cluster of morally neutral qualities which cannot readily be divided into good, i.e., friendly and helpful to whites, or bad, i.e., inimical toward them, but rather a group of core traits—"red gifts," as Natty Bumppo would say—which authors regarded as definitive of Indianness. Thus, all fictive Indians are fine physical specimens, proficient in wilderness skills, stoical, and given to figurative speech. None of these characteristics are moral, according to the special white formulation of good and bad for Indians, but all are to some degree positive and admirable.

The excellent physical condition and appearance of Indians had been remarked by writers from the earliest contact of the two cultures. Robert Beverley notes: "They are straight and well proportion'd, having the cleanest and most exact Limbs in the World: They are so perfect in their outward frame, that I never heard of one single *Indian,* that was either dwarfish, crooked, bandy-legg'd, or otherwise misshapen."[13] Captain John Smith admits that the Virginia Indians "differ very much in stature," but are "generally tall and straight, of a comely proportion."[14] The captivity narratives, on the other hand, were little preoccupied with physical appearance *per se.* At times, the Indians attacking and carrying off captives were described as huge, presumably to render them more fearsome to the reader. They were seldom depicted with anything but a distorted visage, howling, scowling, leering, or otherwise grimacing at the poor victim. Only those aspects of the Indian which contributed to the captivity experience and enhanced the fearful quality of the captors were apt to be part of these narratives.

Writers of fiction continued the tradition of the Indian as a fine physical specimen, ranging from tall to huge or gigantic. Hobomok, for example, has a "tall, athletic form." He "was indeed cast in nature's noblest mould. He was one of the finest specimens of elastic, vigorous elegance of proportion to be found among his tribe." Tecumseh has a "giant form," Tokeah is "colossal," Sanutee is "large and justly proportioned," and the Indian chief in *The Champions of Freedom* is "gigantic. . . . More symmetry of form, regularity of features, and dignity of countenance were never united in man. The prowess of Hercules appeared combined with the grace of Adonis." Tadeuskund is both "gigantic" and "Herculean." If imposing physical attributes alone made a noble savage, few Indians in frontier romances would fail to qualify. Even Poe's Sioux, introduced in *The Journal of Julius Rodman* as "an ugly, ill-made race, their limbs being much too small for the trunk, according to our ideas of human form," capitulate to the stereotype only four pages later when they are described as "presenting a very noble and picturesque appearance. Some of the chiefs . . . were really gallant-looking men." In addition to preeminent size and excellent proportion, fictive Indians are generally attractive physically, dignified in posture, and endowed with keen senses.[15]

In the skills required by their mode of life, particularly hunting, tracking, and surprising an enemy, Indians are portrayed as highly proficient. Within the total context of any frontier romance, however, these abilities are seldom given much emphasis. In the middle of a long diatribe against Indians in a short story by James Hall, a pioneer admits that they are "prime hunters," but the load of opprobrium carried by the larger portion of the speech outweighs this one compliment. Another Hall short story refers to the Indian as a "mere hunter." Presumably Indians hunted to live, but, like most fictive characters, they are rarely seen in the process of acquiring their food; the plot generally calls for more exciting work. Tracking and other forest skills receive some attention, but here again, Indian accomplishments are minimized by the requirements of the fictive design: whites must outperform Indians in order to recover captives, defend themselves, and preserve their superior status.

Indian stoicism, another characteristic common to all stereotypes, ranges from a habitual failure to register facial expression to control over all forms of physical reaction during moments of intense stress, in Emerson Bennett's words, "a custom which is held by the savages to be a great virtue."[16] In a general description of the Indian Weshop, John Brainerd writes: "His fixed features seldom betrayed the working of his passions, or any vicissitudes of feeling." James Fenimore Cooper prefers to display Indian stoicism in its most extreme tests.[17] The first person hero of *Satanstoe* remarks about an Indian being whipped: "The pine stands not more erect or unyielding, in a summer's noontide, than he bore up under the pain." Elsewhere, in *The Prairie*, Natty Bumppo describes an Indian on the verge of death:

"I have been a dweller in forests and in the wilderness for threescore and ten years, and if any can pretend to know the world, or to have seen skeary sights, it is myself! But never before nor since, have I seen human man in such a state of mortal despair as that very savage; and yet he scorned to speak, or to cry out, or to own his forlorn condition! It is their gift, and nobly did he maintain it!"

In both instances the Indians were enemies of the whites, but their stoicism is nevertheless admired. For the Indian-hating Luke in *Kabaosa*, stoicism is the only commendable Indian trait: " 'Neither torture nor imprisonment will wring a word from a full-blooded Indian against his will. If there's anything to admire in the character of them-are savages, 'tis that torture or death will never tempt them to betray a comrade.' "

Exceptions to the rule of the stoical Indian do occur, but in such cases the authors are at pains to remark special circumstances. Eoneguski, who ordinarily has "the dignified composure of a savage," breaks down when his father disowns him: "Feelings too powerful for even the stoicism in which he had been brought up to control, forced the tears in rapid succession down his cheeks, while sobs, frequent and violent, heaved his bosom" (*Eoneguski*). More typically, good Indians, especially women characters, abandon their stoical deportment when they fall in love with whites. Magawisca, an Indian maiden who becomes part of a white family, "had a habitual self-command, that hid the emotions of her heart from common observers, and veiled them even from those who most narrowly watched her" (*Hope Leslie*).

But in the presence of her white beloved, and much to his astonishment, Magawisca "threw herself on the ground, drew her mantle over her face, and wept convulsively." Where an erotic motive is absent, Indian weeping may be used to dramatize white influence. In both *Keep Cool* and *Ish-Noo-Ju-Lut-Sche*, Indians are taught to weep by their white mentors.

Indian speech, the final characteristic which all stereotypes share, created a problem which can be traced back to the earliest reports on the American natives. The impressive English periods in which Powhatan spoke, according to Captain John Smith's writings, seem most incredible. Although Smith does not say so, the likeliest explanation is that they were actually uttered in Powhatan's own language, translated by an interpreter, and then made to conform to typical seventeenth-century written English. Nathaniel Saltonstall, on the other hand, quotes an Indian who was frightened when his English opponent took off his periwig: " 'Umh, Umh me no stawmerre fight Engismon, Engismon got two Hed, Engismon got two Hed; if me cut off un Hed, he got noder, a put on beder as dis' " [emphasis removed].[18] This manner of speaking sounds all too authentic and all too inappropriate for fictive purposes. The heavy accent, the ungrammatical constructions, and the simplicity of utterance which lack of verbal facility entails reduce the character to the level of farce. Whatever the degree of verisimilitude, Indians who speak broken English must appear somewhat foolish to the reader. In the face of two extremes, language which was patently artificial and language which seemed realistic but was aesthetically objectionable, most authors adopted a compromise: the formal, figurative style which they believed to convey Indian thought patterns accurately.[19] Cooper, who is credited with establishing this mode of speaking, was oddly unfaithful to it. Half of his ten Indian novels, including the first of the *Leatherstocking Tales*, have Indians speaking like minstrel-show darkies. With this important exception, fiction written after *The Last of the Mohicans* (1826), the all-time best seller of the frontier romance, conforms to the figurative standard.[20]

An early contributor to the genre, Eliza Lanesford Cushing, remarks in *Saratoga* (1824) an Indian who breaks "at once into the forcible and figurative language peculiar to his race." And James

Kirke Paulding notes in his description of the Indian chief Paskingoe "a singular force, brevity, and richness in his phraseology that partook somewhat of the Indian manner of expression" (*The Dutchman's Fireside*). In actual discourse, the distinctive Indian speech tends to be more formal than figurative: an occasional reference to the "paleface" often suffices to satisfy the metaphoric requirement. More zealous authors usually confine their Indians to short flights of metaphor, like Eoneguski's philosophical comment: " 'The children of men . . . are like leaves scattered over the earth, the winds breathe upon them, and they are gathered in heaps—it blows again, and they are scattered widely asunder.' " Cooper alone carries on in this vein at great length. In *The Deerslayer*, Hist's rejection of a Huron marriage offer is entirely metaphoric:

> "Tell the Hurons, Deerslayer," she said, "that they are as ignorant as moles; they don't know the wolf from the dog. Among my people, the rose dies on the stem where it budded; the tears of the child fall on the graves of its parents; the corn grows where the seed has been planted. The Delaware girls are not messengers to be sent, like belts of wampum, from tribe to tribe. They are honeysuckles, that are sweetest in their own woods; their own young men carry them away in their bosoms, because they are fragrant; they are sweetest when plucked from their native stems."

Hist continues at length without ever plainly answering the question Deerslayer has pressed upon her but evoking his admiration for expressing her "honest, deepest feelin's, in proper words." The reader may sympathize with the patronized Hutter girl, to whom Deerslayer remarks: " 'You don't understand it, I suppose, Judith.' " The degree to which Cooper is committed to figurative Indian speech in *The Last of the Mohicans* and *The Deerslayer* in particular makes the periodic lapses into pidgin English of his frontier romance career all the more puzzling.

William J. Snelling, who envisioned his authorial role as the correction of an inaccurate Indian stereotype, found the typical fictive Indian speech to be "a farrago of metaphor and absurdity." He distinguished between ordinary Indian language, which is "flat and commonplace," and council orations, which are "studied efforts, in which the speaker purposely obscures his meaning with parables and verbiage."[21] James Strange French followed Snelling in discriminating between an "everyday" and an "exalted" manner, adding: "Never as far as my personal experience enabled me to judge, did I hear any expressions more highly wrought or figurative, than such as would be used in ordinary conversation among ourselves." In spite of these remarks neither author qualifies as a dissenter in practice: Snelling seldom gives his Indians any direct discourse, and French's speak metaphorically like other fictive Indians.

3

The Bad Indian

The Indian who is inimical to whites, the bad Indian stereotype, was taken over by fiction from the captivity genre, which in turn originally developed from the same world view and historical circumstances that produced the Puritan chronicle. A more satisfactory enumeration of the salient features of the fictive bad Indian than William Bradford's seventeenth-century chronicle could hardly be found:

> Ye salvage people . . . are cruell, barbarous, and most trecherous, being most furious in their rage, and merciles wher they overcome; not being contente only to kill, and take away life, but delight to tormente men in ye most bloodie manner that may be; fleaing some alive . . . cutting of ye members and joynts of others by peesmeale, and broiling on ye coles, eate ye collops of their flesh in their sight whilst they live; with other cruelties horrible to be related.[22]

The evolution of the captivity narrative in the more than a century before the appearance of the frontier romance did not alter the concept of the evil captor Indian introduced by the Puritan chronicle. Instead, his gothic potentialities were exploited more fully than even Cotton Mather might have relished. Adept at coining epithets and name-calling, Mather lacked the sheer weight of grisly detail which would become commonplace in late eighteenth-century captivity narratives. Nor did Mrs. Rowlandson and other early victims seek to embellish their stark accounts. After the initial horror, which might be little more than a listing of people falling and others being carried off, the early captivity story was primarily the record of a terrible struggle to survive in the wilderness. Benumbed and unprofessional, the seventeenth-century captive might be aware of a dreadful din without distinguishing the "exultant laugh" which became a regular mannerism of the fictive Indian captor.

In appropriating the already existent bad Indian stereotype, writers of fiction merely actualized possibilities already present in the figure to allow him a more varied and ambitious role in his machinations against whites. Women included, the Indians of the Puritan chronicle and the captivity narrative are diabolical monsters, chiefly engaged in the massacre and torture of whites.[23] In this capacity, Indians are given to skulking and lurking, exulting over reeking scalps, uttering chilling cries, and devising fiendish torments for their hapless victims. From the predilection for wanton cruelty illustrated by their aggression against innocent whites, other character traits were readily extrapolated. In addition to practicing a barbaric kind of warfare, bad Indians are treacherous, vengeful, and superstitious.

Above all, bad Indians are defined as implacable enemies of whites, the perpetrators of a monotonously repeated pattern of aggression against them. Throughout the frontier romance they endlessly assault and capture whites, "uttering demonic yells of exultation" which change to "howls of rage and dismay" when intrepid rescuers thwart their final triumph. Epithets in the Matherian spirit are plentiful; attacking Indians are merciless monsters, barbarous wretches, red devils, infernal scamps, murderous hounds, red imps of satan, the fiercely exulting foe, and the devil incarnate. As these examples indicate, the Puritan equation of Indian and devil persisted in fiction. The term *savage*, with its strongly pejorative connotations, is also frequently used as a synonym for *Indian*. In swooping down upon a homestead unexpectedly, the Indians usually have "the most diabolical appearance imaginable," but oddly enough, considering the author's intention of exploiting the terror of the Indian raid, concrete details of appearance are few. The attackers are usually large and are often termed "almost naked" or "hideously painted" without further particulars. Some shooting, tomahawking, and scalping are described, but again, physical detail is scant except in the subgenre of Indian hater fiction. In this specialized fiction, devoted to the deeds of professional Indian killers, the horrors of the massacre are enlarged to motivate the ensuing white vengeance. As James Hall writes in "The Pioneer," one of his many Indian hater tales: "The hell-hounds were literally tearing them in pieces—exulting, shouting, smearing themselves with blood, and trampling on the remains of the wretched victims."

Instead of this kind of elaboration, authors often adopt Mather's practice of referring to gruesome particulars which they are in fact withholding from the reader. In *The Champions of Freedom* Samuel Woodworth simply states: "The barbarities of the Indians are shocking beyond belief." Similarly, Ann Eliza Bleecker ends her description of an Indian atrocity in *The History of Maria Kittle* by noting that there were "many additional circumstances of infernal cruelty." M. C. Hodges offers a concern for the reader's sensibility to excuse his omission of data about an Indian raid: "Here, gentle reader, for your sake, we reject the horrible detail of the process of scalping" (*The Mestico*). Even from a nineteenth-century author, this argument is highly suspect. More reasonably, James McHenry asserts that detail is not needed to flesh out the vague horrors of the experience:

> The threats, the barbarities and exultation of the savages; the terrors, the tears, the lamentations and the actual sufferings of the captives, many of whom, during their rapid and cruel march, died of their wounds or their ill-treatment, might require description if they were not already present to every imagination. (*The Wilderness*)

In all probability, an awareness that Indian attack was already a familiar and conventionalized episode accounts for the almost mechanical and generalized recital of its standard components.

Other than scalping, the feature of Indian warfare which receives the most description is the war whoop. Perhaps because it was utterly foreign to white practice, unlike the actual weaponry used by the Indians, the cry regularly evoked terror: "A sudden wild and startling cry is heard—the Indian's furious yell breaks on their ears, unused to such fierce tones. . . . The woods rolled back the dismal notes and many a heart was chilled with deepest terror, inspired by the savage salutation." This frightening prelude to Braddock's defeat in *Tom Hanson the Avenger* seems to encapsulate the elements of unexpectedness and unfamiliarity which played a major part in routing the British troops.

Most commonly, the war whoop was compared to some animal noise: "The yell that followed was like the bursting forth of a menagerie of wild animals, each one striving to make the most horrible and discordant sound" (*Kabaosa*). John Neal, in his typically heightened fashion, made the most detailed attempt to express the effect of the distinctive Indian cry:

I have heard the sullen roar of the Bengal tiger . . . the echo of the lion's voice in the depth of night; the curdling howl of the native wolf, when the breath of the animal almost seemed to touch my ear. I have heard the worst of all sounds that can be uttered, the suppressed cry of the female catamount; when the crackling of the branches tells you she has just leaped, and that some intended victim has escaped; aye, and I have heard its fierce, shrill voice, from the very top of a barren tree, crowning a tremendous cliff; over a still lake, on a clear, cold night: while it ran along the water and the rocks in countless reverberations; when I could have believed a whole herd were crying; but, never, never, have I heard a sound so perfectly appalling as the deep yell of a single Indian, amid the tomb-like silence of a winter night in Canada. The stoutest heart will shrink, though defended by thousands of bayonets; and wrap itself closer in its folds. . . . I have felt mine quake when I knew it was the cry of a *friend*. (*Keep Cool*)

The power of the war whoop seems to be its embodiment of brute ferocity, like the cries of wild animals which Neal's character cites, coupled with the knowledge that it springs from a human malevolence and a popular belief that it was uttered only when victory was certain. Natty Bumppo, however, is able to retain perspective when the Indian cry is heard. He explains to a frightened novice woodsman that the war whoop is the Indian equivalent of a military marching band: " 'Tis their music, boy; their drum and fife, their trumpets and clarions' " (*The Pathfinder*). But he also accepts it as a natural phenomenon of the wilderness, like the call of the catbird or whippoorwill.

The surprise attack which a war whoop heralds is one manifestation of the treacherous disposition commonly ascribed to bad Indians. Because "he is the child of nature, and her caprice will dictate his course," Snelling writes in *Tales of the Northwest*, the Indian's actions cannot rationally be predicted. At best he is inconsistent, at worst treacherous. In Paulding's description in *The Dutchman's Fireside*, an "unsteady" nature "made their friendship as precarious as their enmity was terrible." And in spite of the several occasions in his fiction when Indians are released on parole and later voluntarily surrender themselves up to death, Cooper allows Pathfinder to ruminate on "how valueless pledges became when put in opposition to interest, where a savage was concerned." Such comments suggest that Indians are thoughtlessly and unintentionally treacherous. Other writers voice the harsher view that Indian treachery is premeditated. The white settler Aymor in *Eoneguski* "was not ignorant of the craft of the savage, and that with him an appearance of friendship, is not unfrequently the fair cluster of flowers beneath which the deadliest malice lies coiled, like a serpent, for a more fatal and effectual spring." A typical instance of this Machiavellianism occurs in one of the works of that stalwart of the frontier romance, Emerson Bennett. Travelling whites encounter a group of Indians who beg presents in a servile fashion and then, after they receive them, fire on their benefactors.

Another negative characteristic commonly attributed to Indians is an extreme degree of vengefulness: "In the savage state the feeling of revenge is perhaps the strongest and most inveterate that actuates the mind" (*The Wilderness*). A murder committed by a bad Indian in "The Two Camps" is explained matter-of-factly as "the old revenge for the killing of his father; for an Indian never forgets that sort of obligation." Often, constancy in both revenge and friendship is granted to Indians: the 1828 edition of Noah Webster's *Dictionary* characterizes Indians as remarkable for "truth, fidelity and gratitude to their friends, but implacably cruel and revengeful toward their enemies." For purposes of fiction, it was more convenient to split up these characteristics: bad Indians exemplify undying vengeance while eternal gratitude is reserved for good Indians. One of the most enthusiastic proponents of the bad Indian stereotype, Joseph C. Hart, cautions the reader that Indians may be vengeful without good cause: "Beware of yielding confidence to the Indian! For an imaginary injury done to his remote ancestor, and handed down to him by tradition, he will wreak vengeance upon some innocent descendant of the wrong-doer, even to the fourth generation" (*Miriam Coffin*).

A rather different interpretation is necessary when whites exercise vengeance. Unlike Cooper's separation of red and white gifts, which classifies revenge as "an Indian feeling," frontier romances and also general defenses of the pioneer use the Indian revenge ethic to justify white practice. A white hunter in *The Hawk Chief* states: " 'I look upon revenge as but nat'ral; blood for blood is my maxim. The Ingens too have an instinct for giving as good as they get! And instinct always ranges close to right.' " Comments like this are never given authorial support, for the danger of frontier whites adopting Indian habits and losing their superior civilized status was implicitly recognized.[24]

Indian superstitiousness, like treachery and vengefulness, had a history in the Puritan chronicles and captivity narratives before it became a mainstay of the fictive Indian stereotype. In seventeenth-century New England, a variety of Indian practices and beliefs objectionable to whites, ranging from religion to medicine, were seriously regarded as commerce with the devil. The more secular frontier romance, while still using "devilish" and "diabolical" as common terms for the Indian, substituted the idea of heathen superstition to cover the same range of concerns.

The chief in *Kabaosa*, a romance which treats Tecumseh's uprising, regards his brother the Prophet as a cunning fraud, "who, by means of the credulity and superstition of the natives, managed to obtain such an ascendancy over them, that his will was law in every respect." In *Elkswatawa* the same Prophet promises his brother several years before the war that he will play on popular superstition to advance their cause: " 'I have considered their plans [other prophets'], I have learned their tricks, their deceptions, their practices.' " Similarly, *The Hawk Chief* describes a medicine man as "one of those whose superior craft or intelligence enables them to bend the wild rabble to their will, by their jugglery and pretended communication with the Deity." Being non-Christians, Indians could only pretend to any kind of true spirituality; nevertheless their medicine always exhibits remarkable healing powers, even when applied to presumably unsuperstitious whites. Authors felt no need to instruct their readers that these good results were attributable to the natural remedies Indians knew of, rather than to the incantations or other practices accompanying their application.

4

The Noble Savage

Although in the aggregate, either as bands raiding the pioneer homesteads or as whole tribes making war on the whites, Indians in the frontier romance usually belong to the bad Indian stereotype, the noble savage concept maintains an uneasy coexistence with the bad Indian image.[25] The guilty conscience which America developed as the Indian declined into probable extinction, the influence of English and European romanticism, and a genuine belief in the admirable qualities of pre-Columbian Indian life are all factors which may explain the unlikely presence of the noble savage in a captivity narrative format.[26] The difficulty in introducing the noble savage into the frontier romance lay in the primal conflict of interest between two cultures: Indians possessed land which whites coveted and seized either outright or by dubious treaty; in retaliation for white encroachment, Indians became the aggressive captors who figure so essentially in the plot of this genre. The elemental struggle of the captivity experience had no room for complex portraiture: the Indian was by definition a scalper and murderer of whites, a completely ignoble being. To find him otherwise without repudiating their commitment to white civilization, authors had to create a fictive situation which partially antedated white-Indian conflict: in isolation, in his Edenic wilderness, the Indian could be approved of as a noble savage, certainly inferior to whites, but suited to the simple and in some ways attractive life of the forest. As Washington Irving writes: "There is something in the character and habits of the North American savage, taken in connexion with the scenery over which he is accustomed to range, its vast lakes, boundless forests, majestic rivers and trackless plains, that is, to my mind, wonderfully striking and sublime."[27]

Because the frontier romance is really about whites, isolation cannot be complete nor can fiction be avoided totally. When the issue is joined, the noble savage is suddenly changed into the enemy: white authors naturally support their white characters and the values they stand for against the Indian.

The rationale which explains this process of transformation is the deterioration of the Indian when he is exposed to white civilization. The frontier romance is full of protestations that the Indian known to white settlements must not be equated with the noble denizen of the wilderness:

> The rude portraits of the red man, as given by those who see him in degrading attitudes only, and in humiliating relation with the whites, must not be taken as a just delineation of the same being in his native woods, unsubdued, a fearless hunter, and without any degrading habits, to make him wretched and ashamed. (*The Yemassee*)

With few exceptions, the degraded settlement Indian holds no interest for writers: he is reality intruding into a romantic literary age, living testimony to the dubious blessings which white civilization brought to the native inhabitants of the continent.[28] In equal measure, writers are anxious to assure the reader that they have accurate knowledge about Indians and that the reader's own information is most likely derived from observations of the sorry half-breeds of white communities. William J. Snelling, who prided himself on having lived among unspoiled western Indians, prefaces his *Tales of the Northwest* with a warning to the reader to distrust "the knowledge that may be acquired by a residence near the degraded race that a constant intercourse with our frontier settlers has made miserable." More specifically, Washington Irving describes the settlement Indians as "drunken, indolent, feeble, thievish and pusillanimous."[29] The Indian whom Snelling and his fellow authors wished to depict was one still living in primitive purity, interacting with whites to some extent but uncorrupted by their ways.

The easiest way to pay homage to the noble savage without disrupting the plot mechanism was to praise Indian virtues as a phenomenon of the past. Because only aggression against whites defined a bad Indian, most writers could safely do this; the torturing and scalping of other Indians which took place in precolonial Indian history could comfortably be assimilated to the noble savage image. Thus, Anna L. Snelling refers to "the persecuted race, who once in lawless freedom could rove unheeded through these beautiful scenes, and quench their thirst from the pure bosom of the flood beneath their feet; but who now turn from the white man's door, satisfied with the few poor crusts of bread dealt out by niggard hands" (*Kabaosa*). Mrs. Snelling's sympathy occasionally gives an Indian character eloquence to defend his way of life, but fails to alter the typical sequence of plot events. Her Indians attack and capture whites and are condemned and defeated like bona fide bad Indians.

A similar development occurs in James Birchett Ransom's *Osceola.* First, the author presents a picture of idyllic Indian life, undisturbed by white infringement: "Give the Indian the forest for his home, the wild sports of the chase for his amusement and support, and he is perfectly happy." The product of such a way of life is even superior to that of civilization:

> [She was] reared in a rude wigwam, among the wildest scenes of nature, a perfect stranger to all the refinements and elegances of life; and yet her artless innocence, and the

intelligence and sweetness of her sprightly countenance revealed a delicacy of feeling, a dignity of spirit, and nobleness of soul, which but few could acquire in the highest and most exalted walks of civilized society.

Once whites have "contaminated [his] rude and simple virtues by frequent examples of deception and fraud," the noble savage is metamorphosed into a Puritan fantasy: "with vengeance in his eye and death upon his lip, like a whirlwind of destruction he swept wildly and madly through the forest." Although they employ treachery, the whites, with the author's approbation, naturally triumph over the Indians. Ransom carries the aborigine from noble savage to bad Indian; Mrs. Snelling suggests the final step of defeat and decline: the degraded settlement Indian.

Although portraying the Indian as a noble savage in some past period of time is not in itself illogical, in practice the necessary compression of time often results in an overly sudden transformation: the worthy aborigine of one page becomes the howling savage of the next.

Another way of introducing the noble savage which writers of the frontier romance often chose is the well-known Cooper approach, the division of Indians into good and bad tribes. Just as the world of the *Leatherstocking Tales* is divided into evil Hurons (Mingos) and Sioux and good Delawares and Pawnees, so *The Shoshonee Valley* contains Shienne *[sic]* and Shoshonee, *Ish-Noo-Ju-Lut-Sche* and *The Scout* separate Mohawks and Hurons, and a number of other works distinguish between tribes fighting for the British (in pre-Revolutionary settings) and for the French, or, after the Revolution, for the Americans and for the British. Under this system, bad tribes, allied with enemy whites or obstreperous on their own initiative, can fill the function of attacker-captors demanded by the captivity plot and receive a strong measure of opprobrium for their treacherous ways. Good tribes, in contrast, may be lauded as noble savages.[30]

The difficulty inherent in this schematization is everywhere apparent in its most popular exponent. Cooper may at times describe the virtuousness of the Delawares and the viciousness of the Hurons,[31] but just as often he describes an Indian nature which is undifferentiated by tribe. Context governs the difference: when Indians are compared to whites, they are homogeneously lumped together; when they are compared with one another, it becomes possible to distinguish between a Delaware and a Huron. A problem arises in trying to reconcile the two kinds of comparative statement. In *The Prairie*, for example, a comparison to whites is explicitly made in the following passage: "Calm, dignified, and yet far from repulsive, they set an example of courtesy, blended with reserve, that many a diplomatist of the most polished court might have striven in vain to imitate." But when Cooper describes the Sioux as "a treacherous and dangerous race," he suggests a comparison with "their neighbors of the prairies"—other tribes. The dilemma for the reader lies in uniting the specific statement about the villainous Sioux with the noble savage qualities asserted by the general statement. Conversely, general statements about the treachery and deceit of the aborigine ill accord with the virtues ascribed to the Delawares. The procedure of dichotomizing into good and bad tribes is continuously defeated by this dual standard of comparison. Like the representation of earlier Indians as noble savages, the attempt to divide Indians into admirable primitives and evil marauders doomed Indians to a Jekyll and Hyde existence unsatisfactorily accounted for by authors. In terms of Indian characterization, the noble savage is only a progenitor, both of the bad Indian and, more directly, of the good Indian.

5

The Good Indian

Fictive Indians always begin as bad Indians, but through contact with benevolent whites, individual Indians may become "good," that is, they can be taught to forego some of the practices and beliefs objectionable to whites and to adopt white values and loyalties. Thus, good Indians enter fiction singly, cut off from their own people to provide an opportunity for extended interaction with whites. In a reversal of the most popular plot action of the frontier romance, the Indian may be a captive of whites, who teach him their ways and gain his devotion. He may come to them of his own volition, the fictive representative of generations of Indian scouts and guides. In other instances, he is cut off from his tribe only metaphorically; although he moves among Indians, some contact with whites has elevated him to a superior position from which he may deplore certain savage usages of his fellows. It is important to note that this figure is not simply a noble savage, but a noble savage upon whom certain aspects of white civilization have been engrafted. Whatever the circumstances, the good Indian has become good primarily through intercourse with whites, and his goodness is expressed chiefly by his services to them. The good Indian is loyal to whites to the point of self-sacrifice, conscious of Indian inferiority to the white man, and susceptible to certain white teachings, particularly Christian ideals. Considering how similar this racist pattern is to a sexist paradigm prevalent at that time, it is hardly surprising that the good Indian of fiction is often a woman.[32]

In the either-or formulation of the good Indian—civilized or dead—almost all authors of the frontier romance declare for civilization, although after they have civilized their good Indians they usually kill them off anyway. Contact with whites only makes bad Indians worse, transforming them into degraded and drunken derelicts on the fringes of a prosperous society, but it operates beneficially on the exceptional Indian. In *Hope Leslie*, for example, when the captured young Indian Magawisca is brought as a servant to the white household, she is told:

> "You should receive it as a signal mercy, child, that you have been taken from the midst of a savage people, and set in a Christian family. . . . You will soon perceive that our civilized life is far easier, far better and happier than your wild wandering ways, which are, indeed . . . but little superior to those of the wolves and foxes."

The enlightenment predicted for Magawisca is regularly alluded to in descriptions of good Indians. In *The Sanfords* Sequod is "a noble specimen of a true Indian chief, uniting in himself all the best traits of their untutored daring character, polished and softened by his superior intelligence and intercourse with the Sanfords." Benjamin Tashima in *Miriam Coffin* is an analogous case: "Though of the true breed, and in his youth a wild ranger of a continental forest, subsequent education, and conformity to the habits of civilization, had wrought an agreeable change in his person and demeanour."

In conformity with white expectations, good Indians are sensible of the benefits of white culture and to some extent reject their own way of life. The sachem of the Mohawks hopes that among his people "the tomahawk and the scalping knife will be exchanged for implements of husbandry and the domestic concerns of life" (*Ish-Noo-Ju-Lut-Sche*). In the same book the Indian girl Manima rejoices that "the dawn of civilization hath arisen on our dark and benighted nation." More frequently, Indian devotion is given to particular whites as much as to their way of life. The Indian Onona in *Kabaosa* had been brought up to hate the whites, but one sight of sleeping white girl disarms her: " 'From the moment I gazed upon the fair Lily as she slept in the wood, my heart began to grow soft, and I wondered how there could be ought but love between the daughters of the red man and those of the white.' " The dying Sequod thanks Geraldine Sanford for his enlightenment: " 'You and yours, kind lady, have taught me a milder spirit, and the poor Indian will die happier in your gentle presence, than if the blaze of villages he had conquered, lighted him to the far country, and the noblest warriors of his race chanted the death-song in his ear' " (*The Sanfords*). *Saratoga* contains a similar picture: "The faithful Ohmeina continued attached to his [Captain Grahame's] household; and till the last moment of a long and happy life, he evinced the same rectitude of principle and conduct, and the same devotion to his master, of which we have given so many instances in the progress of our history."

In addition to their gratitude and devotion to whites, both Sequod and Ohmeina display other characteristics typical of the good Indian stereotype: they are isolates, without family or tribal ties and, however civilized, are unable to convert other Indians. Good Indians can faithfully serve whites but are unable to engender any new birth among their own people. Ultimately, civilization meant death, even to fictive Indians. Only one good Indian actively attempts to raise his whole tribe to his own exceptional level: the old chief Benjamin Tashima in *Miriam Coffin*. He founds a model community for his dwindling Nantucket tribe, but as the author comments:

> It is difficult, however, to change the skin of the Ethiopian; and it did, sometimes, happen that the dogged and loose propensities of the Indian would break forth as of yore. Sullen laziness, drunkenness, petty theft, and cowardly violence—inherent qualities of the race—would prevail for a time among a few of the more dissolute.

When Tashima dies, the tribe "soon relapsed into the beastly habits of the Indian."

For the good Indian, saving the white friend or beloved from bad Indians is the most typical and approved action. Whites reciprocate the affection they receive from Indians and often run risks for them; the difference is that whites, unlike Indians, do not experience suffering and death in these episodes. Eoneguski, who as a child had begged the life of a white man from his father's wrath, lives to see the man's son use his friendship to take both Eoneguski's future wife and the leadership of the tribe. For this betrayal Eoneguski has Christlike forgiveness. When he is commanded to kill a white man in accordance with the Indian revenge code, Eoneguski spares him at the behest of a white girl and is disowned by his father. In *Fort Braddock Letters* the Indian Weshop helps his master against enemy Indians throughout the novel and then is killed fighting at his side against the French and Indians.

A number of unlucky Pocahontas figures populate the frontier romance, saving white beloveds only at the cost of their own lives, or, in the case of Magawisca, limb. She defies her tribe and loses an arm to save the white man she loves from death. He, in turn, is later able to free her from a Puritan prison, but without harm to himself. Numerous variations on the theme of sacrifice of an Indian woman exist. In *The Christian Indian* Miona's death

purchases a white beloved's freedom from an Indian curse; in
Elkswatawa Mishwa and her mother are put to death in place of
the white girl whose escape they have contrived; in *Kabaosa*
Onona is killed shielding the white officer she loves; and in
Miriam Coffin and *Kabaosa* Indian women no longer wanted by
white lovers obligingly free their paramours for pursuit of white
heroines by dying.

The Indian willingness to suffer and die for whites is sometimes lauded as a proof of inherent nobility. More often, in the
context of the frontier romance, it is considered to be a manifestation of natural justice, a value judgment on which Indians and
whites agree. As Joseph C. Hart writes: "From the moment that
the natives felt the ascendancy of the 'Yenghese' on the continent
the spirit of despair and the consciousness of inferiority, un-
nerved the red warrior, and prostrated his wild and savage
nature" (*Miram Coffin*). Indian characters themselves often
express a sense of their own inferiority to whites; they not only
recognize the fait accompli of white supremacy but also approve
it.[33] A Cooper Indian in *The Oak-Openings* states: " 'Injin don't
own 'arth. 'Arth belong to God, and He send whom He like to live
on it. One time He send Injin; now He send Pale-face. His 'arth,
and He do what He please wid it. Nobody any right to com-
plain.' " However subtly it may be communicated, the attachment
of Indian to white is recognized by author and character alike to
be that of inferior to superior. When the time for sacrifice comes,
as it invariably does in a romance, the fitting or natural or inevitable course is for the suffering to fall to the inferior's lot.
According to this rationale, the Indian preserves a life or way of
life more valuable than his own.

Clearly, to become a good Indian is to see Indianness through
white eyes; an awareness of their inferiority is exhibited by most
fictive good Indians. In describing their status, Pope's expression
"the poor Indian" becomes a cliché. One Indian apologizes for
lack of sophistication by saying: " 'The poor Indian has been
trained in the woods.' " Another marvels that a white saved a
"poor Indian" from drowning; the rescued Indian later repays
his benefactor by dying in the service of American troops during
the War of 1812. When asked to state the difference between

Indians and whites, Cooper's Trackless tersely replies: " 'One strong, t'oder weak—one rich, t'oder poor—one great, t'oder little—one drive 'way, t'oder haf to go!' " (*Satanstoe*). Another Cooper Indian despairs of conquering the Puritans: " 'An Indian is but a man! Can he fight with the God of the Yengeese? He is too weak' " (*The Wept of Wish-Ton-Wish*). The humble declaration of a medicine man in *The Shoshonee Valley*—" 'that we know nothing, and that the pale faces know all deep things' "—may be just rhetoric, followed as it is by an effective counter to a white preacher's Calvinism; later, however, a rejected Indian suitor seriously makes the comparison: " 'The pale face is fair and good, and what chances had an untutored red man beside him?' "

The detailed working out of such a statement, the perfect paradigm for the good Indian, occurs in Lydia Maria Child's *Hobomok*. The titular figure, a stereotypical good Indian, is accused of loving a white girl, Mary Conant. His sense of decorum is shaken; like other kinds of forbidden love, this one dare not speak its name: "He had looked upon her with reverence, which almost amounted to adoration. If any dregs of human feelings were mingled with these sentiments, he at least was not aware of it; and now that the idea was forced upon him, he rejected it, as a kind of blasphemy." Religious language is appropriate to convey the *proper* attitude of Hobomok to Mary: the worship of a being beyond his own sphere. When Mary's white lover is reported dead, she marries Hobomok in a state of shock, but gradually recovers under the kind and attentive care of her husband. Hobomok, of course, benefits greatly by the marriage. As Mary's best friend phrases it: " 'Within these three years he has altered so much, that he seems almost like an Englishman.' " Approximation is the best that the Indian can do, but it is never enough: the long-lost white lover returns, and Hobomok willingly relinquishes his wife and child to him. True to the pattern of the good Indian having no future, Hobomok fades into the wilderness where he will presumably die brokenhearted. The son achieves what the father could not—white identity: "When he left that infant university [Harvard], he departed to finish his studies in England." The extinction of Indian identity in his son completes Hobomok's sacrifice.

6

As Lippmann concludes about stereotyping: "Generally it all culminates in the fabrication of a system of all evil, and of another which is the system of all good."[34] Their values reinforced by success in conquering the continent, American whites found their Indian stereotypes comfortable and comforting: as noble savages, Indians could be remembered with a vague regret; as good Indians, they could helpfully initiate whites into the wilderness milieu before falling victim to their inherent inferiority; and as bad Indians, they deserved the harsh fate actively meted out to them by the conquering race. In Simms's view of the Indian: "It is, perhaps, his destiny! He hath a pioneer mission, to prepare the wild for the superior race; and, this duty done, he departs" (*The Cassique of Kiawah*). By employing these stereotypes, writers of the frontier romance felt that they were simultaneously supplying historical and imaginative truth. The bad Indian represented, alas, the reality of the Indian as the white man knew him; the noble savage and the docile good Indian embodied the charitable nostalgia of the victorious whites toward the waning Indians, and, perhaps unconsciously, what D. H. Lawrence would call the "wish fulfillment fantasy" or "yearning myth" of racial harmony.[35]

NOTES

1. William T. Hagan, *The Indian in American History* (New York, 1963), p. 2.
2. Clark Wissler, *The American Indian*, 3rd ed. (New York, 1938), p. 220.
3. Washington Irving, *A Tour on the Prairies* (Oklahoma City, 1955), p. 29; John T. Irving, Jr., *Indian Sketches Taken During an Expedition to the Pawnee Tribes*, ed. John Francis McDermott (Norman, 1955), p. xlii; James Hall, *Sketches of History, Life, and Manners, in the West* (Philadelphia, 1835), vol. I, p. 31; William J. Snelling, *Tales of the Northwest* (Boston, 1830), p. vi.
4. A. Irving Hallowell, "The Backwash of the Frontier: the Impact of the Indian on American Culture," *The Frontier in Perspective*, ed. Walker D. Wyman and Clifton B. Kroeber (Madison, 1957), p. 246.
5. Walter Lippmann, *Public Opinion* (New York, 1949), pp. 54-55.
6. Ibid., p. 64.

7. Ms. of the Rev. W. Ruggles, quoted in Washington Irving, "Philip of Pokanoket, an Indian Memoir," *The Sketch Book* (London, 1821), vol. II, p. 205.

8. Nathaniel Saltonstall voiced a popular opinion when he wrote during King Philip's War: "Care now is taken to satisfie the (reasonable) desires of the Commonalty, concerning Mr. Elliot's Indians, and Capt. Guggin's [Gookin's] Indians. They that wear the Name of Praying Indians, but rather (as Mr. Hezekiah Ushur termed Preying Indians) they have made Preys of much English Blood, but now they are all reduced to their several Confinements; which is much to a general Satisfaction in that Respect" (*The Present State of New-England With Respect To The Indian War* [London, 1675], in *Narratives of the Indian Wars 1675-1699*, ed. Charles H. Lincoln [New York, 1913], p. 49).

9. *A New and Further Narrative of the State of New England by N. S.* (London, 1676), in Lincoln, p. 91.

10. Letter to Samuel Elbert, Dec. 16, 1787, *Writings of Benjamin Franklin*, ed. A. H. Smyth (New York, 1907), vol. IX, p. 625.

11. Roy Harvey Pearce, *Savagism and Civilization*, rev. ed. (Baltimore, 1967), and Bernard W. Sheehan, *Seeds of Extinction* (Chapel Hill, 1973), provide good discussions of eighteenth-century scholarship on the American Indian.

12. Both D. H. Lawrence, *Studies in Classic American Literature* (New York, 1930) and Leslie A. Fiedler, *The Return of the Vanishing American* (New York, 1968) see the mythic significance of the Indian in American literature primarily in terms of a good companion to the white man in an exclusively male wilderness compact.

13. Robert Beverley, *The History and Present State of Virginia* (London, 1705), ed. Louis B. Wright (Chapel Hill, 1947), p. 159.

14. Captain John Smith, *A Map of Virginia: with a Description of the Countrey, the Commodities, People, Government and Religion* (Oxford, 1612), in *Narratives of Early Virginia*, ed. Lyon Gardiner Tyler (New York, 1930), p. 99.

15. The sexual quality of physical appearance is discussed in Chapter Four.

16. William J. Snelling is the only author of frontier romances to take exception to the general attribution of stoicism to Indians. He complains that the typical fictive presentation of the aborigine depicts him inaccurately as "insensible to fear and weakness." One of his tales begins with this declaration: "Those who imagine that the aborigines are all stoics and heroes . . . are informed that there are fops in the forest as well as in Broadway; their intrinsic value pretty much the same in both places."

17. A good discussion of Cooper's Indians, seen along a spectrum from demonism to a wise chief figure, can be found in Kay Seymour House, *Cooper's Americans* (Columbus, 1965).

18. Saltonstall, *The Present State of New England*, p. 39; it should be noted here that captivity narratives rarely report the direct discourse of Indians.

19. John T. Frederick, "Cooper's Eloquent Indians," *PMLA* 81 (1956), pp. 1004-1017, documents the Indian fondness for figurative speech in source materials of the early nineteenth century. His analysis of Cooper's figurative Indian expressions reveals that out of a total of 712, 569 are attributable to other sources, 172 are original but closely patterned on other sources (p. 1014). Ignorant of Indian languages, many writers might have echoed William Gilmore Simms: "I felt the eloquence which I could not understand" ("Oakatibbe or the Choctaw Sampson").

20. Frank Luther Mott, *Golden Multitudes* (New York, 1947), p. 8, classifies *The Last of the Mohicans* as an all-time best seller; other Cooper frontier romance best sellers listed by Mott, pp. 305-306, are *The Pathfinder, The Deerslayer, The Prairie,* and *The Pioneers.*

21. As Hugh Henry Brackenridge's Indian treaty-maker comments: "Indian speeches are nearly all alike. You have only to talk of burying hatchets under large trees, kindling fires, brightening chains; with a demand at the latter end of blankets for the backside, and rum to get drunk with" (*Modern Chivalry,* ed. Lewis Leary [Nw Haven, 1965], p. 74).

22. William Bradford, *Bradford's History "Of Plimoth Plantation"* (Boston, 1901), pp. 33-34.

23. Authors often remark with special condemnation the "unnatural" delight taken by Indian women in torturing prisoners, a stereotype of the captivity narrative which persists into fiction. Robert Montgomery Bird, *Nick of the Woods,* generalizes: "In truth the unlucky captive had always more to apprehend from the squaws of a tribe than from its warriors"; in *The Prairie,* Cooper describes the squaws in similar fashion: "A few of the withered and remorseless crones of the band were clustering together in readiness to lend their fell voices, if needed, to aid in exciting their descendants to an exhibition which their depraved tastes coveted." While age makes little difference in the stereotyping of Indian males, bad female Indians are usually old viragos while good Indian women are young.

24. Washington Irving, *Astoria,* rev. ed. (New York, 1868), p. 5, found that the *coureurs des bois* of the fur trade "became so accustomed to the Indian mode of living . . . that they lost all relish for civilization, and identified themselves with the savages among whom they dwelt." Wilcomb E. Washburn, "A Moral History of Indian-White Relations: Needs and Opportunities for Study," *Ethnohistory* 4 (1957-1958), p. 52, remarks: "An extraordinary number of whites preferred Indian society, while almost no Indians preferred white society."

25. See Hoxie Neale Fairchild, *The Noble Savage: A Study in Romantic Naturalism* (New York, 1961), p. 2: "A Noble Savage is any free and wild being who draws directly from nature virtues which raise doubts as to the value of civilization." The definition of cultural primitivism formulated by Arthur O. Lovejoy and George Boas, *Primitivism and Related Ideas in Antiquity* (New York, 1965), p. 7, is also germane: "the belief of men living in a relatively highly evolved and complex cultural condition that a life far simpler and less sophisticated in some or all respects is a more desirable life." Within the total context of any frontier romance, the Indian's virtues and the desirability of his life style are not so strongly presented.

26. Lovejoy and Boas demonstrate that primitivism is as old as Western literature; as they state, ibid., p. 287: "The idealization of savages is, of course, cultural primitivism isolated from chronological primitivism."

27. Washington Irving, "Traits of Indian Character," *The Sketch Book of Geoffrey Crayon, Gentleman* (London, 1821), vol. II, p. 163.

28. William Gilmore Simms, *The Yemassee,* has the degraded settlement Indian Occonestoga; William Cullen Bryant, "The Indian Spring," contrasts a majestic warrior who appears to him in a vision with the beggar Indian of reality, a "fat, one-eyed vagabond in ragged trousers" (*Prose Writings of William Cullen Bryant,* ed. Parke Goodwin [New York, 1884], vol.I, p. 184].

29. Irving, "Traits of Indian Character," p. 167.
30. Karl Postl's *Tokeah* illustrates a variation of this method. There is no "bad tribe," but the ideal Indians are geographically remote from the novel's action: "A settled abode in the delightful plains of Santa Fe, a mild delicious climate, and a frequent warlike intercourse with the Spaniards, by whom they are respected and considered as an independent nation, has raised their spirits far above the common level of the Indians, and greatly banished from their character that savage ferocity which is so inherent in the oppressed minor tribes."
31. In *The Last of the Mohicans*, Hawkeye says of the Hurons: " 'They are a thievish race . . . you can never make anything of them but skulks and vagabonds' "; in *The Prairie*, he laments the passing of his favorite tribe: " 'Your Delawares were the redskins of which America might boast!' "
32. The popularity of Pocahontas and Sacajawea, historical figures who became mythicized, may be explained by the powerful conjunction of two stereotypes: the good female, totally devoted to the male, and the good Indian, totally devoted to white interests.
33. Bad Indians tend to be more stubborn. They admit white dominance but regard it as unjustifiable usurpation.
34. Lippmann, *Public Opinion*, p. 100.
35. Lawrence, *Studies in Classic American Literature*, p. 73.

4

Whites Vis-A-Vis Indians

The warfare that long existed between the intruders and the Redskins was sanguinary and protracted; but the former at length made good their footing, and the latter drew off their shattered bands, dismayed by the mental superiority and indomitable courage of the white men.

John James Audubon, AUDUBON AND HIS JOURNALS

1

Not until the twentieth century would novels and tales totally devoted to Indian characters be written in any significant number; in the greater part of the nineteenth century, the frontier romance is a special kind of white fiction, the Indian a source of interest not in and of himself, but only vis-à-vis the white man. As Roy Harvey Pearce writes: "Looking at the Indian in his lack of . . . power, the Englishman could be sure of what he himself was; looking at himself, he could be sure of what the Indian should be. In America, from the very beginning the history of the savage is the history of the civilized."[1] Fiction made the same demands as history: both good and bad Indians must play subservient roles to whites, must exemplify white superiority. Robert Strange's preface to *Eoneguski* explicitly states the moral which all frontier romances draw from white-Indian interaction:

From the uniform success attendant in my story on the white

man, in every species of contest with the savage, whether in
love or war, and whether single handed or in numbers, we
may learn to set a just value upon the advantages of civilization. From thence nothing can be more natural than for us to
advance another step, and feel our hearts warmed with
gratitude to Providence, who has cast our own lot in the
fortunate class.

The frontier romance illustrates the blessings of whiteness, which
admits a man into a civilized and progressive culture and destines
him to be superior to dark-skinned people who were born into
lesser orders. As Pearce indicates, Indians are defined by whites;
thus, a study of fictive Indians is unavoidably a study of the white
characters whose interests they serve in both the form and substance of the fictive construct.

The most striking feature of the general white stereotype is the
assumption of white superiority to Indians in all ways. Committed
to progress, materialism, and perfectibility through technology,
nineteenth-century whites perceived a vast gulf between their
own advanced culture and the primitive condition of the Indian.
To render this view in fiction, however, it is not enough to show
whites excelling in civilized arts. To prove their worth conclusive-
ly, white characters must meet the Indian on his own ground as
well: they must best him in wilderness skills.[2]

Through their membership in a superior race and through
their individual abilities, whites are both actively and passively
superior to Indians. "The War Belt," a short story by the prolific
frontier romancer James Hall, illustrates the latter: presence
alone, the white man as representative of his race, overcomes a
formidable Indian threat. The historical Colonel George Rogers
Clarke quells rebellious Indians with nothing more than a force-
ful glance:

He gazed upon that savage band, whose hundred eyes were
bent fiercely and in horrid exultation upon him, as they
stood like a pack of wolves at bay, thirsting for blood. . . . He
spoke, and there was no man bold enough to gainsay him—
none that could return the fierce glance of his eye.

The Indians had planned to turn the peace conference into a white massacre, but are so overwhelmed by Clarke's gaze that they sign a peace treaty instead. Hall attributes Clarke's success to his "moral superiority," a quality which seems to be as much racial as personal. Surely fifty Indians knew they could dispatch a single white, but the will of white expansionism which Clarke embodies is irresistible.

In woodcraft skills and Indian fighting, white frontiersmen have an opportunity to demonstrate actively their superiority. According to Hall: "It is well understood that when the white man is trained to this species of hostility, he is superior to the Indian, because his physical powers are greater, and his courage of a higher and more generous tone" ("The Pioneer"). And in spite of praise for the red man's acute senses and wilderness proficiency, Cooper in practice agrees with the opinion of Hall. As one of his white characters says: "Experience has shown that the white man usually surpasses the Indian even in his own peculiar practices, when there have been opportunities to be taught." Simms's formulation of pioneer ascendancy is in terms of "the superior vigour of their own frames, their greater courage, and better weapons." Elsewhere he works out the comparison of frontiersmen and Indians more thoroughly:

> The Carolinian woodman knew enough of the savages to know that they were no opponents, generally speaking, to be feared in a trial of respective muscular strength. The life of the hunter fits him to endure rather than to contend. The white borderer was taught by his necessities to do both. He could wield the axe and overthrow the tree—a labour to which the Indian is averse. He could delve and dig, and such employment was a subject of scorn and contempt with the haughty aboriginal warrior. At the same time, he practised the same wanderings and the same felicity of aim, and in enduring the toils of the chase, he was fairly the equal of his tawny but less enterprising neighbour. The consciousness of these truths—a consciousness soon acquired from association—was not less familiar to the Indian than to the Carolinian; and the former, in consequence, despaired of

success usually when required to oppose the white man hand to hand. (*The Yemassee*)

Simms suggests that the disparity may partially be accounted for by inclination; the Indian does not choose agricultural labors. This faulty choice, the failure to be enterprising, as Simms calls it, is attributable to an inferior intellect; as well as outperforming him physically, a white man can outthink an Indian. The hero of *The Yemassee*, for example, was

> practised considerably in Indian stratagem—had been with them in conflict, and could anticipate their arts—was resolute as well as daring, and, with much of their circumspection, had learned skilfully to imitate the thousand devices, whether of warfare or of the chase, which make the glory of the Indian brave.

Ultimately, beneath the many comparisons Simms draws, his constantly reiterated theory of white superiority rests on color. Many writers remark the Indian's dusky complexion slightingly,[3] but no one else defines the basic terms of white supremacy so forthrightly: "The very difference between the two, that of colour, perceptible to our most ready sentinel, the sight, must always constitute them an inferior caste in our minds" (*The Yemassee*).

2

Any frontier romance of some length can provide ample illustration of the author's commitment to a many-faceted white supremacy. In a formal running contest in "Pinchon" a Yankton Sioux with a reputation as the swiftest Indian runner is pitted against trader LeDuc, whose previous activities in the story have consisted of drinking and carousing. When LeDuc wins, the Indian remarks in surprise: " 'I was never outrun before; and I did not think there was a man alive who could do it.' " The race arouses the competitive instinct of another white trader, Pinchon, who races the same Indian on the next day. To outdo his friend

LeDuc, Pinchon runs with four guns strapped on his back and wins handily. This time the author has no words to record the Indian runner's surprise.

In hand-to-hand combat, a white always defeats a single Indian, and usually more than one. As a character in *Mount Hope* remarks: " 'Ten Englishmen are a match for thrice that number of savages.' " In *Miriam Coffin* a slender young white boy attacked by a muscular adult Indian defeats his physically superior adversary by stratagem. The author attributes his success to the "obtuse intellect of the Indian (they have thick skulls, like the African negro)." Even more impressive are the exploits of a frontiersman during an Indian ambush:

> Two powerful Indians, hard abreast, weapons in hand, and well mounted, rushed upon him at once, and involuntarily I uttered a cry of horror, for I thought him lost. But no! With an intrepidity equalled only by his activity, a weapon in either hand, he rushed his horse between the two, and dodging by some unaccountable means the blows aimed at his life, buried his knife in the breast of one and at the same moment his tomahawk in the brain of the other. (*The Prairie Flower*)

This energetic Indian fighter is later revealed to be the famous Kit Carson, who might be expected to loom larger than life in a fictive portrait. Other white hunters, however, including those of the same author, are scarcely less accomplished. The Indian hater Lewis Wetzel dispatches a party of three Indians singlehandedly with his aptly named rifle, Killnigger,[4] and then proffers his own version of white superiority: " 'Poor fellow,' he said, giving the dead Indian a kick and again indulging in a low, quiet laugh; 'you mought hev bin a powerful smart chap amongst your own painted brethren, but you ain't o' no account to come agin a white gintleman as knows how to handle powder' " (*The Forest Rose*).

The reference to handling powder is significant for the frontiersman stereotype: although Kit Carson and other Indian fighters can defeat Indians with their own weapons, tomahawk and knife, the white man usually performs his greatest feats of killing with his own distinctive weapon, the gun. It is axiomatic in the frontier romance that Indians cannot use firearms with efficacy. In spite of their keen sight and good physical condition, they seldom hit a target.[5] Moreover, their rifles often misfire, a sign that white technology is beyond them. At their best they fail to equal the white man, as Natty Bumppo ruminates after killing an Indian in a shoot-out: " 'Say what you will for or ag'in 'em, a redskin is by no means as sartain with powder and ball as a white man. Their gifts don't seem to be that a way. Even Chingachgook, great as he is in other matters, isn't downright deadly with the rifle' " (*The Deerslayer*).

Such a restrained formulation of Indian deficiency is foreign to Emerson Bennett, the perpetrator of so many excesses in the frontier romance. All of the writers in this genre subscribe to and exemplify in their work the idea of white superiority, but none reach the zenith of white capabilities—and corresponding Indian stupidities—achieved in Bennett's *The Forest Rose*. From a strategically situated rock fortress, two white frontiersmen hold off hundreds of Indians, who, despite numerous losses, persist in suicidally hurling themselves against the stronghold. The ignominy for the Indians is increased by observing one of the whites run from the forest before their eyes and join the other in the safety of the rocky enclosure: "Leaping boldly from his covert upon the rocks, in full view of the yelling savages, he darted before their astonished eyes like a meteor, and the next moment, amid a shower of rifle bullets, which flew harmlessly past him, he gained a position by the side of the old hunter." The Indians make one of their many futile assaults on the frontiersmen's position:

> The instant a small portion of the body of the foremost became visible to the eye of Wetzel, his finger pressed upon the trigger of his never-failing rifle. . . . Nothing daunted, apparently, by this, the savage next behind pressed forward in the hope of being more successful, and received the contents of Albert's rifle in his abdomen. A third and a fourth made the attempt with like success.

Whites shooting at Indians are always excellent marksmen in the frontier romance, but no one surpasses Bennett in portraying the Indian as a target.

In *Mount Hope*, even a white woman is able to get the better of the Indians, first by force, and then by stratagem. When Dorothea Doolittle's Indian captors want her to travel the gauntlet lines on her horse, righteous indignation gives her the will to ride them down:

> "To be captivated by such vile reptiles is doleful enough, though a decent captivity might be borne. But such infernal capers and devilish doings (may the Lord forgive me!) are not to be exercised on a woman of spirit. I'll ride ye down, squaw and Injin, to the earth e'en now." And flourishing her stick about the head and ears of Davie [her horse], she rode headlong into the midst of her tormentors. The momentum of Davie, as well as the more than aboriginal ferocity of the good Dame's features, that seemed to be instinct with a rage almost supernatural, drove the squaws and papooses from her with a shrill scream.[6]

When the Indians succeed in subduing Mrs. Doolittle, at some cost to themselves, they decide to kill her immediately. A pretence of having "medicine" now saves her; as Hollister records: "The superstition of the savages completed her triumph."

The stereotyped romantic heroines who people the frontier romance are incapable of such direct speech and determined action as Mrs. Doolittle, but she has a prototype in the well-known historical captive, Hannah Duston. Without embellishment, Mrs. Duston's story is a realized myth of feminine pioneer ability. She was carried into captivity only a week after giving birth to her eighth child, a circumstance which caused Nathaniel Hawthorne to comment wryly:

> Our great-great-grandmothers, when taken captive in the old times of Indian warfare, appear, in nine cases out of ten, to have been in pretty much such a delicate situation as Mrs. Duston; notwithstanding which, they were wonderfully

sustained through long, rough, and hurried marches, amid toil, weariness, and starvation, such as the Indians themselves could hardly endure.[7]

Before reaching their destination in the wilderness, Mrs. Duston and two adjunct captives murdered their group of Indians and returned to civilization with ten scalps. Cotton Mather's recounting of the exploit, which compares Mrs. Duston's feat to Jael's murder of Sisera, details approvingly the considerable recompense which the three received from both official and private sources. Hawthorne's retelling of the story, in contrast to Mather's, describes Mrs. Duston as deserving of something other than the acclaim her contemporaries greeted her with: "Would that the bloody old hag had been drowned in crossing Contocook River, or that she had sunk head and ears in a swamp, and been buried there, till summoned forth to confront her victims at the Day of Judgment."[8] Leslie A. Fiedler to the contrary, such a redoubtable figure could have no place among the major characters of the frontier romance: her prowess would have competed far too strongly with the hero's and made the plot staple of heroine-rescue superfluous. The frontier romance reserves such flagrant exhibitions of white superiority for men.[9]

Demonstrations of white superiority in other Indian provinces are dictated by the operation of the captivity plot; captive whites have an opportunity to display their ability to endure torture, pursuing whites to exhibit wilderness skills in effecting a rescue of the captives. According to the general stereotype of the Indian, the stoical endurance of suffering and death is a valued quality. Knowing this, white characters often emulate their Indian captors by enduring torture with fortitude:

A variety of other means were used to torture and intimidate their victim, and to induce him to degrade himself by showing some symptom of alarm. But all to no purpose: Colonel Hendrickson was well acquainted with the habits of his enemies; he had prepared himself to die and faced his savage persecutors with the composure of intrepid resignation. (*The Harpe's Head*)

Characters also follow the Indian manner in shouting defiance at their torturers. An Irish laborer, chosen as a sacrificial victim by the Yemassee, welcomes the torments devised for him with a show of boldness: " 'But it's not Teddy Macnamara, that your fires and your arrows will iver scare, ye divils; so begin, boys, as soon as ye've a mind to, and don't be too dilicate in your doings' " (*The Yemassee*). The white victim not only suffers the Indian torments with unbroken fortitude, taunting the Indians in their accepted fashion, he even escapes for a moment. In recapturing Macnamara, the Indians are forced to kill him prematurely: having won the only victory to be obtained in such a situation, he dies heroically. One other variation on the theme of white stoicism is the appearance of enjoyment of torture, which transcends mere resignation and fortitude. William Ashford, the hero of *Mount Hope*, resolves to counter every torment with the Indians' own stoicism, but his actual behavior is even more impressive:

> The chief raised him by taking hold of both his swollen hands, and lifting him slowly, so as to prolong the keen anguish that the operation inflicted. He then looked scrutinizingly into his face for traces of suffering. But the lip did not quiver, the veins did not swell upon the temple, nor did the perspiration start upon the forehead. The privateer even smiled, as if the sensation was grateful to his nerves.

If for no better reason than the rule of the frontier romance that the hero is not to be killed by Indians, Ashford's superhuman efforts of self-control do not go unrewarded. In this instance, no white rescue party was near, so King Philip himself, acting without explanation or evident motive, saves the hero's life.

Whites who are members of rescue expeditions against the Indians have more active roles tracking, surprising the Indians, and overpowering them in hand-to-hand combat. A chapter heading in *The Prairie Flower* illustrates the nature of the contest: "Cowardice of the Western Indians—Cold-Blooded Mutilation— Coolness and Valor of the Mountaineers." The outcome of any such encounter is predictable: "But though he [the Indian]

moved with all the instinctive craft of his people, he was under the
eye of one [the white hunter], whom many years spent in these
wilds had rendered fully his equal" (*The Hawk Chief*). The Indian's proficiency is merely instinctive; the white man can learn
and adapt himself to new conditions. Coming to the wilderness,
he takes from the Indian those skills needed to survive in that
environment, but he must walk a fine line, like Natty Bumppo in
The Deerslayer: "too proud of his origin to sink into the condition
of the wild Indian, and too much a man of the woods not to
imbibe as much as was at all desirable, from his friends and
companions."[10] If he takes too much, or loses the characteristics of
his own culture entirely, he becomes an object of special horror in
the world of the frontier romance: a renegade white savage.[11]

3

In evil as in goodness, the white man surpasses the Indian.
Sometimes individual white villains direct Indians in machinations against whites; on other occasions nations of whites
—Spanish, French, and British—are held accountable for Indian
depredations against American settlers. Whenever Indians
function as tools of white villainy, they receive a lesser share of
authorial obloquy; however unpleasant, their activities are "in
obedience to the laws of an uncultivated nature" (*Mount Hope*);
the behavior of the inciting whites, directed against their own
kind, is to the fullest extent unnatural. In *Kate Clarendon*, for
example, the rejected suitor Moody disguises himself as an Indian to abduct Kate. For the Indians who comprise his raiding
party the author restricts himself to a brief stereotyped description of "hiderous-looking savages . . . uttering terrific yells of
fury." None are as sinister as Moody, who bears off the heroine
"with a laugh so fiendish it made the blood of all who heard it
curdle." Later, when Kate's intended is also in the villain's power,
the Indian Mugwa admires his bravery and wishes to adopt him.
Moody, in contrast, persuades the other Indians to kill him.
    A more serious case is the historical renegade Simon Girty.
Author and character alike excoriate Girty for his shameful

betrayal of his own color: the renegade not only fights with Indians against whites, he has become a white Indian, a crime attributed to a depraved nature rather than to any positive aspects of Indian life. Like Moody, Girty is more fiendish than his Indian cohorts and more insensitive to the plight of the white prisoners.[12] While Girty pursues his ravaging of the Kentucky settlements, the Indian chief Black Hoof decides to save the captive hero, Algernon Reynolds. With the help of the famous chief Logan but without the author's help in providing a motive for this benevolence, Black Hoof conveys Algernon to the British. Because of the gentleman's code operating among groups of opposing whites in the frontier romance, Algernon can then be ransomed back to the American side.

Another renegade of this genre who has no historical existence to explain his ferocity is Wacousta, born Reginald Morton. In *Wacousta*, this renegade, rather than the Indian leader Pontiac, is the intransigent spirit behind the frontier war of 1763. Endowed with the typical attributes of the stereotype, Wacousta out-Indians the Indians: he performs marvelous physical and military feats, devotes himself wholly to revenge, and is unsurpassingly bloodthirsty and unmerciful to captives. Pontiac is able to conclude a peace with the English only after "his terrible coadjutor and vindictive adviser was no more."

Not surprisingly, the fiction which draws upon stereotypes for its Indians also uses pattern figures for whites.[13] In addition to exhibiting stereotyped attitudes and behavior toward Indians, whites in the frontier romance reveal themselves to be typed characters who embody a romantic tradition in a frontier setting. The young hero and heroine are ideal specimens of physical beauty, moral worth, and sensitivity, exceedingly devoted to their parents (who are apt to be threatened or killed by Indians) and menaced by a villain who wishes to dispatch the hero and seize the heroine for himself. A mystery of identity and fortune surrounds either the hero or the heroine: although either may be penniless and unfortunate at some point, both belong to the gentry and ultimately receive the large inheritance justly due them. The villain is usually a man of gentlemanly birth and depraved nature; in *The Yemassee*, however, he is a lower-class Englishman turned pirate; in *The Mestico,* an ambitious half-breed; and in several Cooper novels, an Indian. Whatever his caste, the villain is a would-be or rejected suitor of the heroine, who plots to possess her by force.

The other significant white character, the woodsman-Indian fighter, comes not from an English literary tradition but directly from the American frontier experience. He is a mediator between the wilderness and civilization, a man who remains arrested in the Indianized condition characteristic of the first encounter between whites and the wilderness. As Frederick Jackson Turner writes: "In short, at the frontier the environment is at first too strong for the man. He must accept the conditions which it furnishes, or perish, and so he fits himself into the Indian clearings and follows the Indian trails."[14] Rather than progressing to the next stage, that of permanent settlement, the frontiersman prefers to be a rootless denizen of the forest, often opposed to the advance of civilized communities. As a master of wilderness skills, he is in a position to aid the hero and heroine in the unfamiliar and hostile environment.

Among white characters, there is a weak reflection of the good-bad schematization for Indians: good whites, particularly the hero and heroine, are sympathetic to the situation of the Indian and may acquire good Indian friends; at the same time, by virtue of the plot mechanism, they often have reason to deplore the actions of bad Indians. Frontiersmen, who are presented as ignorant and bigoted, but not actually villainous, regard Indians as unsalvageable varmints akin to other wilderness beasts of prey.

A variety of positions exists within the general negative attitude, ranging from an extreme of Indian hating which dominates the character's life to a minor blind spot in his total personality. The numerous Indian haters, entirely devoted to the killing of Indians, represent an extreme which is condemned by author and character alike. Next come the pioneers, who lack the Indian hater's preoccupation but kill Indians that menace them as a matter of wilderness necessity. As Daniel Boone comments in *The Renegade*: " 'I don't want anybody to thank me for shooting Indians, for I always do it, whensomever I get a chance.' " Emerson Bennett, the author of *The Renegade,* is notably zealous in championing whites against Indians; most authors endow their good frontiersmen with more restraint. The best formulation of their credo is made by the woodsman Adherbal in *The Hawk Chief*: " 'One of my maxims is, "never to shed blood onnecessary." If an Ingen sends an arrow after me, then I kill him, but I never go out of my path to look for him. It isn't moral.' " The moderation of Adherbal's stand on Indian killing, in contrast to the excesses of several bloodthirsty characters in the romance, is part of a sympathetic characterization.

A virulent contempt for Indians, on the other hand, usually indicates an unadmirable character. In *The Deerslayer* Hurry Harry is contrasted unfavorably with the humane Deerslayer, both in theory and in practice: where Hurry considers Indians to be merely animals, Deerslayer asserts their humanity; where Hurry coldbloodedly goes after Indian scalps for the bounty, Deerslayer kills an Indian only in the extreme of self-defense, and then, regretfully. Balt, the hunter in *Greyslaer*, expresses feelings like Hurry's, but they are not to be taken as the full measure of his character. The author apologetically notes that Balt's "only foible, if so it may be called, was, that he never could abide a *Redskin*." This intolerance is somewhat mitigated by his reluctant fondness for the Indian boy Teondetha: "Aware of his absence, [Balt] felt now a degree of concern about his fate which he was angry at himself at feeling for a "Redskin"; though somehow, almost unknowingly, he had learned to love the youth." Without abandoning his general adherence to a negative stereotype of the "redskin," Balt is able to distinguish one worthy individual among the Indians.

Earth, the modified Indian hater figure in *Elkswatawa*, is a similar case. Although he brags that he has "never spared an Ingen; no, there don't breathe one who can say I ever showed him any favour," he has made one exception, the helpful Indian Oloompa. Like Balt, Earth experiences surprise at finding his stereotyped portrait contradicted: " 'Oloompa has behaved nobly; I didn't think it was in a red skin.' " Both Earth and Balt are good characters whose unfavorable attitude towards Indians is an unhappy result of their frontier encounters with bad Indians. That they are not totally insensitive beings is exemplified by their ability to transcend their prejudices when they meet an Indian who deviates from their stereotyped expectations.

4

Stereotyping of attitudes and relationships pervades the treatment of sexuality as it does other facets of white-Indian contact. Because whites are depicted as superior in all ways, they must be more sexually desirable than Indians. Thus, fictive male Indians often desire white women, although only in exceptional cases do they succeed in possessing them.[15] Similar circumstances obtain for Indian women and white men: the love of the Indian for the superior being is more prevalent in this combination, but despite the popularity of the Pocahontas legend, the results are even more negative. Among major characters in the frontier romance, no Indian girl acquires a white husband.

Of the Indians who love whites, good Indians stoically resign themselves to loving in vain. Aware of their inferiority, they have no expectations of being loved in return. As Lightfoot confesses to a white girl in *Lord Fairfax*: " 'I have done wrong, because I have spoken with my eyes, to the Dove, as a young pale-face may speak, and said, "I love you." I am not a pale-face, I am a poor Indian, and inferior to the tribe beyond the Big Water.' " In expiation, Lightfoot saves the girl's life at the cost of his own; he dies thanking her for converting him to Christianity. A notable characteristic of bad Indians, on the other hand, is a failure to know their place and be properly grateful for the benefits of white civilization; instead, they scheme to possess white heroines and die—unlike Lightfoot—in unwilling expiation of their presumption. It should be added that whites never reciprocate these erotic sentiments, but simply consider Indians to be friendly (good) or inimical (bad). The closest a white comes to recognizing sexual love for an Indian is given as conjecture hedged by the belief that such a feeling would have been wrong. The white hero of *Hope Leslie* confesses about an Indian girl: " 'I might have loved her—might have forgotten that nature had put barriers between us.' "

The "natural barrier" on which most authors were fixated is color. Judgments of any sort which white characters make about Indians refer to some stereotyped quality of Indianness; in the sexual relationship, the characteristic which commands authorial emphasis is color. What is an Indian? A red man. Conversely, in the Indianese of this body of fiction, a white man is a paleface. Simms was fond of arguing that this instant determinant was providentially designed to keep the races apart: "God has made an obvious distinction between certain races of men, setting them apart, and requiring them to be kept so, by subjecting them to the resistance and rebuke of one of the most jealous sentinels of sense which we possess—the eye" (*The Wigwam and the Cabin*). The eye of the writer notes the difference accordingly; Indians may possess physical beauty, but of an inferior sort to that of whites. Beauty of almost every feature is attributed to them in one work or another except the one beauty which they can never possess. Sometimes bluntly, sometimes obliquely, authors convey that the definitive characteristic of perfect beauty is whiteness. The formula "I did not believe an Indian could be————" allows a conclusion of "noble," "loyal," "intelligent," or another of the good adjectives appropriated by whites; the ending it can never take is "white."

The fatal impediment to an Indian attractiveness which can rival that of whites is complexion. To quote that early student of the Indian, Robert Beverley: "Their women are generally Beautiful . . . wanting no Charm, but that of a fair complexion."[16] In its most forthright form in the frontier romance color prejudice is, like Beverley's, openly stated. Timothy Flint writes about the Shoshonees: "Laying the roundness of their faces, their Indian noses, and a slight tinge of copper out of the question, many of them are in fact pretty" (*The Shoshonee Valley*). William J. Snelling describes an Indian girl: "Sheenah Dootah Way, if her color be excepted, was one of the prettiest girls I ever saw" ("The Captive"). In *Elkswatawa* an Indian girl is "as pretty as a dusky maid can be." The author also assures us that Tecumseh's face, "but for its dusky hue, would have been thought handsome, even by the pale faces."

A similar objection is advanced in *Saratoga* by Lieutenant

O'Carroll, who "cannot imagine any beauty in a face where the splendor of the rose and lilly *[sic]* are usurped by the dusky and lifeless hue of the olive." The lieutenant is only a secondary character, however, embodying the typically unenlightened view of the lesser whites in the frontier romance. True to the more sympathetic understanding which the hero ordinarily displays, Colonel Grahame defends the Indian claim to beauty, but without contravening the idea that white skin is superior to dark. The brilliance of the eyes, he asserts, "makes ample compensation for the darkness of the countenance they illumine." O'Carroll remains intransigent on the issue of color; he concedes some beauty to the Indian girl Minoya, but insists that it is marred by a dark complexion.[17] The author lends support to O'Carroll's view when, following the discussion, the white heroine receives Minoya: taking the girl's dark hand, her own appears "dazzlingly white" in contrast.

As the appellation "paleface" might indicate, fictive Indians are also aware of the significance of skin color. Onona, an Indian who loves a white man (and later dies to save his life), rationalizes what she realizes is an unappealing feature: " 'And what though that dark tinge adorn her cheek which fairer maidens scorn? The crimson hue shines through its stain, that speaks of perfect health.' " In reality, her knowledge that even perfect health is no substitute for sexual attractiveness is apparent in the attempt at justification. Disillusioned when her white lover abandons her, the Indian girl in *Miriam Coffin* appraises the situation more candidly: " 'How foolish, not to know that the dark skin of the Indian maid would prove the impassable barrier to my happiness!' "

Some authors hesitate to name the offending feature of Indian appearance quite so specifically. Cooper writes in *Satanstoe*: "Trackless was a singularly handsome Indian, the unpleasant peculiarities of his people being but faintly portrayed in his face and form; while their nobler and finer qualities came out in strong relief." Mrs. Sedgwick makes the same reservation in her description of an Indian girl in *Hope Leslie*: "Her face, although marked by the peculiarities of her race, was beautiful, even to a European eye." The word "peculiarities" suggests a deviation from an accepted norm, in this case the standards of Caucasian beauty. Although the plural is employed, implying a number of undesirable attributes, the great amount of attention paid to complexion by other writers makes it likely that color is the major peculiarity to which these authors refer. In another Cooper romance, the aspects which differentiate a white girl from the Indians among whom she was raised are given in specific terms of color:

> Its lustre [the skin's] having been a little dimmed by exposure, a rich, rosy tint had usurped the natural brightness of a complexion that had once been fair even to brilliancy. The eye was full, sweet, and of a blue that emulated the sky of evening . . . and the hair, instead of dropping in long straight tresses of jet black, broke out of the restraints of a band of beaded wampum, in ringlets of golden yellow. (*The Wept of Wish-ton-Wish*)

Fairness extends itself from its most striking manifestation, skin color, to light eyes and blond hair, all characteristics which a full-blooded Indian would never have. An explicit comparison between Indian and white is made only for the hair, but the positive connotations of the entire description of the white girl imply the missing parts: if her complexion, still fairer than an Indian's, had been dimmed from its natural brightness and brilliancy, how dull and lusterless a darker skin must be. Would an eye that emulated the sky of midnight be equally handsome? The descriptions of white and Indian girls in other frontier romances point to a negative answer.

Should an Indian woman be remarkably beautiful, she is almost certain to stand revealed sooner or later, like Cooper's Ruth, as a white captive.[18] In these cases the difference in complexion is always noted; after describing a mysterious Indian girl as unsurpassingly beautiful, celestial, and with a figure as faultless as that of a Venus, the hero of *The Prairie Flower* comments: "Her skin was dark, but not more so than a Creole's, and with nothing of the brownish or reddish hue of the native Indian." This conjunction of superlative beauty and fairish skin should immediately dissipate the mystery for the reader, although another dozen pages elapse before the hero questions the girl's origin: "Was she of the Indian race? I could not believe it. She seemed too fair and lovely, and without the lineaments which distinguish this people from those nations entitled to the name of pale-face." Similar doubts are shared by the hero of *Tadeuskund* when he encounters the lovely Indian Elluwia: "[He] could not refrain from revolting at the idea that so perfectly beautiful and noble a being should descend from the race of the savage tenants of the woods; and from wishing that it might be discovered that she belonged to his own nation." The author also takes pains to dissociate Elluwia from Indian women: "Her complexion, though in our cities it might have seemed sunburnt, was unusually fair, when compared with the daughters of the forest. Her jet black locks, also contrasted, by their softness, with the coarse hair of the Indian race." Even when she least conforms to the ideal of the pale-complexioned blond heroine, when she is sunburned and dark-haired, the white girl retains a significant advantage over the Indian.

Rather than the overt labeling of the dark complexion or a reference to unappealing features, many authors assert the superiority of white beauty more indirectly. No comparison of white and Indian is made, but a longer and more enthusiastic description of the white heroine serves to establish her preeminence. Or, a mere mention of Indianness reminds the reader that a different and lower standard is in effect. When Gideon M. Hollister remarks of King Philip's wife in *Mount Hope* that "her beauty was of the most perfect aboriginal mould," his further praise of her appearance has been restricted to a lower type than that of white beauty by the qualifying "aboriginal." The white heroine is also perfection, but without reservation: "the rare ideal of feminine loveliness, such as often haunts the dreams of the imaginative and young, but seldom meets us in the walks of life."

Given the positive connotations of white and the negative connotations of dark, it is often enough to employ these and synonymous words in descriptions to convey the superiority of white beauty. Both Nahtorah and Lucy in *The Hawk Chief* are called beautiful, but Lucy has "a neck as white as ivory," Nahtorah "jetty locks" and "jet black eye." The Hawk Chief desires Lucy at first sight and plans to have her supplant Nahtorah in his lodge.

By the nineteenth century, a literary convention of a fair and virginal heroine and an opposing dark temptress figure had been established.[19] Although the dark-haired white woman of this tradition is a sexually vital being, the dark woman of the frontier romance is not. The stigma of darkness remains without the compensating passion, for rather than being the archetypal mistress, the Indian woman is a white heroine manqué, an imitation who outperforms the valued white character in acts of devotion and goodness, but cannot change her "dusky, but irritably red features" (*The Yemassee*). She is uniformly good, self-sacrificing, and virginal, but she can never, of course, be white.

The one instance of an obvious sexual attractiveness bestowed on an Indian is the half-breed girl Nimqua in "Adam Baker, the Renegade." A scarcely veiled sexuality, conveyed by imagery of heat and expansion, permeates her description:

> The vaulting arch of that bold forehead—just a summer evening's tinge of orange on it, enough to make it warm under the intense black of that glossy mass of hair—then the free curve of that classic nose, and the curl of the upper lip, that, with a saucy coyness, brooded over the rich swell of its ambitious twin—and then the burning ebon depths of those large eyes, the shadow of the long, dark lashes seemed to be over them in mercy—for what the full blaze thereof might be, imagination could not compass.

In spite of this description, Nimqua is only a typical white heroine after all; mingled blood, unlike its effect in male characters, does not cause her behavior to deviate from the standard adolescent purity and marriage syndrome of the white heroine.

Because whites have a monopoly on sexual desirability, the white hero attracts Indian women, just as the white heroine arouses desire in Indian males.[20] The white hero is usually oblivious to the sexual element in an Indian woman's devotion; her ministrations when he is wounded and help in escaping from her own people seem to be regarded as characteristic of her sex and race. In the extravagant musings of Harold, the Byronic hero of *Logan,* the Indian girl who prepares to die for him is simply exhibiting the feminine syndrome: " 'How full of womanhood!—the pure divinity of woman!—uncomplaining, patient, meek, silent, and dying!' " White heroines are never put to such extremes, however. In keeping with the aggressive and passive stereotypes of sex role which are little altered by race, Indian males—but not females—can actively pursue whites. The Indian's intentions in these plot machinations are quasi-honorable: force must be used to secure the person of the white heroine, but the Indian wishes to marry her rather than to seduce her. Nevertheless, the white hero is the preferred possessor in the world of the frontier romance, and death is more welcome than miscegenation.

5

Only in some few cases is the interdiction against a white-Indian union set aside, and these are both exceptional and temporary marriages. For two of the three examples, the childhood captivity of the white girl and her residence among Indians until adulthood have made her into a white Indian. Only her superior appearance, especially the definitive characteristic of white skin, differentiates her from the real Indian woman. Hope Leslie's sister Faith, once restored to her white relatives, proves as uncivilizable as an Indian was wont to be. She and her Indian husband finally succeed in escaping to the wilderness, the only interracial couple in the frontier romance to achieve a happy ending. Faith is not the novel's white heroine, however; she is more expendable than Hope Leslie in terms of the plot, and—depicted as almost a moron—in terms of character as well. Cooper, who flirts with the possibility of miscegenation on several occasions, allows it to happen once in *The Wept of Wish-ton-Wish.* The circumstances are similar to those of *Hope Leslie*: Ruth, a white girl captured in childhood, is rediscovered by her real parents as the young bride of an Indian sachem, Conanchet.

Faithful to the white dictum that it is hard to reclaim a captive from "those seducing pleasures which he had once enjoyed in the freedom of the woods,"[21] Ruth proves as intractable as Faith Leslie. To create a more complex situation, Cooper provides Ruth with a child, which, oddly enough, is not accounted for in the concluding summary of the later lives and deaths of the principals. When her Indian husband is executed by the Puritans, Ruth immediately lapses into a state of shock followed closely by her death; her child at that moment lies nearby but unheeded. Most likely, the difficulty in suitably disposing of the "little flower of two colors," as Conanchet refers to his son, played a part in Cooper's oversight. Since he regarded miscegenation as productive of a "race [which] has much of the depravity of civilization without the virtues of the savage,"[22] it is not surprising that Cooper eschewed Mrs. Child's solution in *Hobomok*: the transformation of the half-caste son into a perfect white gentleman.

The last example of a mixed marriage, Mary Conant to Hobomok, has already been discussed to some extent. A typically, although Hobomok already loves her, Mary takes the initiative in proposing marriage. The author makes clear that a combination of trying circumstances had disordered Mary's mind; her superstitious belief that Hobomok was fated to be her husband, the apparent death of her white lover, and her father's harsh Calvinism precipitate her into a shocked stupor at the time of the marriage. To give Hobomok his due as a good Indian, he is properly amazed and hesitant when Mary offers herself. During the several years of the marriage she increasingly values Hobomok's devotion. but does not become Indianized. When the missing lover appears, the central issue is not whether Hobomok should sacrifice his interest, but whether Charles is willing to have a woman who has been married to an Indian. To accomplish the happy ending, all traces of Indianness must be obliterated: Hobomok disappears and his son becomes a well-educated white man.

Because of the strength of the miscegenation taboo, few half-breed characters are found in the frontier romance. As a general rule, authors kill off Indians who covet white heroines before any consummation can take place. Except for Conanchet, who dies afterwards, Cooper follows this practice; in *The Last of the Mohicans*, the woman also dies. Good Indians join with whites in abhorring race mixture. The wise sachem of the Mohawks instructs a chief who loves a white woman in *Ish-Noo-Ju-Lut-Sche*: " 'It is contrary to the law of nature and will be productive of a race of beings, and a state of things, subversive of all order, and destructive to your nation.' " In more metaphoric speech, Magawisca proclaims in *Hope Leslie*: " 'The sunbeam and the shadow cannot mingle.' " For authors, Indian violation of a white woman is suggested as a titillating danger which differs from scalping and torture in that it never occurs in their fiction.

Fictive half-breeds are the product of the more likely union of the lower caste woman and the superior male, i.e., an Indian mother and a white father. Such a forbidden coupling, it was popularly believed, unites the worst of both peoples.[23] In this vein M. C. Hodges describes his half-breed villain, Jim Henry:

> In the character of this half-breed were blended, as in blood, the striking moral and intellectual habitudes of the Indian, with many of the grovelling, vicious propensities of those representatives of our own race with whom he had associated, and who are always more or less conspicuous characters in frontier settlements. (*The Mestico*)[24]

Should the nature of Indian "moral and intellectual habitudes" be in doubt, Hodges goes on to characterize Henry as "vile, drunken, intractable in peace—cruel, base, rapacious in war." Hodges seems to attribute some of Henry's unwholesomeness to the whites he has come in contact with rather than to genetic predisposition; the blending of blood in Henry simply literalizes the blending of cultures which so many of the Indians in settled areas displayed. In the frontier romance, neither racial nor cultural miscegenation can produce legitimate issue. More acceptable to the white community than a full-blooded Indian, the half-breed had worked for white men and learned their ways only to be frustrated in his aspirations by his Indian blood. Prevented from rising in white society, Henry is well suited to lead the troublesome Indians who are resisting removal westward. Once the half-breed is captured, resistance to white encroachment collapses.

Another half-breed to have a significant role in fiction is Arthur Gordon Pym's companion in adventure, Dirk Peters, "the son of an Indian woman of the tribe of Upsarokas. . . . His father was a fur-trader." One of the mutineers on the ill-fated *Grampus*, he begins as a typical Poe grotesque:

> Peters himself was one of the most ferocious-looking men I ever beheld. He was short in stature, not more than four feet eight inches high, but his limbs were of Herculean mould. His hands, especially, were so enormously thick and broad as hardly to retain a human shape. His arms, as well as legs, were bowed in the most singular manner, and appeared to possess no flexibility whatever. His head was equally deformed, being of immense size, with an indentation on the crown (like that on the head of most negroes), and entirely bald. . . . the teeth were exceedingly long and protruding, and never even partially covered, in any instance, by the lips.
> (*The Narrative of A. Gordon Pym*)

Like the hunchback of Notre Dame, Peters turns out to be a monster with a heart of gold. Although the development of his relationship with Pym is sacrificed to a chronicle of adventures, it is clear enough that Peters is no evil half-breed whose distorted form reflects his desire to punish innocent whites for his identity problems. On the contrary, he saves Pym's life on several occasions. Even before Pym's reference to himself and Peters as "the only living white men upon the island," it is apparent that Poe has forgotten about the Indian mother or chosen to ignore the potentialities of such a lineage.[25]

It remained for John Esten Cooke, one of the last writers in the frontier romance tradition, to combine the bizarre appearance which antimiscegenation fantasies spawned in Poe with the evil character that authors commonly attributed to half-breeds. Physically, the grotesque villain of *Lord Fairfax* is a direct descendant of Dirk Peters:

about five feet high, with a deep yellow or sallow complexion, a gigantic breadth of chest, long monkey-like arms, and legs which resembled the crooked and gnarled boughs of a distorted oak. His forehead was scarcely an inch in height; his small eyes, as cunning and cruel as a serpent's, rolled beneath bushy brows; his nose was crooked like a hawk's bill, and the hideous mouth, stretching almost from ear to ear, was disfigured with protruding tusks like those of a wild boar.[26]

Cooke is the first author to attempt a full exploitation of the horrors of miscegenation; unfortunately, his awareness of the subject's potential combines with a lack of writing skill to produce caricature. Illustrating the extreme of his Indian nature, the half-breed orders a white settler quartered and affixed to the four corners of a room. He is no match for the gentleman's daughter, however, and falls so completely under her sway that he becomes the easy dupe of her escape plan and is killed by the romance's frontiersman character. As monster, Cooke's villain exemplifies the beauty and the beast myth which lives on in the numerous film monsters attracted to white heroines. As half-breed, he is the literary progenitor of certain groteque mixed bloods in Faulkner and the misshapen Tom-baby in James Herlihy's *Midnight Cowboy*.

The only other half-breed who is an important character in the frontier romance, Areskoui in *The Shoshonee Valley*, is a special case. His mother is a Creole, but the only effect this has in the romance is to make him better looking: "Though retaining a touch of the copper visage and the distinct black lank locks of his father his countenance was noble and Italian." The heroine Jessy is herself of mixed Chinese and English blood, but by virtue of culture she feels superior to the unteachable Areskoui. Despite the mingled blood, Jessy functions as the stereotyped white heroine and Areskoui as the full-blooded good Indian. Jessy is beset by a veritable moral and cultural spectrum of suitors: Nelesho, a bad Indian; Areskoui, a good Indian; Julius, a white villain of mixed Portuguese-English descent; and Frederic, the white hero whom she prefers.[27] Frederic is capable of appreciating Areskoui to the limits of good Indianhood, regarding him as "a fine fellow for an Indian," but he considers him far beneath Jessy. Somewhat strangely, he and Julius often call Jessy an "Indian girl".

Although the racial mixture does not seem to affect the stereotyped roles of white heroine, good Indian, and villain, it may account for the atypical tragic ending which supplants the customary happy union of white hero and heroine. After Areskoui has nobly committed suicide, realizing himself to be the less valuable lover, Frederic and the recently orphaned Jessy set sail for China and presumably a more secure identity for Jessy among her mother's people. Considering herself responsible for Areskoui's death, Jessy, too, takes her life before they arrive. It seems most unlikely that a completely white heroine would lament an Indian to such a degree, but Jessy was born of Chinese-American parents, raised among Indians, and even called an Indian by the worldly white gentlemen who penetrate and bring misery to the Edenic retreat of the Shoshonee Valley. Her disoriented behavior shortly before she dies indicates a disintegration of identity prepared for by all of these circumstances and triggered by Areskoui's suicide. As a woman of mixed blood, Jessy could play the white heroine among the Indians in the isolated valley, but to white society at large, as Frederic's and Julius's deprecatory references to her as an Indian show, her nonwhite blood is a barrier to acceptance. Because any other society based on racial exclusiveness will similarly reject her, Jessy can never succeed in becoming fully Chinese either; for her death to occur between the two homelands is symbolically fitting. Whether uniting the best or worst of two races, the fictive half-breed experiences the same fate, exclusion from white society and death. Like the full-blooded Indian, he cannot achieve white identity.

6

The character stereotyping which is a salient feature of the frontier romance turns both Indians and whites into representative figures repeatedly reenacting the basic confrontation between their two peoples. Because both groups are defined in terms of each other, the inferiority and savagery of the Indian must constantly be juxtaposed to the superiority and civilization of the white man. Historically, whites vanquished the American Indian; in fiction, they could do no less.

NOTES

1. Roy Harvey Pearce, *Savagism and Civilization*, rev. ed. (Baltimore, 1967), p. 8.
2. Nicholas J. Karolides, *The Pioneer in the American Novel* (Norman, 1967), pp. 20-21, discusses the stereotyped frontiersman as a character who habitually "out-Indians the Indians." Francis Parkman, *The Conspiracy of Pontiac* (Boston, 1899), vol. I, p. 166, voices a dissenting opinion: "There are niceties of the woodsman's craft in which the white man must yield the palm to the savage rival"; cf. the twentieth-century ethnologist Walter S. Campbell, discussing this stereotype as it applies to the Plains Indians. He states that in actuality "[they] could out-ride, out-starve, out-hide, and out-fight nine in ten of the white troopers" ("The Plains Indians in Literature—and in Life," *The Trans-Mississippi West*, ed. James F. Willard and Colin B. Goodykoontz [Boulder, 1930], p. 189).
3. Indians are often called tawnies, first in the captivity narratives and Puritan chronicles and then in the frontier romance. Emerson Bennett also calls them niggers, but I have not found this usage elsewhere.
4. Obviously named after Natty Bumppo's more innocuous Killdeer.
5. *Mount Hope* contains an Indian with a "deadly aim." This is a good Indian, however, fighting with the English settlers against King Philip. In *The Hawk Chief*, the Pawnees' only good rifle shot is a half-breed, and he is readily picked off by a Ranger sharp-shooter.
6. Cf. *Old Hicks the Guide*, in which a Frenchwoman displays similar enterprise: "I perceived him [an Indian] about to throw his lance and was in the act of stepping forward to shoot him, when I saw her stoop suddenly to the earth, and the lance pass harmlessly over her. She then faced about rapidly, and with a quick thrust transfixed the headlong savage, and, leaving the lance in his reeling body, sped past us like an arrow."
7. Nathaniel Hawthorne, "The Duston Family," *Miscellanies Biographical and Other Sketches and Letters, The Complete Writings of Nathaniel Hawthorne* (Boston, 1900), vol. XVII, p. 233.
8. Ibid., p. 238.
9. Leslie A. Fiedler, *The Return of the Vanishing American* (New York, 1968), regards Hannah Duston's experience as one of the basic myths of white-Indian relations. Fiedler describes her, p. 95, as "the great WASP Mother of Us All, who, far from achieving a reconciliation between White men and Red, turns the weapon of the Indian against him in a final act of bloodshed and vengeance." Such a figure does not have a history in American fiction, however, supplanted as she was by the conventional romantic heroine of the

English novel. The fragile and genteel heroine of the frontier romance conforms much more to the "Old World archetype of the Persecuted Maiden" (Fiedler, p. 97) than to Hannah Duston.

10. James Fenimore Cooper, Preface to the Leatherstocking Tales, *The Deerslayer* (New York, 1897), p. v.

11. Washington Irving, *Astoria*, rev. ed. (New York, 1868), p. 275, describes the renegade as follows: "One of those desperadoes of the frontiers, outlawed by their crimes, who combine the vices of civilization and savage life, and are ten times more barbarous than the Indians with whom they consort."

12. Cf. *Old Hicks the Guide*: "He [the renegade Albert] controls these savages because he is the most ferocious and relentless savage of them all."

13. Different nationalities are often stereotyped, too. John Davis, *Walter Kennedy*, asserts: "A Frenchman's vivacity never forsakes him"; similarly, Washington Irving describes the *coureurs des bois*: "They are generally of French descent, and inherit much of the gayety and lightness of heart of their ancestors"; James McHenry, *The Wilderness*, states: "If the French are noted for unthinking frivolity, the Irish are no less so for a fervency of feeling by which they are enabled to suppress the suggestions of care, as effectually as the French can dismiss them." Blacks are invariably comic characters in the frontier romance.

14. Frederick Jackson Turner, "The Significance of the Frontier in American History," *The Frontier in American History* (New York, 1920), p. 4; cf. Abraham Lincoln's cousin, Dennis Hanks, speaking of the Ohio Valley in the second decade of the nineteenth century: "We lived the same as Indians 'ceptin we took an interest in politics and religion" (quoted in Howard H. Peckham, *Captured by Indians* [New Brunswick, 1954], p. xi).

15. The Indians' failure to abuse women sexually is noted by Cadwallader Colden, *The History of the Five Indian Nations Depending on the Province of New-York in America* [1727] (New York, 1902), vol. I, p. xxvi: "I have always been assured, that there is not one instance, of their offering the least Violence to the Chastity of any Woman that was their Captive"; cf. John Heckewelder, *History, Manners, and Customs of The Indian Nations, Who Once Inhabited Pennsylvania and the Neighboring States*, ed. William Reichel (Philadelphia, 1876), p. 339, who claims that Indians treat female prisoners with "moderation, humanity and delicacy." Wilcomb E. Washburn, "A Moral History of Indian-White Relations: Needs and Opportunities for Study," *Ethnohistory* 4 (1957-1958), p. 51, affirms the absence of sexual violation on the part of Indians toward white captives; cf. Edmund Pearson, *Dime Novels* (Boston, 1929), p. 37, for a subliterary treatment of this situation: "A thousand paleface damsels were captured by red-skinned warriors during the progress of the dime novel, but none were ever violated."

16. Robert Beverley, *The History and Present State of Virginia* (London, 1705), ed. Louis B. Wright (Chapel Hill, 1947), p. 159.

17. One of O'Carroll's objections to dark skin is the absence of a blush: " 'I know not by what signs to detect them [emotions], where there are no eloquent blushes, no sweet mutations of countenance, to indicate the feelings of the soul.' " Grahame counters with the observation that a glow is indeed visible " 'through the swarthy complexion of the Indian.' " Cf. *Hope Leslie*: "To an observing eye, the changes of the olive skin are as apparent as those of a fairer complexion." Even as strong a partisan of the noble savage as Henri Sydney in

Keep Cool admits that he loved his Indian friend better for being "lighter than the common copper of his people, scarcely darker than a Spaniard."

18. An Indian's display of any remarkable quality is generally sufficient to provoke this conjecture. Surprised by an Indian's fluent speech, Greyslaer thinks he might be some "disguised renegado white, who, with talents fitted for a better sphere, had induced by caprice or compelled by crime, banished himself from society, and assumed the character of one of the aborigines" (*Greyslaer*).

19. See D. H. Lawrence, *Studies in Classic American Literature* (New York, 1930), p. 85: "the good old division, the dark sensual woman and the clinging, submissive little blonde, who is so 'pure.' "

20. Several authors who depict Indians attempting to gain possession of white heroines make general comments on the safety of white feminine honor among the Indians without any suggestion of anomaly. John T. Irving, Jr., in *The Hawk Chief*, writes: "He well knew that cruel as were the tribes of American Indians, still that with them the honour of a female was never violated." More delicately, Cooper states in *The Oak-Openings*: "The savage American is little addicted to abusing his power over female captives."

21. On three different occasions in his notes to C. F. Volney, *A View of the Soil and Climate of the United States of America* (Philadelphia, 1804), Charles Brockden Brown explains the attachment of both Indians and captives alike to savage life as the result of custom formed in youth (pp. 372, 376, 377).

22. Cooper, *The Prairie*; other references to the propriety of keeping the races separate are scattered throughout Cooper's novels. In *The Deerslayer*, Natty Bumppo tells Judith Hutter, who had asked about a love interest in his life, " 'I am white—have a white heart and can't, in reason, love a red-skinned maiden, who must have a redskin heart and feelin's.' " His central theory of a distinction between white and red gifts militates against race mixture. As Natty remarks in *The Pathfinder*: " 'The white man has his difficulties in getting redskin habits, quite as much as the Injin in getting white-skin ways. As for the raal natur', it is my opinion that neither can actually get that of the other.' " But in *Notions of the Americans* he writes: "As there is little reluctance to mingle the white and red blood, (for the physical difference is far less than in the case of the blacks, and the Indians have never been menial slaves,) I think an amalgamation of the two races would in time occur."

23. Cf. Francis Parkman, *The Oregon Trail* (Boston, 1891), p. 288, for a popular definition of the half-breed: "According to the common saying half Indian, half white man, and half devil." Alexis De Tocqueville, like Beverley and Byrd before him, expresses a view of optimism about miscegenation: "Deriving intelligence from the father's side without entirely losing the savage customs of the mother, the half-blood forms the natural link between civilization and barbarism" (*Democracy in America*, Henry Reeve text, rev. Francis Bowen and Phillips Bradley [New York, 1945], vol. I, p. 345).

24. Although Henry is portrayed as absorbing bad qualities from lower-class whites, he speaks like the traditional white villain-gentleman, calling the heroine "my brave beauty."

25. Fiedler, *The Return of the Vanishing American*, p. 130, suggests that the South Pole, where Pym and Peters's final adventures take place, and its savage Negro-like inhabitants constitute "a world in which Red no longer has an archetypal place."

26. Cf. Hodges's half-breed in *The Mestico* who has "a face of manly beauty" and a "tall, erect and muscular body."

27. Alexander Cowie, *The Rise of the American Novel* (New York, 1948), p. 220, describes this cast of characters as "racially and morally varied enough to form a good nucleus for a study of ethnology and anthropology."

5

A Paradigm for Racism: The Subgenre of Indian Hater Fiction

It is not easy for those living in the tranquility of polished life fully to conceive the depth and force of that unquenchable, indiscriminate hate, which Indian outrages can awaken in those who have suffered them. The chronicles of the American borders are filled with the deeds of men, who, having lost all by the merciless tomahawk, have lived for vengeance alone; and such men will never cease to exist so long as a hostile tribe remains within striking distance of an American settlement.

Francis Parkman, THE CONSPIRACY OF PONTIAC

1

While the frontier romance is predominantly concerned with the white-Indian confrontation along the frontier as background for the development of a conventional genteel love story, the sub-genre of Indian hater fiction has a different emphasis. Using as protagonist the familiar frontier figure of the Indian hater, these works focus upon behavior generated by violent and overt race hatred. The ritualistic behavior of the Indian hater constitutes a paradigm for racism, one which contains a curious set of ambivalences and ironies.

Originally inspired by the killing of their own flesh and blood, Indian haters generalize their personal grievances into a racial conflict and ultimately out-Indian the Indian in revenge. They exist like metaphoric half-breeds between the white and Indian communities, isolated from ordinary men of either race by the intensity of their hatred and the single-mindedness of their commitment. With their resourcefulness, tenacity, and mastery of the wilderness environment, Indian haters are the first New World examples of the abuse of those pioneer gifts which American writers have so often celebrated.

2

In keeping with the racist view of white superiority, the Indian hater's skills in the Indian's own wilderness environment are notably better than those of his foe. James Hall's account of the historical Colonel Moredock describes him as well suited to the vocation he has espoused:

> [He] was expert in the use of the rifle and other weapons; and was complete master of those wonderful and numberless expedients by which the woodsman subsists in the forest, pursues the footsteps of an enemy with unerring sagacity, or conceals himself and his design from the discovery of the watchful foe.[1]

The reputations which fictive Indian haters acquire among whites and Indians alike testify to their proficiency. The Indians imagine the Indian hater in *Nick of the Woods* to be "neither man nor beast, but a great ghost or devil that knife cannot harm nor bullet touch." In *The Forest Rose*, Lewis Wetzel's name "became famous on the frontiers among the whites, and a word of terror to the savages." Such appellations as "Bloody Ben," "Longknife," and "the Dauntless One" further attest to the abilities of Indian haters.

Indian hater exploits, which include revenge on the murderers of their own kin,[2] are in keeping with their fame. It is a rule of frontier fiction that white men are superior to Indians in any kind of reasonable contest, and often in unreasonable ones as well, but Indian haters especially excel because they constantly seek out opportunities to kill Indians. Timothy Weasel, the Indian hater in *The Dutchman's Fireside,* claims to have sacrificed "almost a hecatomb to the manes of his wife and children." More impressively, Hugh Bradley boasts a total of three hundred scalps, " 'taken by my own hands from the sculls *[sic]* of red ruffians!' " (*The Spectre of the Forest*). Most Indian haters promulgate no statistics, but their practice of killing Indians as a full-time occupation seems likely to result in large totals.

Indian haters are also known to be completely inflexible in their cause. The principle of an equitable measure of retaliation, i.e., a rough kind of justice, is incompatible with the racist attitude which informs the Indian hater role. According to this view, all Indians are culpable by virtue of their race, and their total elimination is therefore desirable. Thus, when someone objects to Hugh Bradley's killing of an Indian who had given him helpful information, the Indian hater replies: " 'It is not in my nature to spare an Indian.' " In *Elkswatawa* Earth similarly tells a white hunting party: " 'You all know I never spared an Ingen.' " And Colonel Moredock is described in the short story "The Devoted" as one who "never let slip an opportunity to dip his hands in Indian blood." Tom Quick considers sparing a baby, but the realization that "the child would in a few years become an Indian . . . so enraged him that he instantly dashed out its brains." When asked in later years why he killed children, Tom invariably replied: " 'Nits make lice!' "—a reduction of the enemy to extermination-worthy subhuman status (*Tom Quick, the Indian Slayer*).

3

Some authors believe that the Indian hater's course is both justified by circumstance and beneficial to the white community, but all agree that only a species of madness could cause a man to pursue such a calling. They attempt to make the Indian hater's genocidal mania plausible, and to some degree acceptable, by endowing their protagonists with a tragedy of overwhelming proportions, usually the sudden extinction of all immediate family by marauding Indians. Often, the recollection of this loss is so traumatic that it induces a fit of temporary insanity or frenzy in which the essential madness of the Indian hater's character is clearly seen. When the Indian hater Rogers in *Tadeuskund* shows a party of frontiersmen his own scalped skull, "there was a cast of wild distraction upon his countenance, which impressed the beholders with irresistible horror. His convulsed features spoke the warring passions which his tongue for a time refused to express." Similarly, when the Indian hater Hugh Bradley attempts to describe the incident which provoked his career, he abruptly exclaims: " 'I shall go mad, my brain will burn, if I dwell on the terrible picture!' " (*The Spectre of the Forest*).

Both grisly details of the massacre and the emotional outburst which their recital produces are designed to establish a sympathetic view of the transformation of ordinary man into Indian hater: Indian haters are made, not born. In this vein James Wilmer Dallam writes about his Indian hater figure in *The Deaf Spy*: "Circumstance and suffering—not nature—had planted the hardness in his heart, which had grown upon and cankered it; as one after another of its dearest and fondest ties were snapped in twain." The importance of such a view to the racist attitude of Indian hater fiction is clear: although Indians and Indian haters behave in similar ways within the genre, one is by nature evil while the other—born to kindness, sensitivity, and other good attributes—has been corrupted from his natural state by a tragic experience with Indians.

Extravagant expressions of enjoyment are one sign of the derangement which characterizes the fictive Indian hater. As Hugh Bradley proclaims melodramatically: " 'The scalps of redmen are my glory, and their blood the drink that delighteth my soul' " (*The Spectre of the Forest*). Equally happy in his calling is Tom Quick, who kills Indians "with fewer compunctions of conscience than he would have felt at crushing a reptile" (*Tom Quick*). A further measure of abnormality is provided by the Indian hater's acquisition of the more brutal aspects of Indian behavior.

In *Nick of the Woods*, for example, the Indian-like avenger appears to be a "truculent madman" in the eyes of his fellow whites:

> His Indian garments and decorations contributed somewhat to this effect; but the man, it was soon seen, was more changed in spirit than in outward attire. The bundle of scalps in his hand, the single one, yet reeking with blood, at his belt, and the axe of Wenonga, gory to the helve, and grasped with a hand not less blood-stained, were not more remarkable evidences of transformation than were manifested in his countenance, deportment, and expression. His eye beamed with a wild excitement, with exultation mingled with fury; his step was fierce, active, firm, and elastic, like that of a warrior leaping through the measures of the war-dance.

Whereas this is stereotypical of fictive Indians, it is aberrant for a white character.

Most Indian-like of all is the Indian hater's passion for vengeance.[3] That whites make superior revengers is pointedly illustrated by the contrast between the insatiable Indian hater Tom Hanson and the old Indian he encounters: "He [the Indian] had sworn never to cease until those who had murdered his friends had shared a similar fate; he pursued his vow and fulfilled it. Satisfied in having obtained revenge, he retired to the cave, and ever after lived the life of a hermit" (*Tom Hanson, the Avenger*). Like the historic Logan, the old Indian was able to limit his revenge.[4] In contrast, Indian haters are genocidal, not simply from policy but from the necessity of feeding their habit. As Samuel Monson relates in James Hall's story "The Indian Hater," the propensity to kill Indians is beyond control: " 'I could not quench my thirst for the blood of those monsters. I swore never to forgive them, and when peace came, I continued to make war.' " Indian haters are by nature absolutists, but the sentiment of revenge also seems to have an addictive quality of its own which can never by appeased completely; the exercise of vengeance only whets the Indian hater's appetite for more.

Freedom from the need to kill Indians is usually attained only through death. During the last illness of Tom Quick, "he never expressed a regret that he had killed so many Indians; but was sorry that he had not murdered a greater number!" After repeated urgings by his fiancee, and after several short-lived retirements, Tom Hanson reluctantly settles down at last, but it is difficult for him to overcome his mania. He remarks nostalgically: " 'We haint the fun here we had with the cussed Red Skins. Ah! them was the times!' " Circumstance alone, particularly the imposition of peace on a frontier area, causes Indian haters to relinquish their profession.

While authors are generally sympathetic with their Indian hater protagonists and take great pains, as we have seen, to provide elaborate rationales for their behavior, they sense the dilemma which complete approval of vengeance would entail. Thus, the destructiveness of this all-consuming emotion is spoken of by several Indian haters and illustrated by all. Without overt comment, some Indian hater fiction conveys the same negative view of the effects of revenge. In *Tom Hanson,* for example, the author describes a father returning from the field to find his family massacred: "He pauses. Firm is his resolve. His fields are deserted, his corn arrives to perfection, none are nigh to gather it. The one who tilled it, is far from his once happy home. Vengeance yields an impulse—and he aims to fulfil his threats." Remembering that a prominent argument for white dispossession of the Indian was cultivation, the abandonment of the fields is significant. The white man reverts to a more primitive life; bent on destruction, he becomes a wanderer. His crop will be death rather than the life-sustaining grain he cultivated before.

Tom Hanson himself is much like the Indian avenger Pesquet. While Pesquet harangues his warriors never to let vengeance sleep, Tom is busy recruiting disciples. Predictably, the result of such mutual incitement is that "enemies were increased, while blood flowed freely from the breasts of white men and Indians." *Tom Hanson* is, in fact, a collection of exempla, many of them digressions from Tom's adventures, which illustrate the endless destructive spiral of revenge.

Just as Tom's bloodthirstiness is equated with Pesquet's and contrasted with the humanity of the old Indian who saves the life of a white boy, so other Indian hater works implicitly condemn their protagonists by juxtaposing the Indian hater and a humane character. In *The Spectre of the Forest* people are said to feel that Hugh Bradley's oath "would be better broken, as it leads to blood-spilling, and was taken rashly," but the chief criticism of the Indian hater is the character of his own son. Ephrain Bradley emphatically rejects his father's calling: "Not that he was a coward, for he possessed courage and intrepidity sufficient to meet his foe when called upon by any proper cause; but he did not choose to hunt after adventures of hardship and hazard, for the attainment of no real good. He wished for the enjoyment of domestic comforts."

Two violently opposed characters exemplify the same moral in *Tadeuskund*: the Indian hater Rogers, whose philosophy is "to exist upon destruction," and the Quaker Burton, whose loss at the hands of the Indians has inspired him to work among them for peace. The author depicts Rogers as a fiend and Burton as a saint. In *Nick of the Woods* this contrast is internalized in the dual nature of the Indian hater: as a peace-loving Quaker, Nathan Slaughter (whose name provides a clue to his real predilections) piously refuses to join the frontiersmen in defending the community against Indians; as the dreaded *Jibbenainosay*, he kills, scalps, and mutilates them. Like Brecht's good woman of Setzuan, Nathan finds it impossible to integrate his predatory and pacific impulses into a total personality.

4

The Indian hater's dedication of himself to vengeance is presented as a response to a personal loss of great magnitude; nevertheless, the willingness to embrace such a dubious calling has been developed by the frontier ethos long before this tragedy. In James Hall's explanation, a one-dimensional image of the Indian is inculcated in every backwoodsman:

He [the Indian] had to do with men who had long been taught to consider the savage as a natural enemy, as hateful as the serpent, and as irreconcilable as the wolf; men whose ears had been accustomed from infancy to legends of border warfare, in which the savage was always represented as the aggressor, and as a fiend stimulated by hellish passions, and continually plotting some detestable outrage or horrible revenge. Most of them had witnessed the Indian mode of warfare, which spares neither age nor sex; and many of them had suffered in their own families, or those of their nearest friends. They were familiar with the capture of women and children, the conflagration of houses, and the midnight assassination of the helpless and decrepid [sic]: and they had grown up in hatred of the perpetrators of such enormities, which the philanthropist could hardly condemn, as it originated in generous feelings, and was kept alive by the repeated violation of the most sacred rights and the best affections. ("The Backwoodsman")

What authors of Indian hater fiction convey is that their protagonists differ in degree rather than in kind from other inhabitants of the frontier. The ordinary frontiersman, in Washington Irving's description, "was not naturally a stern or cruel man; but from his boyhood he had lived in the Indian country among Indian traders, and held the life of a savage extremely cheap."[5] The Indian hater simply translates the feelings of the entire community into action: "He hears little from . . . the old chroniclers of the forest, but histories of Indian lying, Indian theft, Indian double-dealing, Indian fraud and perfidy, Indian want of conscience, Indian bloodthirstiness, Indian diabolism." As Melville's narrator in *The Confidence-Man* further asserts: "Indian-hating was no monopoly of Colonel Moredock's; but a passion in one form or other, and to a degree, greater or less, largely shared among the class to which he belonged." The Indian hater is no aberration who can readily be disowned by his peers, but rather the student of community traditions and beliefs who has learned his lesson too well.

This indoctrination is not the only communal force operating on the formation of an Indian hater, however. The logic of frontier survival dictates both unmitigated hatred of the Indian and, ironically, a partial adoption of his way of life: "In his earliest venture, he [the frontiersman] learns and adopts the habits of his enemy, and in some cases it would seem his very nature also; and the result is, that he becomes at last neither more nor less than . . . a civilized savage" (*The Prairie Flower*).[6] The apparent similarity of bitter enemies is not entirely surprising. As Hall notes and Cooper's Natty Bumppo exemplifies, to a certain extent frontiersman and Indian desire the same things: the white woodsman "shuns a crowded population, delights to rove uncontrolled in the woods, and does not believe that an Indian, or any other man has a right to monopolize the hunting grounds, which he considers free to all."[7]

In taking up certain aspects of the Indian life style—wearing moccasins and deerskin clothing, carrying tomahawk and knife, and even scalping the enemy—the frontiersman may be saved from a complete loss of white identity by thinking of the people he emulates as "red niggers," "greasy faces," and "red imps of satan." If he goes too far in emulation, he becomes the most abhorred figure of frontier literature, the renegade or "white Indian."[8] If he carries his hatred of the Indian too far, he becomes equally cut off from the white community as an Indian hater. Although the Indian hater technically remains on the side of civilization, he, too, has effectively lost his white identity.

Scalping, a process which symbolizes commitment to hatred and barbarism in frontier literature, separates Indian haters from the rest of the white population. Good frontiersmen and young heroes are unanimously opposed to it as a gratuitous cruelty. An old and experienced backwoodsman tells a novice in *The Hawk Chief*: " 'The white man slays, but he never scalps. 'Tis against his conscience to mutilate.' " Or, as Natty Bumppo tells the modified Indian hater Hurry Harry in *The Deerslayer*: " 'I'll not unhumanize my natur' by falling into ways that God intended for another race.' " The immoral nature of scalping is also brought out by the admirable character in *The Spectre of the Forest*: " 'It is an unnecessary and cruel practice to mangle the slain; and I should think, is too close an imitation of our barbarous enemies, to be followed by Christians.' "

Writers like Robert Montgomery Bird and Emerson Bennett, who approve of the white man's scalping of Indians, defend it as an inevitable product of frontier hostility. To Bennett, white scalping is a commonplace of the frontier milieu, but he nevertheless admits in *The Prairie Flower* that the man who kills and scalps Indians "with the same indifference and delight that he would shoot a bear or deer . . . [is] a strange compound . . . of good and evil." Bird writes in *Nick of the Woods*:

> Such is the practice of the border, and such it has been ever since the mortal feud, never destined to be really ended but with the annihilation or civilization of the American race, first began between the savage and the white intruder. It was, and is, essentially a measure of retaliation, compelled, if not justified, by the ferocious example of the red-man.

The passage contains the typical formulations of the white-Indian confrontation found throughout Indian hater fiction: the impossibility of coexistence and the initial ferocity of the red man which compels strong retaliation. Ironically, it is the Indians who constitute "the American race" for Bird, but this is a mean advantage compared with the values of white civilization.

The Indians pursued by the Indian hater are uniformly portrayed as the worst variety of the stereotyped howling savage. In *Nick of the Woods* they are "lying devils," "wicked enemies and captivators," and "foul assassins," in short, the familiar figures of the seventeenth-century Puritan chronicles and eighteenth-century captivity narratives. And in the subliterary Ned Buntline story-paper series, a character apologizes for "Merciless Ben, the Hair-Lifter" by explaining: " 'He may be merciless, but it is to a race that knows no mercy! To a race which deserves none. For theirs is a life of falsehood, treachery, and heartless cruelty from their birth to the grave!' "[9] The Indian hater thus regards his quarry not only as subhuman but as the embodiment of evil whose killing extirpates evil from the world.

What distinguishes the Indian hater from other frontiersmen is his adoption of Indian killing as a profession, a vocation which takes priority over the conventions of the civilized community. Deprived of blood relatives by the massacre which launches his career, the Indian hater chooses not to reestablish those ties which bind the human community, Indian and white alike. Although many Indian haters live a peripatetic wilderness existence, free to hunt Indians whenever the opportunity arises, even the Indian hater who lives among his fellows is spiritually isolated from them. Melville's portrait of the archetypal Indian hater, Colonel John Moredock, subtly reveals the ironies of such a position:

> He could be very convivial; told a good story (though never of his more private exploits), and sung a capital song. Hospitable, not backward to help a neighbour, by report benevolent, as retributive, in secret . . . yet with nobody, *Indians excepted*, otherwise than courteous in a manly fashion; a moccasined gentleman admired and loved. [my emphasis]

The description prickles with significant qualifications. Moredock loved a good story, but he could not speak of his life's work and constant preoccupation. He was in all ways sociable—except to Indians. The exception seems to be inserted casually in the list of Moredock's good qualities; in reality, it looms over and effectively negates them. For all his bonhomie Moredock is a man apart, paradoxically a "moccasined gentleman" who cannot run for governor as his friends desire because his passion for killing Indians would impel him into the woods on periodic forays.

The coming of peace illustrates the ambivalent position the Indian hater occupies in relation to the white community. In an exposed frontier situation, where Indians constitute the chief hazard, the double impetus of race prejudice and danger causes the Indian hater to be looked upon as a hero. Applause greets the flourishing of his scalp belt; posterity converts his exploits into legend. After peace is made he becomes a danger himself, an antisocial force operating outside the community's control and against its laws. Because racism persists, the reaction against the Indian hater will never be total. When the narrator of "The Indian Hater" indignantly protests that "in a civilized country, within the reach of our laws, a wretch is permitted to hunt down his fellow creatures like wild beasts, to murder a defenceless Indian who comes into our territory in good faith," he is given the following racist rebuttal: " 'Many of the settlers have had their kin murdered by the savages in early times; and all who have been raised in the backwoods, have been taught to fear and dislike them. Then Monson is an honest fellow . . . and it seems hard to break neighbourhood with him for the matter of an Indian or so.' " Monson's neighbor characterizes the Indian hater's practice as "not exactly permitted"; neither is it condemned. Rather, the community tolerates what ought to be labeled wanton murder as an understandable, if regrettable, act. Although white civilization requires the cessation of personal vengeance, prejudice against the Indian continues to inspire sympathy for the anachronistic Indian hater.

5

In portraying Indian haters, authors show some of the same ambivalence toward them which is found in the fictive white community. They attempt to place the best possible construction on the Indian hater's career by representing Indians as demons, by showing the climate of hatred toward Indians in the frontier milieu, and by then maddening the protagonist with a stunning personal loss inflicted by Indians. The familiar rationale of Indian "outrages" rather than Indian occupation of the land (the root cause of the conflict) is invoked to explain and sanctify white hatred. The Indian hater's asceticism and disinterested devotion to the extirpation of the hated enemy inspire some authorial admiration; nevertheless, the total view which this body of fiction provides is one of terrifying dehumanization, both of the hunter and his victim. Ironically, as Roy Harvey Pearce writes of the Indian hater: "It is this man who has made the frontier safe for civilization; yet, to do so, he has had to become one of the savages whom he would destroy."[10]

For most of the writers of Indian hater fiction, the Indian has an inferior and barbaric nature which makes him understandably evil. In Hall's comparison, while Indians are "ferocious, ignorant and brutal," whites are "civilised and polished." In blurring the distinction between the two races, the Indian hater, like the renegade, threatens the system; he is as bad as an Indian, even bad *like* an Indian, yet he is no benighted savage, but a white man. Born to the purple of racial superiority, he has retrogressed to a life of willful brutality patterned after his own distorted perception of Indian behavior. The Indian hater's savagery combines with the greater resources for destructiveness which white technology affords to become a dreadful and efficient force in the service of genocide.

In the contest for possession of the continent, whites believed that killing the Indian was the necessary action which freed the New World Eden from heathenism and evil and opened it to white settlement. By embracing Indian killing as an end in itself and openly avowing race murder, the atavistic Indian hater makes a mockery of the tenets of white civilization. Exemplifying the code of personal vengeance and blood sacrifice which his society claims to practice no longer, he is the logical embodiment and culmination of those dark feelings of race hatred inherent in the white conquest of North America.

NOTES

1. James Hall, *Sketches of History, Life, and Manners, in the West* (Philadelphia, 1835), vol. II, p. 81.
2. G. Harrison Orians states: "Rarely . . . did the pursuit find the supreme climax, which the novelist gives us in 'Nick of the Woods,' the ultimate ferreting out of the Indian who had caused the original injury" ("The Indian Hater in Early American Fiction," *The Journal of American History* 27 [1933], p. 43.) On the contrary, most fictive Indian haters apprehend and kill the Indians responsible for their own losses.
3. In a list of Indian vices which he compiled, Benjamin Rush writes: "[They] possess a spirit of revenge, which places them upon a footing with infernal spirits" ("An Account of the Vices Peculiar to the Indians of North America," *Essays*, 2nd ed. [Philadelphia, 1806], p. 257). The 1828 edition of Noah Webster's *Dictionary* similarly characterized Indians as "implacably cruel and revengeful toward their enemies."
4. Logan pronounced himself finally satisfied: " 'I have killed many: I have fully glutted my vengeance' " (quoted in Thomas Jefferson, *Notes on the State of Virginia* [New York, 1801], p. 96).
5. Washington Irving, *Astoria*, rev. ed. (New York, 1868), p. 557; cf. Peter Loewenberg, "The Psychology of Racism," *The Great Fear*, ed. Gary B. Nash and Richard Weiss (New York, 1970), p. 187: "A white child coming of age . . . acquires prejudice as a matter of course by living in his environment and

internalizing its values. It is not necessary to teach him any explicit ideology of racism. He has only to observe and participate in his world."

6. Cf. *The Dutchman's Fireside*: the Indian hater Timothy Weasel is described as "a compound of the two races."

7. *Sketches of History, Life, and Manners, in the West*, vol. II, p. 76.

8. In *Nick of the Woods* a renegade comments: " 'I'm a white Injun, and there's nothing more despisable.' "

9. Quoted in Mary Noel, *Villains Galore* (New York, 1954), p. 243.

10. Roy Harvey Pearce, "Melville's Indian-Hater: A Note on a Meaning of *The Confidence-Man*," *PMLA* 67 (1952), p. 944.

PART 2

The Subversive Periphery of the Frontier Romance

It is the spirit of humanity, that which animates both so-called savages and civilized nations . . . that interests us most.
                                        Henry D. Thoreau, JOURNAL

When Hawthorne and Melville began their careers, the frontier romance was well-established and thriving. That neither author chose to write in the genre reflects a dissatisfaction with the hackneyed pattern of white-Indian relations promulgated by so many of their contemporaries rather than a lack of interest in Indians. As Hawthorne wrote in response to Simms's enthusiasm for Indians and events of American history as literary materials:

> We cannot help feeling that the real treasures of his subject have escaped the author's notice. The themes suggested by him, viewed as he views them, would produce nothing but historical novels, cast in the same worn out mould that has been in use these thirty years, and which it is time to break up and fling away.

Perceiving that the pattern had outlived its usefulness, Hawthorne was nevertheless sensible of the "real treasures"

143

which he felt that Simms had overlooked: one result of his efforts to use these materials more meaningfully is *The Scarlet Letter*, another is a pervasive system of references to Indians and their few but significant appearances in his fiction. While writers of the frontier romance repeatedly depict captivity and retaliation sequences intertwined with a love story, Hawthorne and Melville reject the formula but expose its meaning. Where the majority of these romancers mechanically provide large quantities of action with little awareness of the racist and nationalistic chauvinism inherent in their design, Hawthorne, and especially Melville, reverse the proportions: when parts of the pattern appear, as they do in a disjointed and fragmentary fashion, the concern is with the underlying attitudes and implications rather than with the action itself. Their ironic penetration of the stereotyped views found in the frontier romance reveals them to be white rationalizations smoothed over dark truths; the white man's destruction of primitive peoples is the true barbarism which the aggressors avoid recognizing by labeling their victims savages. For both writers, the schematized perspectives of the frontier romance are replaced by a more fluid and ambiguous vision in which all men become the generic man, a mixture of good and evil, irrespective of race.

6

Hawthorne and Puritan Inhumanity

1

Taken out of context, Hawthorne's avowed dislike of "an Indian story" has been interpreted as complete lack of interest in the subject of Indians. A more extensive quotation from the often-cited passage provides a different view. After relating an old Indian legend which a party of travellers had been discussing, Hawthorne comments:

> The hearts of the pale-faces would not thrill to these superstitions of the red men, though we spoke of them in the centre of the haunted region. The habits and sentiments of that departed people were too distinct from those of their successors to find much real sympathy. It has often been a matter of regret to me that I was shut out from the most peculiar field of American fiction by an inability to see any romance, or poetry, or grandeur, or beauty in the Indian character, at least till such traits were pointed out by others. I do abhor an Indian story. Yet no writer can be more secure of a permanent place in our literature than the biographer of the Indian chiefs. His subject, as referring to tribes which have mostly vanished from the earth, gives him a right to be placed on a classic shelf, apart from the merits which will sustain him there. ("Our Evening Party Among the Mountains")[1]

145

Hawthorne refers first of all not to white-Indian relations but to a purely Indian legend, a subject almost never attempted by writers of the period.[2] He rightly concludes that such material has little appeal; at that particular historical moment, whites could not value Indians in and of themselves. Aware of this difficulty, Hawthorne confesses his own inability to see what writers of the frontier romance assumed with such facility. Their creations were, of course, the white man's Indian; the romance, poetry, grandeur, and beauty in the Indian character were placed there by white writers for their own purposes: thus the irony of Hawthorne's remark that he was unable to perceive these qualities until they were "pointed out by others." Given the superficial and totally biased view of Indians found in fiction, it is little wonder that Hawthorne next proclaims his abhorrence of "an Indian story." But distaste for overworked literary conventions hardly entails hatred of Indians. Hawthorne quickly continues with a qualification of his statement: there is a worthy endeavor to be done on the subject of Indians, one which can produce the high reward of "a permanent place in our literature." Indians should be memorialized, but not by the false and trivial pages of numerous Indian stories. Hawthorne's reference to "the biographer of the Indian chiefs" suggests a treatment more historical and more truthful than that provided by novelists; his own practice affords one illustration of how to convey the important truth of Indians for white Americans without writing an Indian story.[3]

Hawthorne's use of Indians is predicated upon an awareness of the white writer's limitations in this area with which most frontier romancers, eager to assert the authenticity of their aboriginal portraits, were unwilling to come to terms. Finding an old letter that describes an Indian squaw making salt, Hawthorne remarks:

It is particularly interesting to find out anything as to the embryo yet stationary arts of life among the red people, their manufactures, their agriculture, their domestic labors. It is partly the lack of this knowledge—the possession of which would establish a ground of sympathy on the part of civilized

men—that makes the Indian race so shadow-like and unreal
to our conception. ("A Book of Autographs")

Given the impossibility of accumulating the knowledge necessary
for understanding and accurately depicting the almost extinct
Indians, Hawthorne confines his own treatment to what Indians
mean and have meant to white Americans and what the confrontation between Indians and settlers revealed in the white
man's character. He understood the message of the frontier
romance and, rather than contributing still another version,
chose instead to analyze it. White-Indian relations for Hawthorne
provide, as they later would for Melville, still another example of
man's inhumanity to man.

2

Indians particularly serve Hawthorne in delineating the
Puritan character. Vaguely troubled as he might have been by
those "stern and black-browed" ancestral shades who accuse him
of being a mere "writer of story-books," an idler and degenerate,
Hawthorne was unequivocal in describing the harsh features of
Puritanism. When the balance sheet is drawn up, "as often as our
imagination lives in the past, we find it a ruder and rougher age
than our own, with hardly any perceptible advantages, and much
that gave life a gloomier tinge."

Almost any Hawthorne treatment of the early New England
experience advances the Indian, along with the Quaker and other
deviants from community norms, as a victim of Puritan intolerance. In one of the most explicit examples, "The Maypole of
Merry Mount," Hawthorne writes:

Not far from Merry Mount was a settlement of Puritans,
most dismal wretches, who said their prayers before daylight,
and then wrought in the forest or the cornfield till evening
made it prayer time again. Their weapons were always at
hand to shoot down the straggling savage. When they met in

conclave, it was never to keep up the old English mirth, but to hear sermons three hours long, or to proclaim bounties on the heads of wolves or scalps of Indians.[4]

In almost all respects, the Merry Mounters are more pleasing and more humane than the "grim Puritans": instead of the whipping post they have the Maypole, instead of toil they have sport, and instead of exterminating the wilderness populace they attempt to work out a harmonious mode of existence with them—"perhaps teaching a bear to dance, or striving to communicate their mirth to the grave Indian." While the denizens of Merry Mount are silken and flower-bedecked, the Puritans are weapon-laden, "each with a horse-load of iron armor to burden his footsteps." Their leader, Endicott, "seemed wrought of iron, gifted with life and thought, yet all of one substance with his headpiece and breastplate."[5] If the dancers around the Maypole seem vain and frivolous in comparison with the gloom of the Puritans, they are also pacific and loving; some of the dancing figures are grotesque, but none are harmful.[6] Some wear wolfskins, but it is the Puritans who manifest a wolfish nature. As Hawthorne formulates it, the choice is either clouded visages, hard toil, and endless sermons, or sunshine, flowers, and the Maypole. If the ending of the story asserts that life must be taken seriously and Eden cannot be reestablished, even in the New World, it does not similarly commend Puritan severity and bigotry.

Those who refuse to conform to the narrow Puritan mores are invariably punished harshly, even when, as in the case of the Indians and the inhabitants of Merry Mount, they wish to maintain their own communities apart from the Puritans. The Indians are killed; the Merry Mounters are zealously whipped and driven off; and in "The Gentle Boy" two Quakers are executed. A variety of punishments is meted out to transgressors within the Puritan ranks from the familiar confinement in stocks for a limited period of time to the lifelong wearing of the letter *A* or a halter, from temporary disfigurement by lashing to permanent mutilation by branding or ear-cropping.

In "Endicott and the Red Cross" such chastisements are represented as gratuitous barbarities which pander to the collective sadism but possess no truly corrective powers.[7] The "Wanton Gospeller" and the woman with a cleft stick on her tongue are eager to resume their unsanctioned speech as soon as their term of punishment ends. Those who have been mutilated, the author insinuates, may be led to despair rather than repentance; the man forced to wear a halter "must have been grievously tempted to affix the other end of the rope to some convenient beam or bough." Upon this scene the severest Puritan of all, as Hawthorne describes Endicott in "The Maypole of Merry Mount," comes to speechify about the blessings of New World freedom. Eloquently cognizant of Old World political and religious tyranny, Endicott is ironically insensitive to the Puritans' own brand of oppression, whose silenced victims surround him as he speaks.

Mingling with these unfortunates are "a few stately savages, in all the pomp and dignity of the primeval Indian." In contrast to Endicott, whose breastplate is "so highly polished that the whole surrounding scene had its image in the glittering steel," the Indians carry far less potent arms: "Their flint-headed arrows were but childish weapons compared with the matchlocks of the Puritans, and would have rattled harmlessly against the steel caps and hammered iron breastplates which enclosed each soldier in an individual fortress."[8] Shortly after Hawthorne makes this comparison he has Endicott say: " 'A howling wilderness it is! The wolf and the bear meet us within halloo of our dwellings. The savage lieth in wait for us in the dismal shadow of the woods.' " In reality—as Hawthorne writes in "Main Street"—wolf, bear, and savage alike must fall before the advance of the iron men: "[Their] heavy tread will find its way over all the land; and . . . the wild woods, the wild wolf, and the wild Indian will be alike trampled beneath it."

The various kinds of victims of Puritan severity are also brought together at the beginning of *The Scarlet Letter*. Hawthorne notes that a number of pleasing spectacles might draw such a large crowd as is assembled before the jail:

> It might be that a sluggish bond-servant, or an undutiful child, whom his parents had given over to the civil authority, was to be corrected at the whipping-post. It might be, that an

Antinomian, a Quaker, or other heterodox religionist, was to be scourged out of the town, or an idle and vagrant Indian, whom the white man's fire-water had made riotous about the streets, was to be driven with stripes into the shadow of the forest.

And later in the novel Pearl sees the Puritan children aping the adults, "playing at going to church, perchance; or at scourging Quakers; or taking scalps in a sham-fight with the Indians; or scaring one another with freaks of imitative witchcraft."

Blunter references to the Puritans' conduct towards Indians can be found in Hawthorne's shorter fiction. Like *The Scarlet Letter*, "Young Goodman Brown" brings together the two most severely treated victims, Quaker and Indian, but suggests further that the Puritan practice was diabolical. When Brown follows typical Puritan thinking in imagining the Indians to be devilish, the devil materializes at his elbow to correct his view: " 'I have been well acquainted with your family as with ever a one of the Puritans; and that's no trifle to say. I helped your grandfather, the constable, when he lashed the Quaker woman so smartly through the streets of Salem; and it was I that brought your father a pitch-pine knot, kindled at my own hearth, to set fire to an Indian village, in King Philip's war.' " These particulars do not, of course, grant the Puritans a monopoly on evil; they simply challenge the comfortable Puritan belief that virtue resides in themselves and diabolism in the Indians. Later, Brown overhears a voice like the deacon's remarking on the expected attendance of " 'several of the Indian powwows, who, after their fashion, know almost as much deviltry as the best of us.' " And in "A Virtuoso's Collection," after the narrator examines various memorabilia of Old World exploits, he comments ironically: "That my own land may not deem itself neglected, let me add that I was favored with a sight of the skull of King Philip, the famous Indian chief, whose head the Puritans smote off and exhibited upon a pole."

Throughout the Hawthorne canon, the Puritans' martial prowess against the Indian is undercut by an insistence on the iron quality of their superiority and inhumanity. Just as Endicott appears ludicrous talking about a savage menace when his men stand in their individual iron fortresses among Indians equipped with stone age implements, so the other Indian fighters who make brief appearances in Hawthorne's pages seem more dishonorable than heroic. In "Main Street," for example, the showman presenting a pageant of the town's history attempts to give everything a heroic dimension which a critical spectator persistently undercuts. Captain Gardner, perpetrator of barbarities against the Narragansetts during King Philip's war, is romantically idealized in the showman's commentary: "His trusty sword, in its steel scabbard, strikes clanking on the doorstep. See how the people throng to their doors and windows, as the cavalier rides past, reining his mettled steed so gallantly, and looking so like the very soul and emblem of martial achievement." But this is not the last word on the Puritan leader. The stubborn critic interrupts the showman's official version of history to protest: " 'The mettled steed looks like a pig . . . and Captain Gardner himself like the Devil.' " In "A Virtuoso's Collection," the weapons appear to be "thrown together without much attempt at arrangement"; not so the author's tour of the heterogeneous group which ends with "the rifle of Daniel Boone." Used exclusively against Indians, this gun provokes the narrator to remark: " 'Enough of weapons.' "

"Roger Malvin's Burial" is another instance of Indian-fighting placed in a dubious light. The story opens as if on an ordinary frontier romance episode: "One of the few incidents of Indian warfare naturally susceptible of the moonlight of romance was that expedition undertaken for the defence of the frontiers in the year 1725, which resulted in the well-remembered 'Lovell's Fight.' " But the battle immediately becomes suspect in the author's next sentence: "Imagination, by casting certain circumstances judicially into the shade, may see much to admire in the heroism of a little band who gave battle to twice their number in the heart of the enemy's country." Recalling the tremendous superiority of weaponry that the iron men possessed over the Indians, the two-to-one ratio against the whites, so typical of the frontier romance, is hardly impressive. Even less so are the unnamed circumstances which must be stifled in order to praise the heroism of the whites. According to Edwin Fussell, one of these particulars would be that "the little band was after scalp bounties."[9] Again, the "howling wilderness" evoked here, as it was by Endicott, suggests white rather than Indian depredations.

The older of the two wounded soldiers, Roger Malvin, had escaped from Indian captivity twenty years earlier; failure to learn from this earlier experience has resulted in a fatal miscalculation. As he tells his younger companion, Reuben Bourne: " 'The Indian bullet was deadlier than I thought.' " Knowing his desperate condition, Malvin entreats Reuben, his prospective son-in-law, to save himself, return when he is recovered, and give his remains a Christian interment. To account for the effect this unfulfilled request will have on Reuben's conscience, Hawthorne explains: "An almost superstitious regard, arising perhaps from the customs of the Indian, whose war was with the dead as well as the living, was paid by the frontier inhabitants to the rite of sepulture." In typically Hawthorne fashion something is left unsaid, but just as a reader would know the circumstances of Lovell's Fight—"history and tradition are unusually minute in their memorials of this affair"—so common knowledge would supply scalping as the usual way in which the Indians desecrated the dead. Thus, the scalp hunter, who sought out the Indians deep in their own territory, is mortally wounded by an Indian bullet and must die fearing that his own scalp will be lifted. It is singularly appropriate that, as Bourne takes reluctant leave of his friend, he imagines: "Death would come like the slow approach of a corpse, stealing gradually towards him through the forest, and showing its ghastly and motionless features from behind a nearer and yet a nearer tree." As Edwin Fussell comments: "Death is an Indian slaughtered by the white man."[10] An Indian bullet has already sealed Roger Malvin's fate; the corpse who approaches in Indian fashion will take his scalp as well as his life.

Malvin pays the penalty for being an Indian fighter by dying, Reuben Bourne by living into a time of peace when Indian fighters are not needed. Although Lovell's Fight was beneficial to the country in bringing about a peace which lasted several years, it was unfortunate for the man whose only talent was killing Indians:

The discouragements to agriculture were greatly lessened by the cessation of Indian war, during which men held the plough in one hand and the musket in the other, and were fortunate if the products of their dangerous labor were not destroyed, either in the field or in the barn, by the savage enemy. But Reuben did not profit by the altered condition of the country.

Unable to practice the arts of peace, the Indian fighter can only return to the scene of his victory and defeat, "a region of which savage beasts and savage men were as yet the sole possessors." In this setting he accidentally kills the son he has raised in his own image: "All who anticipated the return of Indian war spoke of Cyrus Bourne as a future leader of the land." This last barbaric act, the violent killing of his own son, is suited to the savage nature of a man whose only success in life was as an Indian fighter. Bourne's satisfaction with this blood sacrifice as expiation for his failure to bury Malvin is clearly an inappropriate Christian response.

Hawthorne also inverts the conventions of the captivity episode to the advantage of the Indians. In "The Duston Family," the captors of Hannah Duston are touching "in their loneliness and their wanderings, wherever they went among the dark, mysterious woods, still keeping up domestic worship, with all the regularity of a household at its peaceful fireside." Moreover, they share their "scanty food" with the prisoners, "as if they had all been the children of one wigwam." While the Indians say their Catholic prayers together, the captives, true to their Puritan exclusiveness, reject this fellowship and pray apart. When Hannah and her companions butcher the sleeping Indians, Hawthorne interjects the plea: "But, O, the children! Their skins are red; yet spare them, Hannah Duston, spare those seven little ones, for the sake of the seven that have fed at your own breast." Of the one Indian boy who escaped the massacre, Hawthorne remarks: "He did well to flee the raging tigress!" His habitual distrust of aggressive women combining with moral outrage, Hawthorne bestows several other choice epithets on Hannah

Duston, undoubtedly one of the worst of Puritans in his view, and upbraids posterity for according "this awful woman" greater renown than her tenderhearted husband.[11]

In "The Gentle Boy" Hawthorne juxtaposes a reference to the menace of Indians with an exchange which points up the Indians' humanity versus the Puritans' barbarity. Tobias Pearson knocks at his own door: "For at that early period, when savages were wandering everywhere among the settlers, bolt and bar were indispensable to the security of a dwelling." Once inside, Pearson introduces his wife to the Quaker waif he has rescued, and the following conversation takes place:

> "What pale and bright-eyed little boy is this, Tobias?" she inquired. "Is he one whom the wilderness folk have ravished from some Christian mother?"
>
> "No, Dorothy, this poor child is no captive from the wilderness," he replied. "The heathen savage would have given him to eat of his scanty morsel, and to drink of his birchen cup; but Christian men, alas! had cast him out to die."

The Puritans fear the heterodox Quakers and heathen Indians, but clearly, as in so much of Hawthorne, the greatest danger is from the savage within; they themselves are the savages "wandering everywhere among the settlers," persecuting and putting to death the innocent. Little wonder that the Quakers "were accustomed to boast that the inhabitants of the desert [the Indians] were more hospitable to them than civilized man."

Indian captivity also occurs in *The Scarlet Letter* as the explanation for Roger Chillingworth's prolonged failure to join his wife in Boston. He makes his first appearance in the novel with an Indian companion, and is "clad in a strange disarray of civilized and savage costume," an outward appearance which prefigures his later inner state. Later, Chillingworth establishes his ascendancy over Dimmesdale by serving as his physician: "In his Indian captivity . . . he had gained much knowledge of the properties of native herbs and roots; nor did he conceal from his patients that these simple medicines, Nature's boon to the untutored savage, had quite as large a share of his own confidence as the European pharmacopoeia." Nature's gift to the Indians, which they have shared with Chillingworth, is perverted by the civilized man to an evil end. The Puritans, who salved their consciences by believing that Indians were affiliated with the devil, shift the onus from Chillingworth to his savage mentors: "Two or three individuals hinted, that the man of skill, during his Indian captivity, had enlarged his medical attainments by joining in the incantations of the savage priests; who were universally acknowledged to be powerful enchanters, often performing seemingly miraculous cures by their skill in the black art." In Hawthorne's world, characters always prefer to locate evil in an external source.

3

When he writes of the past, Hawthorne usually sees the Indian as one of the many victims of Puritanism. However much the Puritans might lament their vulnerability to savage attacks, their armed might eventually exterminated the Indians. Like other Americans, Hawthorne could not repudiate white conquest. In his history of Salem, he writes: "Even so shall it be. The pavements of the Main Street must be laid over the red man's grave." The same sketch encapsulates in the figure of a drunken Indian "the vast growth and prosperity of one race, and the fated decay of another." Early in his career Hawthorne is content to see the wilderness replaced by the city of Cincinnati:

Until the year 1788, the Indian or the hunter, standing on the circular line of hills, above the valley, of which we have described the outline, would have seen only the gigantic trees, and the river sundering the primeval forest with its tranquil breadth. Nearly twenty years later, from the same position, nothing was visible, save a rough backwoods settlement of five hundred people. But soon a marvellous change was to take place; in 1820, the once solitary vale had become populous with nearly ten thousand souls: and now, if the traveller take a view of Cincinnati from its wall of hills, he will behold busy streets, compact and massive edifices, the spires of churches, the smoke of manufactories, and all other characteristics of a city, containing thirty-five thousand inhabitants. ("Cincinnati")

Later, he has a more personal vision of the transformation of his own home site in Salem. Finding an arrowhead in the vicinity of the Old Manse establishes a rapport between Hawthorne and the red hunter whose hand last touched it centuries ago:

Such an incident builds up again the Indian village and its encircling forest, and recalls to life the painted chiefs and warriors, the squaws at their household toil, and the children sporting among the wigwams, while the little wind-rocked papoose swings from the branch of the tree. It can hardly be told whether it is a joy or a pain, after such a momentary vision, to gaze around in the broad daylight of reality and see stone fences, white houses, potato fields, and men doggedly hoeing in their shirt-sleeves and homespun pantaloons. But this is nonsense. The Old Manse is better than a thousand wigwams. ("The Old Manse")

Hawthorne's love of the moonlight conducive to romance, as opposed to the broad daylight of reality, leads him into a dangerous fantasy in which submerged regret for the vanished Indians momentarily asserts itself. Such subversive thoughts must be dismissed as nonsense and the value of the Old Manse—white civilization and Hawthorne's own homestead—be reaffirmed. When the choice is clearly presented, Hawthorne and his compatriots must find for the white man; their very homes are built on the ruins of Indian communities. But unlike his Puritan forebears, Hawthorne is conscious that their treatment of the Indian imposed a load of guilt on white Americans.

At other times, when he feels no personal threat, Hawthorne strikes the elegiac note so prevalent in the frontier romance. In recounting an Indian belief that the progenitors of their race were saved from a deluge by climbing Mount Washington, Hawthorne notes: "The children of that pair have been overwhelmed, and found no such refuge." An examination of old newspapers furnishes an item about fund-raising for missionaries among the Indians of Massachusetts Bay. Hawthorne remarks ironically: "Easy would be the duties of such a mission now!" A more extended passage contrasts the essential powerlessness of the Indian against the white usurper, this time not in the military terms of the Puritan fiction but in terms of the white man's superior ability to change the physical environment. In recreating Salem's past, Hawthorne conjures up the Indian Wappacowet,

> the priest and magician, whose incantations shall hereafter affright the pale-faced settlers with grisly phantoms, dancing and shrieking in the woods at midnight. But greater would be the affright of the Indian necromancer if, mirrored in the pool of water at his feet, he could catch a prophetic glimpse of the noonday marvels which the white man is destined to achieve; if he could see, as in a dream, the stone front of the stately hall, which will cast its shadow over this very spot; if he could be aware that the future edifice will contain a noble Museum, where, among countless curiosities of earth and sea, a few Indian arrowheads shall be treasured up as memorials of a vanished race! ("Main Street")

Where the Indians had a simple footpath, the whites make a broad thoroughfare; transient wigwams give way to an imposing stone edifice; and the Indians themselves are reduced to a few arrowhead mementos in the local museum. The perspective of history finds the fright of the earliest settlers to be groundless: the noonday sun of white power dispels the midnight phantoms of the Indian necromancer.

Another moonlit occasion prompts Hawthorne's most sympathetic expression of the elegiac motif. As he travels into a wilderness region on an Erie Canal boat, the night scene appears to be "the very land of unsubstantial things." One of the unsubstantial things which would no doubt have to be repudiated in broad daylight is Hawthorne's judgment on the violation of the wilderness by civilized man:

> The wild nature of America had been driven to this desert place by the encroachments of civilized man. And even here, where the savage queen was throned on the ruins of her empire, did we penetrate, a vulgar and worldly throng, intruding on her latest solitude. In other lands decay sits among fallen palaces; but here her home is in the forests. ("The Canal Boat")

Hawthorne's perception contains the startling realization that the West is finite and capable of being destroyed completely. Where the transformation of wilderness into settlement and city is presented as a "marvellous change" in "Cincinnati," Hawthorne can now envision the process as one of decay: the downfall of the forest is equated with the downfall of palaces, each a ruin within its own context. And the settlers who introduced all the accoutrements of material progress into the Ohio territory now appear as "vulgar and worldly" intruders on the native nobility of the wilderness.

4

If Indians are portrayed as almost helpless victims of white conquest in much of Hawthorne's fiction, revealing the savagery of their opponents, they also play a more positive role, that of the traditional noble savage whose free spirit beckons to restricted civilized man. When Hawthorne describes the Puritan settlement of Salem, he observes: "How like an iron cage was that which they called Liberty." It is from this iron confinement into an Indian freedom that Hester Prynne escapes in *The Scarlet Letter*:

> Her intellect and heart had their home, as it were, in desert places, where she roamed as freely as the wild Indian in his woods. For years past she had looked from this estranged

point of view at human institutions, and whatever priests or legislators had established; criticizing all with hardly more reverence than the Indian would feel for the clerical band, the judicial robe, the pillory, the gallows, the fireside, or the church.

Metaphorically, Hester becomes an Indian, substituting intellectual for physical freedom. Cast out of the community, she reserves for herself the right to view it as an outsider, i.e., an Indian. But whereas the Indian is indifferent to white institutions through ignorance of them, Hester has painfully and consciously liberated herself.[12] Because Pearl has been brought up by such a woman, apart from community influence, it is little wonder that her glance makes an Indian "conscious of a nature wilder than his own."

Another aspect of Indian freedom observed in *The Scarlet Letter* is dress:

The picture of human life in the marketplace, though its general tint was the sad gray, brown, or black of the English emigrants, was yet enlivened by some diversity of hue. A party of Indians—in their savage finery of curiously embroidered deerskin robes, wampum-belts, red and yellow ochre, and feathers, and armed with the bow and arrow and stone-headed spear—stood apart, with countenances of inflexible gravity, beyond what even the Puritan aspect could attain.

The restrictiveness of Puritan life is reflected in the sad hues of their garments, just as, in "Endicott and the Red Cross," their iron armor restricts and closes them off from other human beings. Indian weapons, in contrast, do not interfere with either their gay apparel or freedom of movement. Nor does their ornamentation make gravity impossible for the Indians; although the Puritans ban all finery and frivolity, they are unable to equal the serious mien of the Indians.

The lengthiest paean to Indian freedom in Hawthorne is spoken by Septimius Felton's Aunt Keziah on her deathbed:

"But if you could be an Indian, methinks it would be better than this tame life we lead. 'Twould have been better for me, at all events. Oh, how pleasant 'twould have been to spend my life wandering in the woods, smelling the pines and the hemlock all day, and fresh things of all kinds, and no kitchen work to do,—not to rake the fire, nor sweep the room, nor make the beds,—but to sleep on fresh boughs in a wigwam, with the leaves still on the branches of the roof! And then to see the deer brought in by the red hunter, and the blood streaming from the arrow-dart! Ah! and the fight too! and the scalping! and perhaps, a woman might creep into the battle, and steal the wounded enemy away of her tribe and scalp him, and be praised for it! O Seppy, how I hate the thought of the dull life women lead! A white woman's life is so dull! Thank Heaven I'm done with it! If I'm ever to live again, may I be whole Indian, please my Maker!" (*Septimius Felton*)

Although Keziah's speech contains a genuine cry for freedom, its prolixity and exclamatory tone are somehow less effective than the terse irony of Hawthorne's earlier Indian references. The freedom from restrictive institutions which Hester shares with the Indians has degenerated to a freedom from housekeeping; where Hester ventures into the masculine province of philosophical speculation, Keziah longs for the more violent prerogative of killing and scalping. In Keziah's mixture of romantic savagery and release from feminine dullness it is difficult to see more than a superficial perception of Indian freedom.

Hawthorne meditates more seriously on the subject in his sketch "The Old Manse." Idyllic excursions with Ellery Channing, in which the two men consciously emulated the Indians, are recalled with nostalgia: "Strange and happy times were those when we cast aside all irksome forms and strait-laced habitudes, and delivered ourselves up to the free air, to live like the Indians or any less conventional race during one bright semicircle of the sun." Unlike Keziah, Hawthorne deals in no absolutes; his adoption of the natural life-style which he associates with Indians is both temporary and admittedly strange. Nevertheless, he attempts to duplicate the Indian experience during this brief time: "The painted Indian who paddled his canoe along the Assabeth three hundred years ago could hardly have seen a wilder gentleness displayed upon its banks and reflected in its bosom that we did. Nor could the same Indian have prepared his noontide meal with more simplicity." As the conclusion of the episode demonstrates, however, Indianness has a deeper meaning for Hawthorne than paddling a canoe and cooking out:

We were so free to-day that it was impossible to be slaves again to-morrow. When we crossed the threshold of the house or trod the thronged pavements of a city, still the leaves of the trees that overhang the Assabeth were whispering to us, "Be free! be free!" Therefore along that shady riverbank there are spots, marked with a heap of ashes and half-consumed brands, only less sacred in my remembrance than the hearth of a household fire.

Even if they constitute slavery, the priorities of civilized life remain of the first importance for Hawthorne, but the appeal of the Indian life-style, as he conceives of it, is both strong and treasured. He knows, as Keziah does not, the impossibility of becoming an Indian, nor does he wish this for a permanent state. The freedom which the leaves enjoin is more than a rapport with nature: it is a state of irresponsibility and exclusively masculine camaraderie as little typical of Indian as of white society. Those spots where Hawthorne's Indian-like fires burned will be, like his arrowheads, remembrances of what cannot be sustained or restored, and what is, from the point of view of the civilized white man, only desirable as a holiday from his ordinary existence. The hearth, symbolic of domesticity and the nuclear family unit, must be placed above this beguiling freedom *in vacuo*.

5

So inextricably a part of the past, Indians are seldom found in

Hawthorne's fiction in a modern setting. Their few appearances as part of a contemporary scene show him to be concerned with their adjustment to a white-dominated world. Passing a boat manned by three Indians on the Erie Canal, he speculates: "Perhaps these three alone, among the ancient possessors of the land, had attempted to derive benefit from the white man's mighty projects and float along the current of his enterprise." Similarly, in speaking about eastern rivers, he reports: "There they paddle their birch canoes among the coasting-schooners and build their wigwam beside some roaring mill-dam, and drive a little trade in basket-work where their fathers hunted deer." In his description of the Indian in "The Seven Vagabonds," Hawthorne passes from commonplace observation to a more meaningful appraisal of the contemporary Indian:

> Fate was summoning a parliament of these free spirits; unconscious of the impulse which directed them to a common centre, they had come hither from far and near, and last of all appeared the representative of those mighty vagrants who had chased the deer during thousands of years, and were chasing it now in the Spirit Land. Wandering down through the waste of ages, the woods had vanished around his path; his arm had lost somewhat of its strength, his foot of its fleetness, his mien of its wild regality, his heart and mind of their savage virtue and uncultured force; but here, untamable to the routine of artificial life, roving now along the dusty road as of old over the forest leaves, here was the Indian still.

Although modern life has vitiated his good qualities to a certain extent, the Indian still has credentials as a free spirit; something, perhaps his thousand-year forest heritage, makes him resistant enough to change to preserve his Indianness. This is not the familiar figure of the degenerate red man, but an Indian, like those glimpsed on rivers, who had adapted a recognizably Indian identity to white culture. If this Penobscot Indian is indeed "the representative modern hero and surrogate of the indigenous artist" that Fussell finds him to be, it is suitable for the would-be novelist-narrator to form an alliance with him in their journey toward the "distant city."[13] In like fashion, Hawthorne relates in "My Visit to Niagara" that he bought a stick made by a Tuscarora Indian: "I selected one of curled maple, curiously convoluted and adorned with the carved images of a snake and a fish. Using this as my pilgrim's staff I crossed the bridge." Either the Indian himself or his stick may serve as an apt guide into the region— nature, past, or mystical body of America—which the novelist wishes to appropriate for his art.

6

Hawthorne's last and most ambitious attempt to use the Indian as guide into long-ago America is also his most disappointing. The unfinished *Septimius Felton* employs a number of clichés of the frontier romance without the usual plot machinations of the genre, but also without Hawthorne's habitual thoughtful delving beneath the surface of a convention or stereotype. In giving Septimius a small but potent amount of Indian blood, Hawthorne apparently intended him to embody a distinctively American attitude, Indianness made articulate and refined by its contact with white culture: in addition to his Indian ancestors, Septimius boasts Puritan divines and remarkable pioneers among his forefathers. This reasonable aesthetic purpose emerges only fit-fully and far too didactically during the novel's course. When the Old World in the guise of the evil Dr. Portsoaken tempts Septimius with the prospect of aristocratic lineage and ancestral wealth, the youth replies: " 'That strain of Indian blood is in me yet . . . and it makes me despise,—no, not despise; for I can see their desirableness for other people,—but it makes me reject for myself what you think so valuable.' "

While this response is a plausible manifestation of Indian attitudes, elsewhere Hawthorne finds it desirable to resort to the stereotype of the bad Indian to characterize his protagonist. Septimius is descended from "that strange wild lineage of Indian chiefs, whose blood was like that of persons not quite human, intermixed with civilized blood." In his confrontation with the

British soldier, "Septimius's fierce Indian blood stirred in him and gave a murderous excitement"; as they quarrel, "that Indian fierceness that was in him [was] arousing itself, and thrusting up its malign head like a snake." His blood has a "wild stream that the Indian priest had contributed"; reference is made almost constantly to his "wild ancestors," and "something in Septimius, in his wild, mixed nature, the monstrousness that had grown out of his hybrid race" makes his beloved shudder. At one moment proud that "the race had been redeemed from barbarism" in the person of a remote mixed-blood ancestor, at the next Septimius declares: " 'There is in me the wild, natural blood of the Indian, the instinctive, the animal nature, which has ways of warning that civilized life polishes away and cuts out.' "[14] None of these traits is convincingly realized in Septimius's behavior: his desire to concoct the Elixir of Life and live forever seems far more the product of a Western Faustian tradition than any wild Indian heritage. The reiteration of "wild" and "savage" never bears fruit, for Septimius is only a pale shadow of Hawthorne's numerous demonic questers.

NOTES

1. All quotations from Hawthorne are from *The Complete Writings of Nathaniel Hawthorne*, 22 vols. (Boston, 1900).
2. Both William Gilmore Simms and James Hall wrote short stories based on Indian legends, but in each case these stories constitute an insignificant portion of their total production of frontier fiction. No novel devoted exclusively to Indians appears in the pre-Civil War period.
3. In 1832, three years before Hawthorne first published this sketch in *The New England Magazine*, Benjamin Bissell Thatcher's *Indian Biography*, an account of the lives of famous Indian chiefs, was a popular work. Hawthorne could be referring to this well-known book, but most likely he had something more imaginative in mind.
4. Q. D. Leavis, "Hawthorne as Poet," *Sewanee Review* 59 (1951), p. 191 enjoins: "The force of the cunning phrase, 'to proclaim bounties on the heads of wolves and the scalps of Indians,' charged with a sense of the inhumanity that leveled the Indian with the wolf, should not be overlooked."
5. Numerous references in Hawthorne link the Puritans and iron; in addition to the above, the Puritans are further described as "men of iron"; in *The Scarlet Letter* Hester refers to them as "iron men"; in "The Gentle Boy" they have "iron hearts"; Puritan weaponry is often emphasized, as it is in "The Maypole

of Merry Mount"; cf. "Endicott and the Red Cross" and the description of Governor Bellingham's mansion in *The Scarlet Letter.*

6. One of the number is a counterfeit Indian, a figure who recurs in the masquerade in *The Blithedale Romance.*

7. It may be argued that the Puritans' punishment of Hester is regenerative: she becomes known for good works although never reintegrated into the community. This is counteracted, however, by her free-thinking spirit and insistence that her act with Dimmesdale "had a consecration of its own." Obviously, in contrasting Hester's and Dimmesdale's development in the novel, public expiation has value, but in the earlier mention of the embroidered *A* in "Endicott," the embellishment is symptomatic of hopelessness, its wearer referred to as a "lost and desperate creature." Hawthorne never shows such punishments bringing about the sincere Christian repentance which the Puritans presumably hoped to effect.

8. Leavis, *Swanee Review,* p. 428, comments: "They [the Indians] suggest that their conquerors differ from them chiefly in having matchlocks and iron armor and that 'pomp and dignity' are not proofs of civilization"; cf. a similar situation in "Sir William Phips," where an assembly on Boston Common includes "a few dark Indians in their blankets, dull spectators of the strength that has swept away their race."

9. Edwin Fussell, *Frontier: American Literature and the American West* (Princeton, 1965), p. 75; how Hawthorne felt about this frontier activity might be inferred from his description of the woodsman in "Sir William Phips": "On his head he wears a trophy which we would not venture to record without good evidence of the fact,—a wig made of the long and straight black hair of his slain savage enemies."

10. Fussell, *Frontier,* p. 76.

11. Hawthorne also castigates Cotton Mather, his source for the Hannah Duston story, as "the representative of all the hateful features of his time; the one bloodthirsty man, in whom were concentrated those vices of spirit and errors of opinion that sufficed to madden the whole surrounding multitude."

12. There were, of course, Indian counterparts to the Puritan institutions which Hester disregards; enthusiasts of the noble savage seldom notice that he is governed by social restrictions as binding as those of civilized society; the real freedom of the Indian—from materiality and technology—is often overlooked.

13. Fussell, *Frontier,* p. 78.

14. Fussell, *Frontier,* p. 369, comments: "The young enthusiast possesses no such instincts, and few fictional characters have ever displayed less animal nature."

7

Melville and the Universal Paradigm of White Domination

1

In Melville's fictive worlds, references to Indians comprise one aspect of an anticivilization theme which also finds expression in Pierre's urban tragedy, the predatory commercialism which walks the decks of the *Fidèle*, and the harsh system of naval discipline in *White-Jacket* and *Billy Budd*. Where Hawthorne depicts the Indian as first Puritan and then American victim, Melville more universally delineates the paradigm of white racial imperialism: the native American, the Polynesian, and occasionally the black man are portrayed as common victims of white oppression and exploitation. This is the way of the white world, whether embodied in a French frigate in the Marquesas or in an American gunboat on a Florida river. But the saving grace for humanity in a fallen world is a commitment to fraternity and communality which transcends national and even racial divisions among men; thus, Melville uses Indians to illustrate the drawing together of culturally diverse peoples. If the white man could truly perceive his duty as a Christian and become aware of the superficiality of cultural differences, Melville says, he would extend the hand of fellowship rather than the sword. In both good and evil man must recognize his essential kinship with all men.

Melville often equates the various kinds of dark-skinned peoples who have suffered from the white man.[1] Although his earliest works describe experiences in the South Seas, Polynesians are always suggestive of American Indians and at times are explicitly identified with them. In a discussion of the disastrous consequences to the Polynesians of their encounter with white civilization, Melville writes:

Let the savages be civilized, but civilize them with benefits, and not with evils; and let heathenism be destroyed, but not by destroying the heathen. The Anglo-Saxon hive have extirpated Paganism from the greater part of the North

American continent; but with it they have likewise extirpated the greater portion of the Red race. (*Typee*)[2]

Falling under the rubric of heathen savage, Polynesian and American Indian alike are objectionable to the white man. Numerous references to the South Sea Islanders as savages, pagans, and heathens reinforce their identification with the North American tribes.

2

Whereas for most writers of the frontier romance the spectacle of the degenerate savage induces contemplation of the unfortunate failure of the Indian to become civilized, Melville's reasoning leads to an indictment of civilization itself. The inferiority of primitive peoples so unquestioned by frontier romancers is assailed by Melville from two directions: the horrors of civilization make its claim to superiority suspect while the felicity and even virtue of "those we call savages" challenge the white man's patronizing view of their state. Melville constantly questions the standard definition of such concepts as "savage" and "civilized":

How often is the term "savages" incorrectly applied! None really deserving of it were ever yet discovered by voyagers or by travellers. They have discovered heathens and barbarians, whom by horrible cruelties they have exasperated into savages. (*Typee*)

The term "Savage" is, I conceive, often misapplied, and indeed when I consider the vices, cruelties, and enormities of every kind that spring up in the tainted atmosphere of a feverish civilization, I am inclined to think that so far as the relative wickedness of the parties is concerned, four or five Marquesan Islanders sent to the United States as Missionaries might be quite as useful as an equal number of Americans despatched to the Islands in a similar capacity. (Ibid.)[3]

That civilization excels in what it commonly defines as savagery is the burden of numerous Melvillian reflections. Describing the French conquest of the Marquesas, Melville marvels at the anomaly of a people who pride themselves on humanity and cultural attainments committing such a flagrant violation of human rights. He continues: "A high degree of refinement, however, does not seem to subdue our wicked propensities so much after all; and were civilization itself to be estimated by some of its results, it would seem perhaps better for what we call the barbarous part of the world to remain unchanged" (*Typee*).

Far from subduing man's evil inclinations, civilization provides him with the technology to implement them far more effectively than the primitive aborigine can. The superiority in evil which writers of the frontier romance reserve for the aberrant white man, whether Indian hater, renegade, or melodramatic villain, Melville distributes among the race at large:

The fiend-like skill we display in the invention of all manner of death-dealing engines, the vindictiveness with which we carry on our wars, and the misery and desolation that follow in their train, are enough of themselves to distinguish the white civilized man as the most ferocious animal on the face of the earth. (*Typee*)

Like Hawthorne juxtaposing the Puritans' iron fortress of

armaments and the Indians' stone-age weapons, Melville contrasts the Polynesians' spears and arrows with the white man's
guns. His account of the origin of hostilities between white man
and native in the Pacific is little different from the encounter
between white and Indian on the North American continent.
Washington Irving describes the same inevitable process on the
western frontier:

> Outrages are frequently committed on the natives by
> thoughtless or mischievous white men; the Indians retaliate
> . . . their act, of what with them is pious vengeance, resounds
> throughout the land, and is represented as wanton and un-
> provoked; the neighborhood is roused to arms; a war ensues,
> which ends in the destruction of half the tribe, the ruin of the
> rest, and their expulsion from their hereditary homes. Such
> is too often the real history of Indian warfare, which in
> general is traced up only to some vindictive act of a savage;
> while the outrage of the scoundrel white man that provoked
> it is sunk in silence.[4]

Carried a step further, Irving's exemplum might have concluded
like Melville's story of French atrocities toward the Typees: "Thus
it is that they whom we denominate 'savages' are made to deserve
the title." For Melville, the paradigm outlined by Irving applies
just as readily to the South Seas: petty traders voyage from island
to island, leaving a trail of gratuitous depredations which, if
they become known, are only mildly censured by the public. As he
goes on to relate, the natives are victims of a double standard:

> How different is our tone when we read the highly-wrought
> description of the massacre of the crew of the Hobomok by
> the Feejees; how we sympathise for the unhappy victims, and
> with what horror do we regard the diabolical heathens, who,
> after all, have but avenged the unprovoked injuries which
> they have received. We breathe nothing but vengeance, and
> equip armed vessels to traverse thousands of miles of ocean
> in order to execute summary punishment upon the

offenders. On arriving at their destination, they burn, slaughter, and destroy, according to the tenor of written instructions, and sailing away from the scene of devastation, call upon all Christendom to applaud their courage and their justice. (*Typee*)

Here, as elsewhere, Melville insists that moral outrages are committed in the name of Christianity and justice; played against the whites' misguided feelings of horror and self-righteousness, his indignation surpasses even Irving's. Although the incident was well known, Melville's choice of the Hobomok disaster was hardly fortuitous: the author who would later name his ill-fated whaler after an extinct Indian tribe must have seen a similar irony in this ship with an Indian name bearing a crew of predatory white men to savage deaths.

In *Redburn* the spokesman of civilization is the obnoxious Gun-Deck, a sailor who "had seen the civilized world, and loved it; found it good, and a comfortable place to live in." This easy acceptance is combined with an overt racism and brutality which informs his account of "popping off Indians" during the Seminole War in Florida: "It was a rat-killing war, he said." Similarly, in *White-Jacket* some of the narrator's messmates, characterized as "rather gentlemanly," regale their companions with exploits from the same war in which Gun-Deck had such sport: "They now enlivened their salt fare with stories of wild ambushes in the everglades; and one of them related a surprising tale of his hand-to-hand encounter with Osceola, the Indian chief, whom he fought one morning from daybreak till breakfast time." To the unthinking veterans, the campaign which destroyed the Seminoles is merely the seasoning for their otherwise dull dinner; to Melville's narrator, in contrast to the attitude of frontier romancers, the typical anecdote of combat with a famous chief lacks credibility. Melville is right to point out that Indian fighters are "native born Americans"; the willingness to acquire land by the violent slaughter of its original inhabitants is an unspoken definition of an American in the frontier romance.

3

Unaware that they were applying racist stereotypes when they found Indians to be the total and irredeemable inferiors of whites, authors of the frontier romance never attained Melville's insights into the workings of prejudice. In *Typee*, willing to see the white-Polynesian confrontation from the natives' point of view, Melville continued to analyze the relationship of the two races in later works. His review of Parkman's *Oregon Trail* took the author to task for a belittling portrait of the Indians: "It is too often the case, that civilized beings sojourning among savages soon come to regard them with disdain and contempt. But though in many cases this feeling is almost natural, it is not defensible; and it is wholly wrong."[5] Describing some acts of wanton cruelty against the natives in *Omoo*, Melville comments: "Indeed, it is almost incredible, the light in which many sailors regard these naked heathens. They hardly consider them human. But it is a curious fact, that the more ignorant and degraded men are, the more contemptuously they look upon those whom they deem their inferiors." The same reasoning prompts White-Jacket to rejoice in his whiteness when he sees a black man flogged, even though white sailors were equally liable to, and often did receive, such punishment. White-Jacket, or Melville, realizes: "There is something in us, somehow, that in the most degraded condition, we snatch at a chance to deceive ourselves into a fancied superiority to others, whom we suppose lower in the scale than ourselves."

Pursuing the matter more deeply, Melville discovered that the unwarranted assumption of superiority or difference came about through a distortion of perception. In *Moby-Dick* the flames of the *Pequod's* try-works change the earthly into the hellish:

> The harpooners wildly gesticulated with their huge pronged forks and dippers; as the wind howled on, and the sea leaped, and the ship groaned and dived, and yet steadfastly shot her red hell further and further into the blackness of the sea and the night, and scornfully champed the white bone in her mouth, and viciously spat round her on all sides; then the

rushing Pequod, freighted with savages, and laden with fire, and burning a corpse, and plunging into that blackness of darkness, seemed the material counterpart of her monomaniac commander's soul.

But this vision, which transforms the dark harpooners into devils and the crew as a whole into savages, is an "unnatural hallucination." After a faulty perception almost causes catastrophe, Ishmael warns the reader:

Believe not the artificial fire, when its redness makes all things look ghastly. To-morrow, in the natural sun, the skies will be bright; those who glared like devils in the forking flames, the morn will show in far other, at least gentler, relief; the glorious, golden, glad sun, the only true lamp—all others but liars!

One kind of light is a false and artificial distortion of reality, the other not necessarily rosy, but natural and truthful. To see by sunlight is not to ignore the evil and griefs of the world, as Ishmael goes on to explain, but to see them both as they are and in context. The dark-skinned harpooners, seen by the artificial or man-made light of prejudiced perceptions, seem to be devils and strange beings; by natural light they are mates, fellow workers, friends—in short, men of the same species as the rest of the crew. Evil exists in the world and savagery in man, but failure to retain perspective leads to disaster.

The false light engendered by the try-works reappears in *Moby-Dick* as the corpusants. Again, this unnatural fire, identified with Ahab's mad quest, induces a sinister vision of the harpooners:

Relieved against the ghostly light, the gigantic jet negro, Daggoo, loomed up to thrice his real stature, and seemed the black cloud from which the thunder had come. The parted mouth of Tashtego revealed his shark-white teeth, which strangely gleamed as if they too had been tipped by corpusants; while lit up by the preternatural light, Queequeg's tatooing burned like Satanic blue flames on his body.

The artificial fire in *Moby-Dick* magnifies the dark-skinned harpooners into devils; of the *Pequod's* crew, Ishmael alone ultimately resists the powerful transfiguring vision of the deluded Ahab. For the generality of men, however, shunning the forces which distort perception and impose false visions is impossible. In *Redburn* Melville had already written of "those local and social prejudices, that are the marring of most men, and from which, for the mass, there seems no possible escape."

In addition to out-and-out extermination and deprivation of human rights, civilization has employed other weapons against primitive populations. The Christian conquerors have bestowed drunkenness, smallpox, and venereal disease, evils "solely of foreign origin," on the Polynesians while withholding the blessings of civilization: "Years ago brought to a stand, where all that is corrupt in barbarism and civilization unite, to the exclusion of all virtues of either state; like other uncivilized beings, brought into contact with Europeans, they must here remain stationary until utterly extinct" (*Omoo*). From what other unfortunate aborigines could Melville so readily predict the future of the South Sea Islanders than the vanished Indians of his own native region? As he wrote in *Mardi*:

Not yet wholly extinct in Vivenza, were its aboriginal people, a race of wild Nimrods and hunters, who year by year were driven further and further into remoteness, till, as one of their sad warriors said, after continual removes along the log, his race was on the point of being remorselessly pushed off the end.[6]

The savagery of civilization operates inexorably in both places.

4

If Melville demonstrates the barbaric practices and the uncivilizing effects of the introduction of white civilization to the Pacific islands, he also exhibits the positive side of so-called savagery. The Typees occasionally indulge in headhunting and cannibalism, but their land strikes the author as the "Happy Valley" in comparison with the "world of care and anxiety" which he has left. Lacking the material resources of Western life, they nevertheless have one valuable commodity of human existence—happiness.

> The Polynesian savage, surrounded by all the luxurious provisions of nature, enjoyed an infinitely happier, though certainly a less intellectual existence, than the self-complacent European. . . . What has he to desire at the hands of Civilization? She may "cultivate his mind"—may "elevate his thoughts,"—these I believe are the established phrases—but will he be the happier? (*Typee*)

Like his attempts to redefine the concepts of savagery and civilization, and his suggestion of missionaries for the Christians, Melville's reference to the conventional shibboleths invoked to sanction the oppression of primitive peoples is an attempt to alter the reader's perception, to explode the official stereotype and reveal the far different reality beneath. Although the Typean chief Mehevi is a cannibal, he is seldom named without the qualifying epithet "noble." It may be, Melville insinuates, that there are worse practices than cannibalism and better qualities than those displayed in white society:[7]

> Civilization does not engross all the virtues of humanity: she has not even her full share of them. They flourish in greater abundance and attain greater strength among many barbarous people. The hospitality of the wild Arab, the courage of the North American Indian, and the faithful friendships of some of the Polynesian nations, far surpass any thing of a similar kind among the polished communities of Europe. (*Typee*)[8]

Significantly, what emerges as the greater virtue among the Typees is the fraternal feeling which Melville would continue to value highly but seldom find again: "There was one admirable trait in the general character of the Typees which more than any thing else, secured my admiration: it was the unanimity of feeling they displayed on every occasion. . . . They showed this spirit of unanimity in every action of life: every thing was done in concert and good fellowship." Considering the permutations of the divided community which populate Melville's later fiction—the coerciveness of military and commercial vessels, the fraudulence permeating the *Fidèle,* the lack of genuine community in the office of Bartleby's employer or on Benito Cereno's *San Dominick*—the perfect accord of the Typees seems to be unattainable in a civilized society.

What emerges from Melville's extended contemplation of civilization and savagery is a more generalized usage of the terms, a rejection of their automatic identification with particular races. When Ahab calls his men a "savage crew," he refers to their wild and reckless willingness to place his quest for the white whale above the material, i.e., civilized aims of an ordinary whaling voyage. In *Omoo,* when the Polynesian harpooner Bembo tries to sink the *Julia* out of revenge for the sailors' insults, Melville characterizes him as possessing "a heart irreclaimably savage, and at no time fraternally disposed toward the crew." Obviously, "savage" in this context refers not to Bembo's race or culture, but to a cruel temperament shared with such white villains as Bland and Claggart, but notably lacking in the three dark-skinned harpooners of *Moby-Dick.*

For Melville, the cherishing of a fraternal feeling towards one's fellow man is the value which transcends superficial distinctions among humankind, a lesson that some Melvillian protagonists learn in opposition to the "civilized" majority view. The narrator of *Typee* comes to admire the cannibals he takes refuge among, Redburn realizes that a black man has a "claim to humanity and normal equality," and Ishmael discovers that Queequeg's tatooed face is "only his outside; a man can be honest in any sort of skin." Reversing the propaganda of the missionaries, Melville offers salvation to the white man through the aborigine. In Ishmael's imagination Queequeg thinks: "It's a mutual, joint-stock world, in all meridians. We cannibals must help these Christians." And, in fact, Queequeg's friendship repairs Ishmael's "splintered heart" just as his coffin sustains Ishmael's body after the *Pequod* sinks. But if Queequeg is a conventional good Indian, Ishmael is not the typical white protagonist who unthinkingly accepts Indian devotion as his due.

Although Queequeg is a Polynesian, he also calls to mind the American Indian: his mat is ornamented with "little twinkling tags something like the stained porcupine quills round an Indian moccasin." A conflation of Polynesian and native American is also implied by Melville's description of the *Pequod,* named, he reminds us, after "a celebrated tribe of Massachusetts Indians," but appearing to be "a cannibal of a craft." Whaling itself, Melville notes, was first engaged in by "those aboriginal whalemen, the Red-Men." The markings on a sperm whale remind Ishmael of "old Indian characters chiselled on the famous hieroglyphic palisades on the banks of the Upper Mississippi," and a stone lancehead found in a whale recalls the aboriginal industry which existed before America was discovered. Furthermore, "all whale-boats carry certain curious contrivances, originally invented by the Nantucket Indians, called druggs."

Just as Melville merges Polynesian and Indian into an archetypal primitive man, so he further asserts, in his review of Parkman, that white and savage partake of the same basic nature: "We are all of us—Anglo-Saxons, Dyaks, and Indians—sprung from one head and made in one image. And if we regret this brotherhood now, we shall be forced to join hands hereafter."[9] Underlying the acceptance of universal brotherhood is the premise that a common human nature is shared by all peoples. Men only appear to be separated by insurmountable barriers: the savage crewman in *White-Jacket,* for example, is so totally foreign that he seems like "a being from some other sphere" to the white sailors. White man and Polynesian regard each other's tastes and creeds as abominable, "a fact proving that neither was wrong, but both right." Disparate customs, Melville tells us repeatedly, are only different expressions of a common impulse. Thus, in the archipelago of Mardi: "Strings of teeth . . . [are] regarded . . . very much as belts of wampum among the Winnebagoes of the North; or cowries, among the Bengalese." In *White-Jacket* a wider sampling tends to the same kind of conclusion: "Metropolitan gentlemen have their club; provincial gossipers their newsroom;

village quidnuncs their barber's shop; and Chinese their opium-houses; American Indians their council-fire; and even cannibals their *Noojona,* or Talk-Stone, where they assemble at times to discuss the affairs of the day."

In addition to enumerating such innocuous and essentially superficial similarities among peoples, Melville trenchantly assails the assumed moral superiority of civilized men. For this purpose he invokes in *White-Jacket* the typical associations of savagery which were rejected in *Typee* and *Omoo.* War is "unchristian, barbarous, brutal, and savoring of the Feejee Islands, cannibalism, saltpetre, and the devil." Never mind that in *Typee* the Feejee Islanders were used as an example of rightful retaliation for white injuries, here "war almost makes blasphemers of the best of men, and brings them all down to the Feejee standard of humanity." When White-Jacket sees ships captured in battle, his recollection of a pioneer village scene furnishes the material for an extended comparison. In this western anecdote Melville utilizes a number of the clichès common to the frontier romance: the Indian warrior is the stereotyped "gigantic red-man, erect as a pine, with his glittering tomahawk, big as a broad-ax."[10] The moccasin-wearing frontiersman is both accepting of the Indian's barbarous practice and faintly patronizing when he explains the sight to White-Jacket:

"That warrior is the *Red-Hot Coal.* . . . He marches here to show off his last trophy; every one of those hands attests a foe scalped by his tomahawk; and he has just emerged from Ben Brown's, the painter, who has sketched the last red hand that you see; for last night this *Red-Hot Coal* outburned the *Yellow Torch,* the chief of a band of the Foxes."

White-Jacket seems to be similarly condescending when he exclaims: "Poor savage! and you account it so glorious, do you, to mutilate and destroy what God himself was more than a quarter of a century in building?" But suddenly the story comes home: "And yet, fellow Christians, what is the American frigate Macedonian, or the English frigate President, but as two bloody red hands painted on this poor Savage's blanket?" The brotherhood of man may rest as solidly on a common propensity for murder as upon the universal social rituals Melville describes elsewhere.

The desire to bring men together into a fraternal fellowship is also responsible for the Whitmanesque assemblages of people Melville creates. The crews of the *Pequod* and the *Bellipotent* and the passengers of the *Fidèle* are described as an Anacharsis Clootz congress, but none truly illustrates the fellowship of man symbolized by the original group. The *Pequod's* diverse nationalities are united by their captain's mad, destructive purpose; the *Bellipotent's* crew is committed to war. The *Fidèle's* anticommunity is a collection of con-men and their gulls. Similarly, the loving relationship between Benito Cereno and his blacks turns out to be a sham, the civilized paradise of Saddle Meadows a fraud. Beyond the Happy Valley and short of the hereafter, Melville was forced to conclude that the true community he believed in could not be sustained.

In his Polynesian works, Melville attributes the failure of community to whites who have provoked the natives into savagery by barbarous actions toward them. If civilized and primitive peoples regard each other's customs with equal abhorrence, only the white man is powerful enough to demand conformity to his set of values (a pattern fruitfully reversed in the Ishmael/Queequeg relationship). The white civilizer may perceive a vast gulf between himself and those who must be coerced into civilization; to Melville, however, white accomplishments are accretions to the natural man which may be stripped off to reveal the Indian beneath. As he describes the crew in *Moby-Dick*: "Long exile from Christendom and civilization inevitably restores a man to that condition in which God placed him, i.e. what is called savagery. Your true whale-hunter is as much a savage as an Iroquois." The crew's lack of reverence for Moby-Dick distinguishes them from real Iroquois, whose "mid-winter sacrifice of the sacred White Dog was by far the holiest festival of their theology."

A number of other references in *Moby-Dick* join Indian and white.[11] In the whaling boats the men are seated "like Ontario Indians": later, the setting sun "sent back its reflection into every face, so that they all glowed to each other like red men." Ahab is like "the last of the Grisly Bears," which in turn is a "wild Logan of the woods"; the sailor Hemp is "a dusky, dark fellow, a sort of Indian"; Captain Peleg sits on deck in "a strange sort of tent, or rather wigwam." Real Indians, embodying an instinctive wisdom lost to whites, are also part of the *Pequod's* world. The old squaw Tistig has accurately prophesied that Ahab's name would be significant, and an old Gay-Head Indian among the crew seems to know how Ahab was branded. In keeping with his people's long past as hunters on land and sea, "the eager Indian" Tashtego leads the other dark-skinned harpooners in crying out during the whale chase, "raising some old war-whoop to the skies." When Tashtego serves as lookout, Ishmael is startled by a sound "so strange, long drawn, and musically wild and unearthly" that he thinks: "From few of those lungs could that accustomed old cry have derived such a marvellous cadence as from Tashtego the Indian's."

By placing his hunting skills in the service of the quest for Moby-Dick, Tashtego becomes the typical good Indian of the frontier romance. In the chapter on "The Whiteness of the Whale," Ishmael relates an Indian tradition about the White Steed of the Prairies: "In whatever aspect he presented himself, always to the bravest Indians he was the object of trembling reverence and awe." Pursuing the white whale, in contrast, is a violation of the divinity of nature which Indians have always respected. Coopted by Ahab, Tashtego is like an Indian scouting other Indians for the white man, as one of Melville's similes makes clear. Certain whales have been systematically hunted down, Melville writes, "as in setting out through the Narragansett Woods, Captain Butler of old had it in mind to capture that notorious murderous savage Annawon, the headmost warrior of the Indian King Philip."[12] In the white man's unholy pursuit of Moby-Dick, Tashtego is the hired tool, whose head, when both he and Ahab are lookouts for the whale, "was almost on a level with Ahab's heel."

Considering the convention of the frontier romance that good Indians die serving their white masters, it is fitting that Ahab's last order is given to Tashtego, and that the Indian is still attempting to carry it out at the moment of his death. Out of the diverse multitude who go down with the ship, Melville chooses Tashtego for the last action and final moment of consciousness; that Indian, American flag, and imperial eagle should be conjoined and submerged with the *Pequod,* named for a tribe which was utterly exterminated by the white man, suggests some act of expiation for the destruction of the Indians.[13] The symbols of America, flag and eagle, are pulled down by the atrocities committed under their aegis; victim and victimizer are alike destroyed.

If Tashtego is a special version of the good Indian stereotype, translated from a land to a sea wilderness, the avengers in *Mardi* are the bad Indians of the captivity tradition placed in a Polynesian setting. Three voyagers, urged by their white leader, rescue a blonde and blue-eyed heroine from fifteen tawny captors—reasonable odds for the frontier romance.[14] Some of the natives, including their priest-leader Aleema, are killed; vowing vengeance for his death, the remnant gives chase. A comparison of the pursuers to Indians invites the assimilation of captors and rescuers to the North American whites and Indians of the captivity pattern. When the rescuers outdistance and lose the natives, Taji states: "Let the Oregon Indian through brush, bramble, and brier, hunt his enemy's trail, far over the mountains and down in the vales; comes he to the water, he snuffs idly in air." Taji falls in love with the rescued maiden Yillah, but now the familiar captivity story undergoes a Melvillian change: Yillah vanishes, the avengers reappear and, after killing two of the original three attackers, continue their pursuit of Taji. The happy ending of frontier romance captivity is eschewed: Yillah is never recovered, and "pursuers and pursued flew on, over an endless sea." The blood guilt incurred during the clash of Indian and white cannot be overcome so easily.

5

The meeting of civilized whites and primitive dark-skinned peoples always reflects dishonor on the white man in Melville's eyes, but, as his career progressed, he increasingly viewed it as a special American infamy. Americans may be no worse than their

European brothers, but the contradictions between their idealistic proclamations and expediential actions are more glaring than European examples. When Redburn sees a black sailor accepted by the English in Liverpool, he first recoils, and then is led through understanding of his reaction to a criticism of the United States: "In some things, we Americans leave to other countries the carrying out of the principle that stands at the head of our Declaration of Independence."

Like other American believers in a manifest destiny of spiritual ascendancy, Melville was disillusioned by his nation's failure to see its mandate in other than material terms. How high his early hopes were is revealed by a passage in *Redburn*:

> We are the heirs of all time, and with all nations we divide our inheritance. On this Western Hemisphere all tribes and people are forming into one federated whole; and there is a future which shall see the estranged children of Adam restored as to the old hearthstone in Eden.
>
> The other world beyond this, which was longed for by the devout before Columbus' time, was found in the New; and the deep-sea-lead, that first struck these soundings, brought up the soil of Earth's Paradise.

The union of peoples in America, Melville discovered, would be restricted to those with white skin: blacks were enslaved and Indians exterminated in the New World Eden. In *Mardi*, the self-satisfied people of Vivenza (the United States) have a statue whose inscription reads: "In—this—re—publi—can—land—all—men—are—born—free—and—equal," but a postscript adds, "Except—the—tribe—of—Hamo." The visiting King Media quickly perceives that the exception nullifies the lofty rule.

In his last novel, *The Confidence-Man*, Melville embraces the reality of the marketplace to expose its complete corruption. As Stubb had explained in *Moby-Dick*: "Though man loves his fellow, yet man is a money-making animal, which propensity too often interferes with his benevolence." In *The Confidence-Man* the interference is complete: the confidence-man's game perverts all human relationships; a totally commercial world destroys the genuine confidence upon which human commitment depends.

In this milieu the confidence-man uses stereotyped views of the Indian in whatever way will further his own interest. He creates sympathy for the Indian as victim in order to solicit funds for a fictitious Seminole Widow and Orphan Asylum. A lady's donation for "those cruelly used Indians" assuages her portion of the national guilt. On the other hand, the confidence-man engenders pity for the "unfortunate man" by endowing his evil wife Goneril with Indian characteristics: " 'She had hard, steady health like a squaw's, with as firm a spirit and resolution. Some other points about her were likewise such as pertain to the women of savage life. Lithe though she was, she loved supineness, but upon occasion could endure like a stoic. She was taciturn, too.' " Calling upon still another connotation of Indianness, the confidence-man as herb doctor claims kinship with "true Indian doctors." Later, as the Cosmopolitan, he wears "a sort of Indian belt" and smokes a "calumet." The two pledges of confidence and good fellowship between Frank Goodman and Charles Noble, wine and cigars, are brought to their table in Indian craft products: the bottle "in a little bark basket, braided with porcupine quills, gaily tinted in the Indian fashion"; the cigars "in a pretty little bit of western pottery, representing some kind of Indian utensil."

The confidence-man's Indian accessories and his professed love of Indians, like all of his other stances and props, are simply part of his game and not to be interpreted as Melville's identification of Indians with evil.[15] Nor is the man who champions Indian haters to be admired; he gets the better of the confidence-man, but his attitude of no confidence precludes any rapport with another human being. The story he tells of the Indian hater is metaphorically his own: "In the settlements he will not be seen again . . . babes are born and leap in their mothers' arms; but, the Indian hater is good as gone to his long home, and 'Terror' is his epitaph." Like Ahab, and like Hawthorne's Puritans, the Indian hater wrongheadedly locates evil in some external source and rejects the fellowship of man in order to hunt it down.[16] This is always the worst sin in Melville's fictive worlds.

The meaningful poles of human behavior for Melville are not

savagery and civilization, but savage isolation and fraternal harmony. Whatever his culture, man has the choice of espousing the human values which assert the brotherhood of man or the savagery which denies it. As Melville wrote to Hawthorne, the first course may offer the only means of experiencing God: "I feel that the Godhead is broken up like the bread at the Supper, and that we are the pieces. Hence this infinite fraternity of feeling."[17] When man rejects fraternal feeling in order to pursue a lonely quest, or violates it by acts of warfare and oppression, he becomes dehumanized and ultimately mad.

The America which Melville describes in *The Confidence-Man* is just such a dehumanized and mad world, a society of predatory materialism in which confidence has been reduced to foolish credulity, Indians reduced to a few artifacts and stories, and meaningful human commitment negated because man has become solely a money-making animal. The extinction of the solar lamp on the novel's last page may well be the quenching of all human warmth and fraternity in a world where confidence-men triumph and real trust cannot survive.

NOTES

1. Cf. Staughton Lynd, *Intellectual Origins of American Radicalism* (New York, 1968), p. 131, who notes that Thoreau united the slave, the Mexican prisoner, and the Indian at the jail in "Civil Disobedience" (1849), thus drawing together examples of American oppression of dark-skinned peoples.

2. Quotations from Melville are taken from the following editions: *Typee, Omoo, Mardi, Redburn,* and *White-Jacket* in *The Writings of Herman Melville,* ed. Harrison Hayford (Evanston, 1968-1970), vols. I-V; *Moby-Dick,* ed. Harrison Hayford and Hershel Parker (New York, 1967); *The Confidence-Man: His Masquerade,* ed. Elizabeth S. Foster (New York, 1954).

3. Similarly, in *White-Jacket,* Melville asks: "Are there no Moravians in the Moon, that not a missionary has yet visited this poor pagan planet of ours, to civilize civilization and christianize Christendom?"

4. Washington Irving, *Astoria,* rev. ed. (New York, 1868), p. 222.

5. Herman Melville, "Mr. Parkman's Tour," *The Literary World* 4 (March 31, 1849), p. 291.

6. Cf. Melville's introduction to *John Marr and Other Sailors:* "The remnant of Indians thereabouts—all but exterminated in their recent and final war with regular white troops, a war waged by the Red Men for their native soil and natural rights—had been coerced into occupancy of wilds not very far beyond the Mississippi."

7. Cf. *Moby-Dick*; Ishmael thinks: "Better sleep with a sober cannibal than a drunken Christian."

8. Another pointed comparison occurs in *Mardi*: "Civilization has not ever been the brother of equality. Freedom was born among the wild eyries in the mountains; and barbarous tribes have sheltered under her wings, when the enlightened people of the plain have nestled under different pinions."

9. Melville, "Mr. Parkman's Tour," p. 291.

10. Edwin Fussell, *Frontier: American Literature and the American West* (Princeton, 1965), p. 254, points out the significance of this comparison: the similarity of tomahawk to broad axe underlines the common nature of warrior and frontiersman.

11. Similar references to Indians are found throughout Melville's fiction. Fussell collects a number of them in his chapter on Melville, *Frontier*, pp. 232-326.

12. "Notorious murderous savage" is the standard image of the bad Indian, used by whites to justify their actions against Indians. Melville's often-expressed view that so-called savage retaliation was called forth by initial white atrocities makes the expression ironic here. It may also be applied to the whale hunt: had Ahab not sought out Moby-Dick, he would not have been subjected to the whale's savage attack.

13. Fussell, *Frontier*, p. 272, identifies Ahab's flag with Old Glory and the sky-hawk with the imperial eagle.

14. Two of the voyagers, Taji and Jarl, are white men; Samoa is the familiar good native mercenary.

15. As some critics do: cf. Walter Dubler, "Theme and Structure in Melville's *The Confidence-Man*," *American Literature* 33 (1961-62), p. 315; John W. Shroeder, "Sources and Symbols for Melville's *Confidence-Man*," *PMLA* 66 (1951), p. 378. Roy Harvey Pearce, "Melville's Indian-Hater: A Note on a Meaning of *The Confidence-Man*," *PMLA* 67 (1952), p. 943, describes the Indians rightly as "natural men, who are good and evil in a way in which nature is good and evil."

16. Cf. the seer Babbalanja in *Mardi*: " 'The essence of all good and evil is in us, not out of us.' "

17. Melville, Letter to Nathaniel Hawthorne, 17(?) November 1851, *The Letters of Herman Melville*, ed. Merrel R. Davis and William H. Gilman (New Haven, 1960), p. 142.

EPILOGUE

I'm comin' down. Watch out! I'm goin' to rape your wagon
Trail woman on TV, scalp the Pulitzer jury. Goin'
 into the liquor business
Maybe. Sell dope, become Commissioner of the BIA, get in
 big
With the Smithsonian. But right now I gotta go to Anthology
Jailhouse. But don't change, white man, I'll be back
Sap's risin', ole wooden Indian's burstin' out with leaves
And the birds are goin' to be singin' in my wooden lung—
I'll be back. But right now
I'm doin' time, doin' time.

John Lefeather, "HI, PALEFACE!"

With the exception of the *Leatherstocking Tales,* the frontier romance is today—even for specialists in American literature—both unreadable and unread. And although we can substitute D. H. Lawrence's mythic interpretation of Natty, Chingachgook, and the American frontier for some of the strictures of "Fenimore Cooper's Literary Offences," a number of Mark Twain's points remain well taken by our own contemporary standards: we must condemn just as adamantly as he a man who "wrote about the poorest English that exists in our language."[1] This criticism holds true for the frontier romance as a whole. The men and women who wrote in the genre were not, in Twain's metaphor, "word-musicians": their "literary flatting and sharping,"[2] their awkward constructions and artificial dialogue, constantly irritate rather than please the reader. In addition to this inability to write, surely a serious defect in a writer, these authors were tiresomely addicted to hackneyed plots, enamoured of Old World conventions badly suited to the American scene, and unable to create convincing characters of any race, creed, or color.

These aesthetic failings account for the perishability of much of the forgotten fiction of the age, but this discussion will only be concerned with the distinctive shortcomings of the frontier romance.

Because they restrict themselves to such narrowly conceived stereotypes of the Indian, the writers of the frontier romance exclude from their imaginary worlds much that is essential to the human experience. Their white characters are seldom successfully drawn, their Indians uniformly even less so. Regarding whites, there is some rapprochement between author and character; the character's thoughts and feelings are described, even dwelt on; his thought processes and emotions are assumed to be like the author's (and the reader's). The same amount of authorial attention may not be lavished on all the white characters, of course, but it will invariably be expended on some, the hero and heroine especially. An Indian, no matter how prominent his role is supposed to be, is always depicted from the outside, the assumption being that his thoughts and feelings are vastly different from those of the white man. Certainly they may be different, but the denial of a common basis of humanity shared by all men, the very hallmark of Hawthorne's and Melville's treatment of Indians, was disastrous to the writers of the frontier romance. The writers' refusal to grant Indians a human status commensurate with their own, to make them more than mere creatures of white-oriented fictive exigencies, produces characters which are little different from that once familiar figure, the wooden cigar-store Indian.

Nevertheless, the failure of the frontier romance as art is a more complex matter than the lack of realism everywhere apparent in Indian portraiture. While the historian may be criticized legitimately for a disregard of ethnology in writing about Indians, the artist—as Howard Mumford Jones's defense of Cooper contends—cannot be judged by this standard:

> His noble savage has been endlessly attacked as anthropological nonsense; and yet if Uncas is idealized, if Magua is too much an incarnation of villainy, yet how excellent they are as imaginative creations! To reduce them to the test and measurement of the social scientist or the

historian is like taking the Jean Valjean of Victor Hugo as a case study in the French labor movement.[3]

It would be a mistake to evaluate Jean Valjean as a "case study in the French labor movement" or Magua as a faithful representative of real eighteenth-century Hurons, but surely these examples beg the question; what we have a right to expect of created personages is that they are convincing as human beings within the given context of the fictive world which each inhabits. As Henry James best describes the issue: "Humanity is immense, and reality has a myriad forms; the most one can affirm is that some of the flowers of fiction have the odour of it, and others have not."[4]

In James's view, the means of achieving this condition are unimportant variables, a judgment equally pertinent to the failures to achieve it. Among the writers of the frontier romance, those who lived among Indians and those who had never seen any, those who had read the well-known historians of the Indian and those who had not, alike fail to convey a sense of felt experience in their characterization of Indians. As James asserts, experience is itself sensibility; lacking the sensibility, or the intellectual rigor, to see through or beyond the stereotypes created by racist assumptions, these writers could not profit from whatever experience came their way.

In my judgment, Uncas and Magua are not the excellent imaginative creations that Jones finds them to be, but are completely *un*imaginative: "just Natty Bumppo, daubed over with red," as James Russell Lowell characterized Cooper's Indians in *A Fable for Critics.* If they and their fictive brethren embody a mythic vision, it is less D. H. Lawrence's hopeful dream of harmonious companionship between the races and more the fantasy of perfect superiority, using inferiors when they are useful and discarding or, more dramatically, sacrificing them when they are no longer so. If the mundane master-servant relationship seems like a harsh reduction of Natty and Chingachgook's celebrated friendship, it is nevertheless borne out by the action of the *Leatherstocking Tales.* At the behest of Natty, Uncas and Chingachgook devote their energies in *The Last of the Mohicans* to rescuing a party of whites from hostile Indians. No matter that *The Deerslayer* begins with Natty committed to helping Chingachgook rescue his Indian betrothed; all are soon caught up in the standard pattern of white captivity and rescue. In *The Pioneers* Chingachgook wills his own death after seeing his people decline into nothingness, Indian land usurped by settlers, and himself a victim of the white man's rum.[5]

<h2 style="text-align:center">2</h2>

The defense of white policies toward the Indians, primarily the assumption that the white man had rightfully and fairly settled an empty continent, shaped the conventions of the frontier romance.[6] Individual bad whites of the lawless frontier might have transgressed on Indian rights at times, but the official national self-image produced no guilt. As De Tocqueville marvelled: "The Americans of the United States have accomplished this twofold purpose [reduction of the Indian population and deprivation of the remnant's rights] with singular felicity, tranquilly, legally, philanthropically."[7] And Cooper writes in *Notions of the Americans*:

> The Indians have never been slain except in battle, unless by lawless individuals; never hunted by bloodhounds, or in any manner aggrieved, except in the general, and perhaps, in some degree, justifiable invasion of a territory that they did not want, nor could not use.[8]

Enmeshed in exceptions and qualifications, Cooper's brief apology for white conduct toward the Indian evokes the violence and injustice it tries to deny. His attempt to create a benign picture of Indian decline is vaguer, and thus more successful; as Cooper describes it, the phenomenon seems to be self-induced and almost painless: "As a rule, the red man disappears before the superior moral and physical influence of the white."[9] This was the pleasing fantasy to which writers of the frontier romance subscribed.

Another version, troublesome in varying degrees, obtruded

itself from time to time in almost all these writers: a vision of violent dispossession and white guilt, of sin committed and absolution demanded. This is the mood of Cooper's very last frontier romance, *The Oak-Openings* (1848). Unwilling to confront temporal realities, the author looks to the religious sphere for relief; having converted Scalping Peter to Christianity, he moralizes:

> The ways of Divine Providence are past the investigations of human reason. How often, in turning over the pages of history, do we find civilization, the arts, moral improvement, nay, Christianity itself, following the bloody train left by the conqueror's car, and good pouring in upon a nation by avenues that at first were teeming only with the approaches of seeming evils! In this way there is now reason to hope that America is about to pay the debt she owes to Africa; and in this way will the invasion of the forests and prairies and "openings" of the redmen be made to atone for itself by carrying with it the blessings of the gospel, and a juster view of the relations which man bears to his Creator.

Thus, even the more truthful version of white-Indian history could be stripped of its horrors by invoking the standard rationale of western imperialism: in exchange for this world, the natives received what was far more valuable, the world to come.

More often, writers were less easily satisfied with a God's-eye view than the Cooper of *The Oak-Openings*. Although one and all believed in white superiority, they could not entirely dismiss the figure of the Indian as victim or the feelings of pity and guilt engendered by him. The conventions of the frontier romance militated against coming to terms with this attitude, however. Other than those occasional laments for the departing red man, interjected rather than incorporated into the real substance of their fiction, writers had no way of translating their sympathy or guilt into fictive terms. Even Indian hater fiction, which specifically treats the worst excesses of white *realpolitik* toward the Indian, avoids a direct confrontation with the underlying racist climate which made Indian killing acceptable and even laudatory.

James might have said of the frontier romancers that they were men on whom a great deal was lost; what remained in their field of vision was insufficient to create enduring literature. Unlike Hawthorne and Melville, who eschewed the fictive design and stereotypes of the genre and uncovered the presence of white racism and savagery, the frontier romancers repeatedly refused to push beyond the conventional attitudes of their day. Rather than the "direct impression of life" which James insisted upon,[10] they rendered a false and expediential version, one which left no place for Indianness on the North American continent. Their fictive Indians are thus ignoble savages in a twofold sense, as inferior beings who must be subjugated and "civilized," and as monuments to the lack of understanding and generosity of their creators. As Thoreau wrote in his *Journal*: "It frequently happens that the historian, though he professes more humanity than the trapper, mountain man, or golddigger, who shoots one [Indian] as a wild beast, really exhibits and practices a similar inhumanity to him, wielding a pen instead of a rifle."[11] Failing to transcend or transform American society's hackneyed image of the Indian, the work of the frontier romancers is persistently uncreative and deservedly forgotten.

3

During the post-Civil War period of the nineteenth century, historical, scientific, and literary developments combined to influence the portrayal of Indians in fiction. In the West, as the frontier entered its final phase, Indians made their last efforts to resist white expansion by force.[12] One by one, the western tribes underwent the metamorphosis which surviving Indians in other sections of the country had already experienced: from independent nations to United States Government wards, from sovereign powers which posed a threat to the new nation to mere nuisances maintained by the charity of the now all-powerful white man. Subjugation of the remaining Indians did not ameliorate white attitudes so much as transform them from one kind of negative vision to another. Rather than hated and feared enemies who retained at least the respect accorded to their destructive capabilities, Indians were now toothless tigers, still hated but no longer feared. As Philip Borden writes: "The nineteenth century had opened with Americans holding a notion of the Indian as a beast. It was closing with the idea of the Indian as a retarded child."[13] To the bitter memories of past violence, still regarded by whites as wrongs against themselves, was added the opprobrium which the Protestant work ethic reserves for the nonproductive members of society.

Even before the Civil War, the frontier romance had worn itself out, a victim of its own uncreative repetition. As the frontier milieu became increasingly exotic for most Americans and Indian captivity only an implausible adventure, the genre lost its viability. With physical Indians no longer much in evidence, it was still too early in the last quarter of the nineteenth century for that nostalgia which would later focus on the "vanishing American" as a mythic and symbolic figure. In time the modern historical novel would emerge as the heritor of the defunct form, but for the remainder of the century what interest existed in literary Indians was not expressed in serious fiction.

Only one work in this period, Adolf F. Bandelier's *The Delight Makers* (1890), exemplifies a new approach to the Indian in fiction, one based on anthropological data. A disciple of the anthropologist Lewis Henry Morgan, Bandelier was thoroughly steeped in the culture of the Pueblo Indians and eager to describe their way of life accurately:

> We have, Mr. Morgan, and I under his directions, unsettled the Romantic School of Science; now the same thing must be in literature on the American aborigine. Prescott's Aztec is a myth, it remains to show that Fenimore Cooper's Indian is a fraud. . . . The cigar-store man and the statuesque Pocahontas of the "vuelta abajo" trade as they are paraded in literature . . . pervert the public conceptions about the Indians—these I want to destroy first if possible.[14]

Bandelier appears to proceed auspiciously to challenge the prevalent distorted conceptions of which he complains. His story takes place before the coming of the white man; thus, interaction to the disadvantage of the Indian does not occur. The complicated plot, focusing on the transgression of tribal taboos by a strong-willed individual, is engrossing, and the characters' thoughts and feelings are often elaborately described. Nevertheless, the encumbrance of the explanatory paraphernalia constantly necessary to make sense of it all to non-Pueblos quickly begins to burden the narrative. As the intrigue among the tribal power centers deepens, the reader must continually distinguish among the *tapop, maseua, hishtanyi chayan, shkuy chayan, shikama chayan,* and literally dozens more. The welter of clans, titles, people, and relationships becomes overwhelming: by insisting on long Pueblo names, Bandelier sacrifices readability for authenticity. This weight of explanation, clearly the author's favorite technique for correcting public misconceptions about Indians, ultimately sinks the fiction.

More damaging to the revision of the Indian's image which Bandelier undertook is the attitude his explanations convey. Although there are no white characters in the novel, the author's own persona suggests more kinship with that earlier tribe of frontier romancers than with the Pueblos. Bandelier's Indians are not the "stolid, mentally squalid brutes"[15] which he says they may appear to be to whites, nor are they the noble savages which he believes earlier writers imposed on the public imagination. They are children—and, by implication, whites are the adults of the world. Provided with this key, Bandelier sets about patiently unlocking all the mysteries of Indian behavior.

Generalizations like the following abound: "To beg pardon for an offence committed is to him a very difficult task. He is a child, and children rarely make atonement unless compelled" (p. 303).[16] When a woman sees a rainbow:

> [She] did not, she could not, reason as we should under similar circumstances. . . . The Indian is a child whose life is ruled by a feeling of complete dependence, by a desire to accommodate every action to the wills and decrees of countless supernatural beings. (p. 208)

This melange of accurate observation and prejudiced attitude is more insidious than the extravagant vituperation directed towards Indians by white characters in the frontier romance or the heavy-handed condescension of its genteel authors. Bandelier's kernel of truth is the Pueblos' totally religious view of life; however, it is almost completely devalued by the surrounding commentary. Clearly, the child is no Wordsworthian ideal but a name for limitation and arrested growth. The Indian not only does not reason as we do, he *cannot*; his "complete dependence" is the bondage of superstition, not the resignation of the truly religious to divine will.

Similarly, to explain Indian speech, Bandelier writes: "The Indian speaks like a child, using figures of speech, not in order to embellish, but because he lacks abstract terms and is compelled to borrow equivalents from comparisons with surrounding nature" (p. 165). Again, the kernel of truth—the Indian's life is nature-saturated and his speech reflects this condition—is obscured by the manner in which Bandelier has presented it and the compulsion to seek in nature what the Indian by reason of his arrested development cannot supply by mental efforts of a higher order. What an impartial observer might find appropriate and natural to the Indian's way of life must always be seen as inferior; hence, Indian speech is designated childlike although the process Bandelier goes on to describe in no way resembles the speech of children.

For all that Bandelier knows his subject and wishes to provide an accurate description of Pueblo life, his wealth of details suggests paucity rather than richness; his preoccupation with explaining Indian customs in white terms, which unfortunately does not extend to his characters' names, must always contrast the meagerness of Indian resources with the complexity of white culture. Indian gossip, he begins, is "as genuine as any that is spoken in modern society" (p. 286). But it is always necessary to go further: "with this difference only, that the circle of facts and ideas accessible to the Indian mind is exceedingly narrow, and that the gossip applies itself therefore to a much smaller number of persons and things" (p. 286). What begins as similarity inevitably ends in difference; just as what begins as factual account becomes evidence for the narrow and circumscribed nature of Indian life.

Elsewhere, Bandelier comments on a moment of crisis by telling us what a white person would do in contrast to what an Indian is able to do:

Under such circumstance many a one sends a short prayer to
Heaven for assistance in his hour of need. Not so the Indian;
he has only formulas and ritualistic performances . . . .
(p. 330)

When the comparison is not overtly made, we are, of course,
capable of supplying the missing term. The Indian protagonist,
for example, is described as "fond of his mother at the bottom of
his heart, as fond as any Indian can be" (p. 200).

In place of the white characters of the frontier romance, *The
Delight Makers* contains a white authorial presence which
effectively negates the supposed value of focusing exclusively on
Indians. Providing white equivalents for Indian behavior seems
to lead Bandelier almost unconsciously into value judgments
which reveal traditional white attitudes garbed in knowledgeabili-
ty. At times this seeming objectivity disappears altogether, as if
Bandelier cannot resist the temptation of comic irony in the
treatment of such data. The morning regimen of an Indian
woman is this kind of occasion:

When the sun rose on the fourth day, it found Shotaye just
about to take her morning meal. That was soon over, for
there was no coffee, no hot rolls, no butter. It consisted
merely of cold corn-cakes. When she had satisfied her
appetite, she rose, shook the crumbs from her wrap, and
went out. She had made a full toilet; that is, she had rubbed
her face with her moistened hands and dried it with a
deerskin, whereby a little more dust was added to her cheeks.
(pp. 307-308)

The patronizing author is conspicuously at work reminding the
reader that the meal which both call breakfast is superior to
Shotaye's mere corncakes, that her "full toilet" is laughably inadequate by white standards and foolishly counterproductive.

We might find Bandelier's attitude toward Indians, as Melville
found Parkman's, "almost natural" but "wholly indefensible."[17] It
comes as a shock to discover C. W. Ceram praising *The Delight
Makers* as "unique" and Edwin W. Gaston, Jr., hailing it as "possib-

ly the foremost nineteenth century work dealing with the American Indian," until we remember the frontier romance.[18] Bandelier's novel *is* a genuine departure in a number of respects, a vivid account of real people and believable power struggles, but beneath the surface of painstaking detail, racism makes its familiar appeal.

4

In the twentieth century, fictive Indians appear in a number of different contexts. Although using somewhat more savvy Indians, works of historical fiction have returned to some of the old plot mechanisms and time periods of the frontier romance. Following the example of Bandelier, anthropological fiction has created Indian worlds which are either independent of whites or in which whites play only subordinate roles. In contrast to both of these identifiable genres, the contemporary novel has brought individual Indians into the present-day white world or placed them in historical milieus which mix the serious with the tongue in cheek.[19] This Indian vantage point functions both as a comic perspective on American society and as a serious alternative to it. Well before the new Indian militancy of the late sixties and the ecological movement which has praised Indian reverence toward nature, writers began to portray the Indian as a repository of wisdom now lost to whites—an updated noble savage founded on a more secure basis of understanding.

In addition to these new white points of view, Indians have begun to create their own image in literature. Whether or not it is up to Indians themselves "to write the final chapter of the American Indian upon this continent,"[20] as Vine Deloria, Jr., urges, the racist stereotypes perpetuated by whites in the frontier romance and its twentieth-century heirs are now being challenged from more than one direction. Having realized their intention of possessing the New World, whites may now be ready to accommodate a dissenting perspective.

NOTES

1. Mark Twain, "Fenimore Cooper's Literary Offences," *North American Review* 161 (1895), p. 12.
2. Ibid., p. 11.
3. Howard Mumford Jones, *The Frontier in American Fiction* (Jerusalem, 1956), p. 38.
4. Henry James, "The Art of Fiction," *Partial Portraits* (London, 1911), pp. 387-388.
5. It is only fair to note that the controlling spirit of the pair, Natty Bumppo, suffers a similar fate in *The Prairie*: he, too, sees the passing of the wilderness milieu he loves, but he is in no way degraded like Chingachgook.
6. As Henry Nash Smith writes in *Virgin Land* (Cambridge, Mass., 1950), p. 3: "One of the most persistent generalizations concerning American life and character is the notion that our society has been shaped by the pull of a vacant continent drawing population westward." Similarly, Thomas D. Clark, *Frontier America: The Story of the Westward Movement* (New York, 1959), p. 7: "Almost from the beginning, frontiersmen came to regard the huge virginal domain as a God-given heritage which was theirs for the taking."
7. Alexis De Tocqueville, *Democracy in America*, Henry Reeve text, rev. Francis Bowen and Phillips Bradley (New York, 1945), p. 355.
8. James Fenimore Cooper, *Notions of the Americans* (Philadelphia, 1841), vol. II, p. 285.
9. Ibid., vol, II, p. 277.
10. James, "The Art of Fiction," p. 384.
11. *The Journal of Henry D. Thoreau*, ed. Bradford Torrey and Francis H. Allen (Boston, 1906), vol. XI, pp. 437-438.
12. A compelling account of this process is given by Dee Brown, *Bury My Heart at Wounded Knee* (New York, 1971).
13. Philip Borden, "Found Cumbering the Soil: Manifest Destiny and the Indian in the Nineteenth Century," *The Great Fear*, ed. Gary B. Nash and Richard Weiss (New York, 1970), p. 96.
14. Adolf F. Bandelier, Letter to Thomas Janvier, September 2, 1888, *The Unpublished Letters of Adolf F. Bandelier* (El Paso, 1942), p. 3. Elémire Zolla, *The Writer and the Shaman*, trans. Raymond Rosenthal (New York, 1973), p. 167, remarks that "Morgan's prejudices hold undisputed sway in Bandelier's mind."
15. Adolf F. Bandelier, *The Delight Makers* (New York, 1971), p. 13. Further references will appear in the text.
16. B. J. Stern, in a laudatory retrospective on Bandelier, states that Bandelier's way of carrying on ethnological research involved learning to think like an Indian. He next remarks that "in personality Bandelier was as simple as a child" (*Social Forces* [March 1928], p. 355).
17. Herman Melville, "Mr. Parkman's Tour," *The Literary World* 4 (March 31, 1849), p. 291.
18. C. W. Ceram, *The First American* (New York, 1971), p. 67; Edwin W. Gaston, Jr., *The Early Novel of the Southwest* (Albuquerque, 1961), pp. 191-192.
19. For an excellent overview of this period see Elémire Zolla; see also Leslie A. Fiedler, *The Return of the Vanishing American* (New York, 1968).
20. Vine Deloria, Jr., *Custer Died for Your Sins* (New York, 1970), p. 272.

APPENDIX A

CHRONOLOGY OF FRONTIER ROMANCES

1793   Ann Eliza Bleecker, *The History of Maria Kittle.*
1798   Susannah Rowson, *Reuben and Rachel.*
1799   Charles Brockden Brown, *Edgar Huntly.*
1802   John Davis, *The First Settlers of Virginia.*
1805   John Davis, *Walter Kennedy.**
1810   Jesse L. Holman, *The Prisoners of Niagara.*
1813   *St. Herbert.*
1816   Samuel Woodworth, *The Champions of Freedom.*
1817   John Neal, *Keep Cool.*
1822   John Neal, *Logan.*
1823   James Fenimore Cooper, *The Pioneers.*
        James McHenry, *The Spectre of the Forest; The Wilderness.*
        James Kirke Paulding, *Koningsmarke.*
1824   Harriet V. Cheney, *A Peep at the Pilgrims.*
        Lydia Maria Child, *Hobomok.*
        Eliza Lanesford Cushing, *Saratoga.*
        The Witch of New England.
1825   *The Christian Indian.*
        Nicholas Marcellus Hentz, *Tadeuskund.*
1826   James Fenimore Cooper, *The Last of the Mohicans.*
1827   John Brainerd, *Fort Braddock Letters.*
        James Fenimore Cooper, *The Prairie.*
        Catharine Maria Sedgwick, *Hope Leslie.*
1829   James Fenimore Cooper, *The Wept of Wish-ton-Wish.*
        Karl Postl, *Tokeah.*
1830   Timothy Flint, *The Shoshonee Valley.*

*First published in London.

L. Larned, *The Sanfords.*

James McHenry, *The Betrothed of Wyoming.*

William J. Snelling, *Tales of the Northwest.*

1831   James Kirke Paulding, *The Dutchman's Fireside.*

1832   James Hall, *Legends of the West.*

1833   James Hall, *The Harpe's Head.*

1834   Joseph C. Hart, *Miriam Coffin.*

1835   James Hall, *Tales of the Border.*

William Gilmore Simms, *The Yemassee.*

1836   James Strange French, *Elkswatawa.*

1837   Robert Montgomery Bird, *Nick of the Woods.*

John T. Irving, Jr., *The Hawk Chief.*

1838   James Birchett Ransom, *Osceola.*

1839   Robert Strange, *Eoneguski.*

1840   Charles Fenno Hoffman, *Greyslaer.*

Edgar Allan Poe, *The Journal of Julius Rodman.*

1841   James Fenimore Cooper, *The Deerslayer; The Pathfinder.*

John Shecut, *Ish-Noo-Ju-Lut-Sche.*

1842   Anna L. Snelling, *Kabaosa.*

1843   James Fenimore Cooper, *Wyandotté.*

Charles Fenno Hoffman, *Wild Scenes in the Forest and Prairie.*

1844   John Shecut, *The Scout.*

1845   James Fenimore Cooper, *The Chainbearer; Satanstoe.*

William Gilmore Simms, *The Wigwam and the Cabin.*

1846   James Fenimore Cooper, *The Redskins.*

James Hall, *The Wilderness and the Warpath.*

Sir William Drummond Stewart, *Altowan.*

1847   Samuel Young, *Tom Hanson, the Avenger.*

1848   Emerson Bennett, *Kate Clarendon; The Renegade.*

James Fenimore Cooper, *The Oak-Openings.*

James Wilmer Dallam, *The Deaf Spy.*

Charles Wilkins Webber, *Old Hicks the Guide.*

1849   Emerson Bennett, *Leni Leoti; The Prairie Flower.*

1850   Emerson Bennett, *The Forest Rose.*

M. C. Hodges, *The Mestico.*

1851   Samuel B. Hanson, *Tom Quick, the Indian Slayer.*
        Gideon M. Hollister, *Mount Hope.*
        John Richardson, *Wacousta.*
1853   Charles Wilkins Webber, *Tales of the Southern Border.*
1859   William Gilmore Simms, *The Cassique of Kiawah.*
1860   Daniel Thompson, *The Doomed Chief.*
1868   John Esten Cooke, *Lord Fairfax.*

APPENDIX B

The Harpe's Head, James Hall
The Hawk Chief, John T. Irving, Jr.
The History of Maria Kittle, Ann Eliza Bleecker
Hobomok, Lydia Maria Child
Hope Leslie, Catharine Maria Sedgwick

"The Indian Hater, " James Hall
"The Indian Spring," William Cullen Bryant
Ish-Noo-Ju-Lut-Sche, John Shecut

The Journal of Julius Rodman, Edgar Allan Poe

Kabaosa, Anna L. Snelling
Kate Clarendon, Emerson Bennett
Koningsmarke, James Kirke Paulding

The Last of the Mohicans, James Fenimore Cooper
Legends of the West, James Hall
Leni Leoti, Emerson Bennett
Logan, John Neal
Lord Fairfax, John Esten Cooke

The Mestico, M. C. Hodges
Miriam Coffin, Joseph C. Hart
Mount Hope, Gideon M. Hollister

Nick of the Woods, Robert Montgomery Bird

"Oakatibbe or the Choctaw Sampson," William Gilmore Simms
The Oak-Openings, James Fenimore Cooper
Old Hicks the Guide, Charles Wilkins Webber
Osceola, James Birchett Ransom

The Pathfinder, James Fenimore Cooper
A Peep at the Pilgrims, Harriet V. Cheney
"Pinchon," William J. Snelling

"The Pioneer," James Hall
The Pioneers, James Fenimore Cooper
The Prairie, James Fenimore Cooper
The Prairie Flower, Emerson Bennett
The Prisoners of Niagara, Jesse L. Holman

"Queen Meg," Charles Fenno Hoffman

The Redskins, James Fenimore Cooper
The Renegade, Emerson Bennett
Reuben and Rachel, Susannah Rowson

St. Herbert, anonymous
The Sanfords, L. Larned
Saratoga, Eliza Lanesford Cushing
Satanstoe, James Fenimore Cooper
The Scout, John Shecut
The Shoshonee Valley, Timothy Flint
The Spectre of the Forest, James McHenry

Tadeuskund, Nicholas Marcellus Hentz
Tales of the Border, James Hall
Tales of the Northwest, William J. Snelling
Tales of the Southern Border, Charles Wilkins Webber
Tokeah, Karl Postl
Tom Hanson, the Avenger, Samuel Young
Tom Quick, the Indian Slayer, Samuel B. Hanson
"The Two Camps," William Gilmore Simms

Wacousta, John Richardson
Walter Kennedy, John Davis
"The War Belt," James Hall
The Wept of Wish-ton-Wish, James Fenimore Cooper
The Wigwam and the Cabin, James Hall
Wild Scenes in the Forest and Prairie, Charles Fenno Hoffman
The Wilderness, James McHenry
The Wilderness and the Warpath, James Hall

The Witch of New England, anonymous
Wyandotté, James Fenimore Cooper

The Yemassee, William Gilmore Simms

BIBLIOGRAPHY

Anon. Review of *Escalala, an American Tale. North American Review* 20 (1825): 210-214.

Anon. Review of "A Vindication of the Rev. Mr. Heckewelder's History of the Indian Nations." *North American Review* 26 (1828): 366-386.

Audubon, John James, *Audubon and His Journals.* Edited by Maria R. Audubon. New York: Charles Scribner's Sons, 1897.

Bandelier, Adolf F. *The Delight Makers.* New York: Harcourt Brace Jovanovich, 1971.

————. *The Unpublished Letters of Adolf F. Bandelier.* El Paso: C. Herzog, 1942.

Bennett, Emerson. *The Forest Rose.* Cincinnati: J. A. and U. P. James, 1850.

————. *Kate Clarendon.* Cincinnati: Stratton and Barnard, 1848.

————. *Leni Leoti.* Cincinnati: J. A. and U. P. James, 1851.

————. *The Prairie Flower.* Cincinnati: J. A. and U. P. James, 1850.

————. *The Renegade.* Cincinnati: Robinson and Jones, 1848.

Bernbaum, Ernest. *Guide Through the Romantic Movement.* 2nd ed. New York: The Ronald Press Company, 1949.

Beverley, Robert. *The History and Present Sate of Virginia* [London, 1705] Edited by Louis B. Wright. Chapel Hill: University of North Carolina Press, 1947.

Bierce, Ambrose. *The Collected Works of Ambrose Bierce.* 12 vols. New York: Gordian Press, 1966.

Bird, Robert Montgomery. *Nick of the Woods.* Chicago: N. B. Conkey Company, 1853.

Bleecker, Ann Eliza. *The History of Maria Kittle.* Hartford: E. Babcock, 1797.

Borden, Philip. "Found Cumbering the Soil: Manifest Destiny and the Indian in the Nineteenth Century." *The Great Fear.* Edited by Gary B. Nash and Richard Weiss. New York: Holt, Rinehart and Winston, 1970.

Brackenridge, Hugh Henry. *Modern Chivalry.* Edited by Lewis Leary. New Haven: College and University Press, 1965.

Bradford, William. *Bradford's History "Of Plimouth Plantation."* Boston: Wright and Potter, 1901.

Brainerd, John. *Fort Braddock Letters.* Worcester, Mass: Dorr and Howland, 1827.

Bristed, John. *Resources of the United States of America.* New York: James Eastburn and Company, 1818.

Brown, Charles Brockden. *Edgar Huntly.* Philadelphia: David McKay, 1887.

Brown, Dee. *Bury My Heart At Wounded Knee.* New York: Holt, Rinehart and Winston, 1971.

Brown, Herbert Ross. *The Sentimental Novel In America 1789-1860.* Durham, N. C.: Duke University Press, 1940.

Bryant, William Cullen. *Prose Writings of William Cullen Bryant.* Edited by Parke Godwin. 6 vols. New York: D. Appleton and Company, 1884.

Byrd, William. *The Prose Works of William Byrd of Westover.* Edited by Louis B. Wright. Cambridge, Mass: Harvard University Press, 1966.

Campbell, Walter S. "The Plains Indians in Literature—and in Life." *The Trans-Mississippi West.* Edited by James F. Willard and Colin B. Goodykoontz. Boulder, Col.: University of Colorado Press, 1930.

Carleton, Phillips D. "The Indian Captivity," *American Literature* 15 (1943-44): 169-180.

Cheney, Harriet V. *A Peep at the Pilgrims.* Boston: Wells and Lilly, 1824.

Child, Lydia Maria. *Hobomok.* Boston: Cummings, Hilliard and Company, 1824.

The Christian Indian. New York: Collins and Hannay, 1825.

Clark, Thomas D. *Frontier America: The Story of the Westward Movement.* New York: Charles Scribner's Sons, 1959.

Clemens, Samuel L. *Contributions to the Galaxy, 1868-1871 by Mark Twain.* Edited by Bruce R. McElderry, Jr. Gainesville: University of Florida Press, 1961.

———. "Fenimore Cooper's Literary Offences," *North American Review* 161 (1895): 1-12.

Colden, Cadwallader. *The History of the Five Indian Nations Depending on the Province of New-York in America.* 2 vols. New York: New Amsterdam Book Company, 1902.

Cooke, John Esten. *Lord Fairfax.* New York: G. W. Dillingham Company, 1868.

Cooper, James Fenimore. *Home As Found.* 2 vols. Philadelphia: Lea and Blanchard, 1838.

———. *Notions of the Americans.* 2 vols. Philadelphia: Lea and Blanchard, 1841.

——— *The Works of James Fenimore Cooper.* 32 vols. New York: D. Appleton and Company, 1901.

Cowie, Alexander. *The Rise of the American Novel.* New York: American Book Company, 1948.

Cushing, Eliza Lanesford. *Saratoga.* 2 vols. Boston: Cummings, Hilliard and Company, 1824.

Dallam, James Wilmer. *The Deaf Spy.* Baltimore: William Taylor and Company, 1848.

Davis, David Brion. "The Deerslayer, A Democratic Knight of the Wilderness: Cooper, 1841," *Twelve Original Essays on Great American Novels.* Edited by Charles Shapiro. Detroit: Wayne State University Press, 1958, pp.1-22.

Davis, John. *The First Settlers of Virginia.* 2nd ed. New York: I. Riley and Company, 1806.

————. *Walter Kennedy.* London: J. F. Hughes, 1808.

Deloria, Vine, Jr. *Custer Died for Your Sins.* New York: The Macmillan Company, 1969.

De Voto, Bernard. *The Course of Empire.* Boston: Houghton Mifflin, 1952.

Dubler, Walter. "Theme and Structure in Melville's *The Confidence Man.*" *American Literature* 33 (1961-62): 307-319.

Emerson, Ralph Waldo. *The Works of Ralph Waldo Emerson.* 14 vols. Boston: Houghton Mifflin, 1883-1899.

Fairchild, Hoxie Neale. *The Noble Savage: A Study in Romantic Naturalism.* New York: Russell and Russell, 1961.

Fiedler, Leslie A. *The Return of the Vanishing American.* New York: Stein and Day, 1968.

Flint, Timothy. *The Shoshonee Valley.* 2 vols. Cincinnati: E. H. Fleet, 1830.

Franklin, Benjamin. *Writings of Benjamin Franklin.* Edited by A. H. Smyth. 10 vols. New York: The Macmillan Company, 1905-1907.

Frederick, John T. "Cooper's Eloquent Indians." *PMLA* 81 (1956): 1004-1017.

French, James Strange, *Elkswatawa.* 2 vols. New York: Harper and Brothers, 1836.

Fussell, Edwin. *Frontier: American Literature and the American West.* Princeton: Princeton University Press, 1965.

Gardiner, William Howard. Review of *The Spy. North American Review* 15 (1822): 250-282.

Gaston, Edwin W., Jr. *The Early Novel of the Southwest.* Albuquerque: University of New Mexico Press, 1961.

Gray, Robert. *A Good Speed to Virginia.* [London, 1609] Facsimile rpt. Edited by Wesley F. Craven. New York: n. p., 1937.

Hagan, William T. *American Indians.* Chicago: University of Chicago Press, 1961.

————. *The Indian in American History.* New York: The Macmillan Company, 1963.

Hall, James. *The Harpe's Head.* Philadelphia: Key and Biddle, 1833.

————. *Legends of the West.* Philadelphia: Key and Biddle, 1833.

————. *Sketches of History, Life, and Manners, in the West.* 2 vols. Philadelphia: Harrison Hall, 1835.

————. *Tales of the Border.* Philadelphia: Harison Hall, 1835.

————. *The Wilderness and the Warpath.* New York: Wiley and Putnam, 1846.

Hallowell, A. Irving. "The Backwash of the Frontier: The Impact of the Indian on American Culture." *The Frontier in Perspective.* Edited by Walker D. Wyman and Clifton B. Kroeber. Madison: University of Wisconsin Press, 1957.

Hanson, Samuel B. *Tom Quick, the Indian Slayer.* Monticello, New York: DeVoe and Quinlan, 1851.

Hart, Joseph C. *Miriam Coffin.* 2 vols. New York: G. and C. and H. Carvill, 1834.

Hawthorne, Nathaniel. *The Complete Writings of Nathaniel Hawthorne.* 22 vols. Boston: Houghton Mifflin, 1900.

Hazard, Lucy Lockwood. *The Frontier in American Literature.* New York: Thomas Y. Crowell Company, 1927.

Heckewelder, John. *History, Manners, and Customs of The Indian Nations, Who Once Inhabited Pennsylvania and the Neighboring States.* Rev. ed. Edited by William Reichel. Philadelphia: The Historical Society of Pennsylvania, 1876.

Hentz, Nicholas Marcellus. *Tadeuskund, the Last King of the Lenape.* Boston: Cummings, Hilliard, and Company, 1825.

Hodges, M. C. *The Mestico.* New York: William H. Graham, 1850.

Hoffman, Charles Fenno. *Greyslaer.* 2 vols. New York: Harper and Brothers, 1840.

———. *Wild Scenes in the Forest and Prairie.* 2 vols. New York: William H. Colyer, 1843.

Hollister, Gideon H. *Mount Hope.* New York: Harper and Brothers, 1851.

Holman, Jesse L. *The Prisoners of Niagara.* Frankfort, Ky.: William Gerard, 1810.

House, Kay Seymour. *Cooper's Americans.* Columbus, Ohio: Ohio State University Press, 1965.

Imlay, Gilbert. *The Emigrants.* [Dublin, 1794] Facsimile rpt. Edited by Robert R. Hare. Gainesville: University of Florida Press, 1964.

Irving, John T., Jr. *The Hawk Chief: A Tale of the Indian Country.* 2 vols. Philadelphia: Carey, Lea and Blanchard, 1837.

———. *Indian Sketches.* Edited by John Francis McDermott. Norman: University of Oklahoma Press, 1955.

Irving, Washington. *Astoria.* Rev. ed. New York: G. P. Putnam's Sons, 1868.

——— *The Sketch Book of Geoffrey Crayon, Gentleman.* 2 vols. London: John Murray, 1821.

——— *A Tour on the Prairies.* Oklahoma City: Harlow Publishing Corporation, 1955.

James, Henry. *Partial Portraits.* London: Macmillan and Company, Limited, 1911.

Jefferson, Thomas. *Letters and Addresses of Thomas Jefferson.* Edited by William B. Parker and Jonas Viles. New York: The Sun Dial Classics Company, 1905.

———. *Notes on the State of Virginia.* New York: Furman and London, 1801.

Jones, Howard Mumford. *The Frontier in American Fiction.* Jerusalem: Magness Press, 1956.

Karolides, Nicholas J. *The Pioneer in the American Novel 1900-1950.* Norman: University of Oklahoma Press, 1967.

Keiser, Albert. *The Indian in American Literature.* New York: Oxford University Press, 1933.

Larned, L. *The Sanfords.* 2 vols. New York: Elam Bliss, 1830.

Lawrence, D. H. *Mornings in Mexico.* New York: A. A. Knopf, 1927.

———. *Studies in Classic American Literature.* New York: Albert and Charles Boni, 1930.

Leavis, Q. D. "Hawthorne as Poet." *Sewanee Review* 59 (1951): 179-205; 426-458.

Leisy, Ernest E. *The American Historical Novel.* Norman: University of Oklahoma Press, 1950.

Lewis, R. W. B. *The American Adam.* Chicago: University of Chicago Press, 1955.

Lippmann, Walter. *Public Opinion.* New York: The Macmillan Company, 1949.

Loewenberg, Peter. "The Psychology of Racism." *The Great Fear*. Edited by Gary B. Nash and Richard Weiss. New York: Holt, Rinehart and Winston, Inc., 1970, pp. 186-201.

Loshe, Lillie Deming. *The Early American Novel*. New York: The Columbia University Press, 1907.

Lovejoy, Arthur O., and George Boas. *Primitivism and Related Ideas in Antiquity*. New York: Octagon Books, 1965.

Lowell, James Russell. *A Fable for Critics*. Boston: Ticknor, 1856.

Lynd, Staughton. *Intellectual Origins of American Radicalism*. New York: Pantheon Books, 1968.

McHenry, James. *The Betrothed of Wyoming*. Philadelphia: n. p., 1830.

———. *The Spectre of the Forest*. 2 vols. New York: E. Bliss and E. White, 1823.

———. *The Wilderness*. 2 vols. New York: E. Bliss and E. White, 1823.

Marek, Kurt W. [C. W. Ceram] *The First American*. Trans. Richard and Clara Winston. New York: Harcourt Brace Jovanovich, 1971.

Mather, Cotton. *Decennium Luctuosum*. [Boston, 1699] rpt. in *Narratives of the Indian Wars, 1675-1699*. Edited by Charles H. Lincoln. New York: Charles Scribner's Sons, 1913, pp. 169-300.

———. *Magnalia Christi Americana*. [London, 1702] 2 vols. New York: Russell and Russell, 1967.

Mathews, Cornelius. *Behemoth*. New York: J. and H. G. Langley, 1839.

Mellen, Granville. Review of *The Red Rover*. *North American Review* 27 (1828): 139-154.

Melville, Herman. *Collected Poems of Herman Melville*. Edited Howard P. Vincent. Chicago: Packard and Company, 1947.

———. *The Confidence-Man: His Masquerade*. Edited by Elizabeth S. Foster. New York: Hendricks House, 1954.

———. *The Letters of Herman Melville*. Edited by Merrell R. Davis and William H. Gilman. New Haven: Yale University Press, 1960.

———. "Mr. Parkman's Tour." *The Literary World* 4 (March 31, 1849): 291-292.

———. *Moby-Dick*. Edited by Harrison Hayford and Hershel Parker. New York: W. W. Norton and Company, Inc., 1967.

———. *The Writings of Herman Melville*. Edited by Harrison Hayford. 7 vols. Evanston: Northwestern University Press and the Newberry Library, 1968-1971.

Mott, Frank Luther. *Golden Multitudes*. New York: The Macmillan Company, 1947.

Mourt. *A Relation or Journall of the beginning and proceedings of the English Plantation settled at Plimoth in New England*. [London, 1622] Facsimile rpt. Edited by Henry Martyn Dexter. Boston: J. K. Wiggin, 1865.

Neal, John. *Keep Cool*. 2 vols. Baltimore: J. Cushing, 1817.

———. *Logan, A Family History*. 2 vols. Philadelphia: H. C. Carey and I. Lea, 1822.

Noel, Mary. *Villains Galore*. New York: The Macmillan Company, 1954.

Orians, G. Harrison. "The Indian Hater in Early American Fiction." *The Journal of American History* 27 (1933): 34-44.

————. "The Rise of Romanticism, 1805-1855." *Transitions in American Literary History.* Edited by Harry Hayden Clark. New York: Octagon Books, 1967, pp. 161-244.

————. "The Romantic Ferment after *Waverley.*" *American Literature* 3 (1931-32): 408-431.

Palfrey, John Gorham. *History of New England During the Stuart Dynasty.* 3 vols. Boston: Little, Brown, and Company, 1865.

————. Review of *Yamoyden, a Tale of the Wars of King Philip in Six Cantos. North American Review* 12 (1821): 466-488.

Parkman, Francis. *The Conspiracy of Pontiac and the Indian War after the Conquest of Canada.* 2 vols. Boston: Little, Brown, and Company, 1899.

————. *The Oregon Trail.* Boston: Little, Brown, and Company, 1891.

Pattee, Fred Lewis. *The First Century of American Literature.* New York: D. Appleton-Century Company, Inc., 1935.

Paulding, James Kirke. *The Dutchman's Fireside.* 2 vols. New York: Harper and Brothers, 1837.

————. *Koningsmarke.* 2 vols. New York: Harper and Brothers, 1836.

Pearce, Roy Harvey. "Melville's Indian-Haters: A Note on a Meaning of *The Confidence-Man.*" *PMLA* 67 (1952): 942-948.

————. *Savagism and Civilization.* Rev. ed. Baltimore: Johns Hopkins Press, 1965.

————. "The Significances of the Captivity Narrative." *American Literature* 19 (1946-47): 1-20.

Pearson, Edmund. *Dime Novels.* Boston: Little, Brown, and Company, 1929.

Peckham, Howard H. *Captured by Indians.* New Brunswick: Rutgers University Press, 1954.

Poe, Edgar Allan. *The Complete Works of Edgar Allan Poe.* 10 vols. Boston: Desmond Publishing Company, 1908.

Postl, Karl. *Tokeah.* 2 vols. Philadelphia: Carey, Lea, and Carey, 1829.

Quinn, Arthur Hobson. *American Fiction.* New York: D. Appleton-Century Company, 1936.

Ransom, James Birchett. *Osceola.* New York: Harper and Brothers, 1838.

Richardson, John. *Wacousta.* New York: Dewitt and Davenport, 1851.

Roosevelt, Theodore. *The Winning of the West.* 4 vols. New York and London: G. P. Putnam's Sons, 1889-1896.

Rowlandson, Mary. *The Captivity of Mrs. Mary Rowlandson.* [Cambridge, Mass., 1682] Rpt. in *Narratives of the Indian Wars, 1675-1699.* Edited by Charles H. Lincoln. New York: Charles Scribner's Sons, 1913, pp. 107-167.

Rowson, Susannah. *Reuben and Rachel.* Boston: Manning and Loring, 1798.

Rush, Benjamin. *Essays.* 2nd ed. Philadelphia: Thomas and William Bradford, 1806.

St. Herbert. Windsor: n. p., 1813.

Saltonstall, Nathaniel. *A New and Further Narrative of the State of New-England.* [London, 1676] Rpt. in *Narratives of the Indian Wars, 1675-1699.* Edited by Charles H. Lincoln. New York: Charles Scribner's Sons, 1913, pp. 75-99.

————. *The Present State of New-England with Respect to the Indian War.* [London,

1675] Rpt. In *Narratives of Indian Wars, 1675-1699.* Edited by Charles H. Lincoln. New York: Charles Scribner's Sons, 1913, pp. 51-74.

Schoolcraft, Henry Rowe. *Algic Researches.* 2 vols. New York: Harper and Brothers, 1839.

Scott, Sir Walter. *The Journal of Sir Walter Scott.* 2 vols. New York: Harper and Brothers, 1891.

———. *The Waverley Novels.* 12 vols. Philadelphia: J. B. Lippincott and Company, 1873.

Sedgwick, Catharine Maria. *Hope Leslie.* 2 vols. New York: Harper and Brothers, 1842.

Select Tales. Charlottesville: Joseph Martin, 1833.

Shecut, John. *Ish-Noo-Ju-Lut-Sche.* 2 vols. New York: P. Price, 1841.

———. *The Scout.* New York: C. L. Stickney, 1844.

Sheehan, Bernard W. *Seeds of Extinction.* Chapel Hill: University of North Carolina Press, 1973.

Shroeder, John W. "Sources and Symbols for Melville's *Confidence-Man.*" *PMLA* 66 (1951): 363-380.

Simms, William Gilmore. *The Cassique of Kiawah.* New York and Chicago: Butler Brothers Incorporated, 1859.

———. *Views and Reviews in American Literature, History and Fiction, First Series.* Edited by C. Hugh Holman. Cambridge, Mass: Harvard University Press, 1950.

———. *The Wigwam and the Cabin.* Philadelphia: Lippincott, Grambo, and Company, 1853.

———. *The Yemassee.* Edited by C. Hugh Holman. Boston: Houghton Mifflin Company, 1961.

Slotkin, Richard. *Regeneration Through Violence.* Middletown, Conn.: Wesleyan University Press, 1973.

Smith, Captain John. *A Map of Virginia: with a Description of the Countrey, the Commodities, People, Government and Religion.* [Oxford, 1612] Rpt. in *Narratives of Early Virginia, 1606-1625.* Edited by Lyon Gardiner Tyler. New York: Charles Scribner's Sons, 1930, pp. 73-118.

———. *A True Relation.* [London, 1608] Rpt. in *Narratives of Early Virginia, 1606-1625.* Edited by Lyon Gardiner Tyler. New York: Charles Scribner's Sons, 1930, pp. 25-71.

Smith, Henry Nash, *Virgin Land.* Cambridge, Mass.: Harvard University Press, 1950.

Snelling, Anna L. *Kabaosa.* New York: D. Adee, 1842.

Snelling, William J. *Tales of the Northwest.* Boston: Hilliard, Gray, Little, and Wilkins, 1830.

Spencer, Benjamin T. *The Quest for Nationality.* Syracuse: Syracuse University Press, 1957.

Spicer, Edward H. *A Short History of the Indians of the United States.* New York: Van Nostrand Reinhold Company, 1969.

Sproat, P. W. *The Savage Beauty.* Philadelphia: S. Roberts, 1822.

Stewart, Randall. "Hawthorne's Contributions to *The Salem Advertiser.*" *American Literature* 5 (1933-34): 327-341.

Stewart, Sir William Drummond. *Altowan.* 2 vols. New York: Harper and Brothers, 1846.

Strange, Robert. *Eoneguski.* [Charlotte, 1839] Facsimile rpt. Charlotte: McNally, 1960.

Ten Kate, Herman F. C. "The Indian in Literature." *Annual Report of the Board of Regents of the Smithsonian Institution (1921).* Washington: Smithsonian Institution Press, 1922, pp. 507-528.

Thompson, Daniel. *The Doomed Chief.* Philadelphia: J. W. Bradley, 1860.

Thoreau, Henry David. *The Journal of Henry D. Thoreau.* Edited by Bradford Torrey and Francis H. Allen. 14 vols. Boston: Houghton Mifflin, 1906.

Tocqueville, Alexis De. *Democracy in America.* Translated by Henry Reeve. Revised by Francis Bowen and Phillips Bradley. New York: A. A. Knopf, 1945.

Tudor, William, Jr. "An Address delivered to the Phi Beta Kappa Society, at their anniversary meeting at Cambridge." *North American Review* 2 (1815): 13-32.

———. Review of *Moral Pieces in Prose and Verse* by Lydia Huntley. *North American Review* 1 (1815): 111-121.

Turner, Frederick Jackson. *The Character and Influence of the Indian Trade in Wisconsin.* Baltimore: Johns Hopkins Press, 1891.

———. *The Frontier in American History.* New York: Henry Holt and Company, 1920.

Tyler, Moses Coit. *A History of American Literature.* 2 vols. New York: G. P. Putnam's Sons, 1879.

Vail, R. W. G. *The Voice of the Old Frontier.* Philadelphia: University of Pennsylvania Press, 1949.

Van Der Beets, Richard. "The Indian Captivity Narrative as Ritual." *American Literature* 43 (1972): 548-562.

Volney, C. F. *A View of the Soil and Climate of the United State of America.* Translated with notes by C. B. Brown. Philadelphia: J. Conrad and Company, 1804.

Walker, Warren S. "The Frontiersman as Recluse and Redeemer." *New York Folklore Quarterly* 16 (1960): 110-122.

Washburn, Wilcomb E. "The Moral and Legal Justification for Dispossessing the Indians." *Seventeenth Century America.* Edited by Morton Smith. Chapel Hill: University of North Carolina Press, 1959, pp. 15-32.

———. "A Moral History of Indian-White Relations; Needs and Opportunities for Study." *Ethnohistory* 4 (1957-58): 47-61.

———. *Red Man's Land/White Man's Law.* New York: Charles Scribner's Sons, 1971.

Webber, Charles Wilkins. *Old Hicks the Guide.* New York: Harper and Brothers, 1848.

———. *Tales of the Southern Border.* Philadelphia: J. B. Lippincott and Company, 1856.

Whittier, John Greenleaf. *Legends of New England.* Hartford: Hammer and Phelps, 1831.

Willison, George F. *Saints and Strangers.* New York: Reynal and Hitchcock, 1945.

Wissler, Clark. *The American Indian.* 3rd ed. New York: Oxford University Press, 1938.

The Witch of New England. Philadelphia: N. C. Carey and I. Lea, 1824.

Woodworth, Samuel. *The Champions of Freedom.* 2 vols. New York: Charles N. Baldwin, 1816.

Young, Samuel. *Tom Hanson, the Avenger.* Pittsburgh: J. W. Cook, 1847.

Zolla, Elemire. *The Writer and the Shaman.* Translated by Raymond Rosenthal. New York: Harcourt Brace Jovanovich, 1973.

INDEX

215